Mr. + Mrs. Shiraza,

Thank you for all the support.

SHATTERED

THE SECTARIAN DIVIDE AND START OF THE FEMINIST REVOLUTION IN ISLAM

BY

SYED ABBAS RIZVI AND S. KHASIM T. RIZVI

authorHOUSE®

AuthorHouse™
1663 Liberty Drive, Suite 200
Bloomington, IN 47403
www.authorhouse.com
Phone: 1-800-839-8640

©2008 Syed Abbas Rizvi and S. Khasim T. Rizvi. All rights reserved.

No part of this book may be reproduced, stored in a retrieval system, or transmitted by any means without the written permission of the author.

First published by AuthorHouse   8/18/2008

ISBN: 978-1-4343-4238-6 (sc)
ISBN: 978-1-4389-0422-1 (hc)

Printed in the United States of America
Bloomington, Indiana

This book is printed on acid-free paper.

DEDICATIONS

Syed Abbas Rizvi:
This book is dedicated to Janabe Fatima Zehra, the beloved daughter of Hazrat Muhammad, prophet of Islam, who led a revolutionary movement for women's rights in the 7th century A.D.

S. Khasim T. Rizvi:
I would like to dedicate this book to my family: My grandmother, Yousuf Zehra Begum Rizvi, who was a guiding light in my life, Asghar Rizvi, Zehra Rizvi, and my father, Abbas Rizvi, who has, and always will, remain an inspirational force of determination and fortitude in my life.

A Special Note From the Authors

We submit apologetically to the almighty Allah for our myopic manifestation of reaching out to those who are unfamiliar with the truth with hope that an impartial and unbiased approach would appeal to the intellectuals with optimistic foray. In so doing, we have reluctantly relied on a path for which we ask Allah for forgiveness. At the mention of the word Allah, Muslims automatically say *"Subhanahu wa taalah."* Similarly, before the mention of the names of Aadam(Adam), Ibrahim (Abraham), Musa (Moses), Muhammad, Ali, Fatima, Hasan, and Husain, the preposition *hazrat* is inserted, and after the name, *Aleha salaam* is said. For females, as in the case of Fatima, the preposition *Janabe* is said before the name, and *Salamullah aleha* is recited after the name. We hope our actions are understood with the best of intentions for the sake of propagating the truth by taking such a course.

We humbly request to all the believers to add the above prepositions and postpositional phrases as they come across these important names in the book.

PREFACE

Iraq has now turned into a battleground for the rebellious and the seditious, with forces from all sides trying desperately to disintegrate the already fragile government. Human bombs to bolster the arsenal behind the sectarian violence have been responsible for thousands of deaths. The indiscriminate onslaught of Muslims against Muslims has proven a reminder of a bloody past. Body parts have been scattered on streets and in mosques, marketplaces, offices, shrines, and even hospitals, while sacred days of the religion have proven to coax even further bloodletting. Freedom has become a mockery in the face of a fallen standard. Safety and security have become victims of their own people.

Sectarian violence has been an unwelcome guest in the Muslim world for centuries. The explosive growth of such violence, particularly in this region, bares political overtones that have been a topic of discourse for all key players. The magnitude of disaster appears to be frustratingly boundless. The Muslim nations surrounding Iraq have major vested interests in the outcome of a newly reborn Iraq, while its birth wounds are positioned to be their political and economic gain or downfall. The sectarian feud has risen after the fall of the brutal dictatorship in Iraq, and the death toll has been beyond anyone's imagination. The UNAMI (UN Assistance Mission for Iraq) reported in their human rights report that 34,452 Iraqi civilians were murdered in cold blood in 2006 alone. In the month of August 2007, more than 1,800 Iraqi civilians were brutally massacred in cold blood for a religious divide used to fuel political undercurrents.

The differences between the two major sects of Islam, the Shi'as and the Sunnis, are significantly deep rooted and go back

to the beginning of Islam, starting at the time of the death of Muhammad. I will try to expand on these differences and trace the events that triggered this split. My focus will be on some of the sensitivities that have escalated into explosive outbursts of sectarian nature, as those seen in Iraq.

My experience of *Hajj* (required pilgrimage to Mecca that every Muslim has to perform at least once in his or her lifetime) demonstrated the fragile nature of the differences between the different sects of Islam. I was eagerly looking forward to my travel to Mecca and Medina to fulfill my lifelong dream to be part of a massive congregation demonstrating solidarity and oneness irrespective of ethnicity and nationality.

I had traveled to Mecca and Medina to fulfill the required part of my obligation for Hajj with great excitement. My first Hajj was a surge of moral excellence. The spiritual upliftment and emotional stimulus were overwhelming and real. I was engulfed in devotion. The entire process of Hajj captivated me, as did the powerful message encapsulated in its concept. Life seemed to sparkle with love, mercy, and compassion. I was in a complex matrix of faith in which I was enticed by strong feeling of total submission—Islam. I was a ball of energy following Newton's laws of motion under ideal conditions. As we flew into Madina, the aerial view of Masjid-e-Nabavi (a mosque built by Muhammad) mesmerized my ocular senses. I was beginning to feel the 1,400 years of history pass by as we landed on the grounds on which every icon of Islam had walked. My imagination zoomed back about ten thousand years to Aadam (Adam) and then shifted to the times of Nooh(Noah), Ibraheem (Abraham), Musa (Moses), Eisa (Jesus), Muhammad, Khadija, Fatima, and Ali, and then it moved on to the devoted followers of Muhammad who sacrificed

their lives to forward this pure and clean message of an ideal way of living to us.

The drama began to unfold as I entered the Masjid-e-Nabavi. Hundreds of thousands of people were streaming in to find a spot to pray, and the lucky ones were able to find spots somewhere inside the main building. The architecture and grandeur both outside and inside reflected the extraordinary effort put into the design and construction of this monumental structure. It was *Tahajud* (midnight) prayer, which was non-obligatory. I finished my prayer and decided to stay inside the Masjid for the *Fajar*, the morning prayer. I had been there about an hour when I decided to go around and look at the inside of Masjid. As I started to walk, I saw throngs of people rushing toward the burial place of Muhammad, and I decided to push my way forward to get the honor of being able to look at and touch the past. After an hour of struggling, I elbowed myself up to the actual shrine of Muhammad and attempted to touch the monument. Suddenly, I felt somebody pushing my hand away. Luckily, I managed to touch the shrine while the crowd behind me spun me out of the stream; I was once again out of the main flow and out of range. I found another spot and finished my Fajar prayer.

I went out and I saw a number of people rushing toward another monument close by. I heard a voice saying, "They opened the door of Baqui (a cemetery) just a few minutes back; let's go; hurry, hurry." I followed a nearby group toward the flight of stairs leading to the entrance. I was excited, although just looking at the mob made me think it would be impossible to make it to the entrance. The crowd was unbelievably out of control. People were being crushed as they tried to move toward the flight of stairs. I heard screams, but nothing deterred the oncoming crowd. I finally decided to inject myself into this stream. I was barely

moving when suddenly I felt a push and was moved forward a few feet. I heard a thud behind me, and I was suddenly pulled from the back. I lost control and fell down upon several fallen bodies. I attempted to roll over when someone helped me with a forward push. I was lucky I had gotten out of the stampede. I was back in the stream, and I inched forward until I reached the entrance. The door closed.

I was sweating and panting from all the pain I had gone through. Disappointedly, I asked the guard when the door would open next. He shook his head with arrogance and gestured me toward the exit. Nobody knew when the door would open again. Someone from behind said, "They may open the door tomorrow after Fajar".

I was dying to go inside, so the next day I was there before Fajar. I did the Fajar prayer and stood by the entrance in the front line, hoping that it would be easier to enter this time. We waited for about forty-five minutes, and then the door opened. We rushed, almost running up the stairs to the entrance, and entered *Baqui,* the burial ground of some of the most important personalities of Islam. Baqui is a huge burial ground divided into sections with some of the graveyards barricaded with chains and walls. Guards were all over Baqui, preventing people from going near the graves. I looked at the map I had received from the head of our group. I was standing by an iron fence about one hundred feet from an area where I saw a row of graves that was the center of attention of the crowd. The person standing next to me pointed at a single grave away from the rest and said: "That is the grave of Fatima Binte Muhammad, the only daughter of Muhammad,[1] and the four graves in a row are those of her son Hasan Ibn Ali, Ali ibn Husain (her grandson), Muhammad Baquir (her great-grandson), and Jafer-e-Sadiq (Muhammad Baquir's son)." In front of these

was the grave of Abbas ibn Muttalib (Muhammad's uncle). The condition in which these graves were kept was appalling.

I asked one of the guards: "Why are these graves poorly maintained"?

He started to explain it to me by saying, "These graves have no value. These people are dead and gone. People venerate and get carried away emotionally. That is why they have these barriers. Moreover, what can these dead people do now?"

I said: "Brother, Islam is a practical, realistic, and intention-driven religion that cannot be shaken by non-obligatory actions. Emotions that are expressions of love and sorrow are non-obligatory. Intent plays a key role in all our faith-based actions. For example, Kaaba is a structure made of stone. Every Muslim is required to bow down and lie prostrate toward it. Are they worshipping the stone structure? The answer is, absolutely not. As long as one does not cross the line in violation of the principle of Tauheed (belief in one supreme being—Allah), one has the freedom of expression of pain, love, and all other elements relating to emotions."

He said, "Emotions are not allowed."

I said, "What is wrong in venting emotions? Where does it say that emotions are not allowed? It is part of human nature to show emotions. More importantly brother," I said, pointing at the graves, "they are providing you and me the reason to remain on the right path, stay Muslim, and practice Islam."

He said "What?" and gave me a blank stare.

I said, "Their teachings, writings, sermons, and speeches are providing us guidance, direction, education, spirituality, confidence

building, and role playing. That is why they are important, and that is why we need them to remind us and reinforce our faith."

He looked at me with a confused stare and said "No!"

I said, "These are not ordinary people; unlike you and me, they have given their lives to propagate Islam. You are here because of them. Moreover, this was the only daughter of Muhammad that he said was a part of him. Don't you think she should have been buried next to him?"

He shoved me aside and asked me to move forward.

I said to him, "You are pushing me away from here because you have no logical explanation to defend your views."

"Go read history," he said.

I said, "History, ahadith and the Quran have taught me one of the most powerful concepts of Islam: 'Be with the *Ahel az Zikr*.'"

At this point I quoted the Quran.

> "And we sent not (as Our messengers) before
> thee other than men whom We inspired--Ask the
> followers of the Remembrance if ye know not!"
> (Quran 16:43)

Then I continued, saying, "In that respect, Fatima was not only special and unique to Muhammad, but the rightfully guided one according to the Quran. The bonds between Muhammad and Fatima are well established. You need to read the Quran and history brother!"

His face turned red in anger as he started to move away. A man listening to our conversation said, while turning toward me, "Brother, he is paid to do what he is doing. You are asking for trouble; move on."

I went back to my hotel trying to understand the logic behind his beliefs and views about Islam. I was wondering where and how this convoluted set of beliefs slid into the world of Islam.

The one and a half million pilgrims who were there were all Muslims, yet they were all different. The philosophy of Hajj, as I understood it, was to bring the entire Muslim *Umma* (community) under one banner to perform the ritual of Hajj and to foster uniformity, equality, and synchronization of one's thoughts and beliefs. The shaved-headed pilgrims wearing ihram (two white pieces of cloth worn by all males) and performing identical rituals irrespective of class, creed, color, and nationality was a perfect setup to exhibit love, friendship, and brotherhood. Even the attitude and behavior employed in the ritual is intended to promote peace and respect. I was in a state of confusion as I tried to delineate the basis of the differences between these two sects, because both Sunnis and Shias follow the exact same Quran, face the same direction toward the *Kaabah,* perform their prayers five times a day at about the same time, fast during Ramadan for one month, and perform Hajj as required in nearly the same fashion, with there just being some minor variations.

I tried to de-convolute in my mind these complexities that have emerged over 1,400 years. I was afraid that this would be a monumental task, but I was determined to do research and get a realistic historic perspective of who or what brought about these modifications and how and when they were brought about, and I wanted to do so through a process and system that was intended to be simple, clean, and pure. My experiences at Arafath,

Musdalifa, Minnah, and Mecca (required sequence of rituals of Hajj at different locations in Saudi Arabia) were thrilling, as were my encounters at Uhad, Khandaq (landmark historic sights of two important wars), and the burial places of Khadija (Muhammad's first wife) and Abu Talib (Muhammad's uncle who raised and protected him throughout his life). I was still reflecting upon my conflict at *Baqui* and was determined to explore and find all the details about why the family of Muhammad was singled out. I spent almost four years investigating histories and *ahadith* (plural of hadith, or traditions) within the framework of the Quran. To my surprise, I was not able to find any literature originally written in English about *Fadak*, a landmark movement in the history of Islam dealing with women's rights; it was only available as translations of articles and lectures. As a result, I collected all data pertinent to this topic in whatever languages it was available (Arabic, Persian, and Urdu).

I was aware of most of the events from the sermons, lectures, and speeches I had attended and benefited from in the past. But this time I wanted to discover everything on my own. This became my first priority. The sacrifices I had to make were significant, because I wanted to make sure that nothing was left unexamined.

This project was driven by my desire to seek the truth. This was my life, and my faith was under scrutiny. I had to use all my efforts to go after facts, even if they turned out to be against my beliefs. I was firm in my commitment to not become a victim of desires and impulses. This was important because I would someday have to answer to Allah, and furthermore, I wanted to spend the rest of my life following the true Islam—the Islam of Allah, and not some fabricated version of it. This effort was supposed to lead me to the right path, and I was hoping that the

end results were going to fix me on solid ground if I obtained the real Islam from the right sources. My criteria were that the sources had to be verifiable, that the Quran would be my primary means to identify these sources, and that if history and ahadith could support my queries, my understanding would be consolidated.

My limitations were severe because of my lack of expertise in Arabic. But I was able to overcome some of the difficulties, because a lot of the material has already been translated into English. In the last few years, I started to develop the habit of reading Arabic, particularly the Quran and its translations, interpretations, hermeneutics, and exegesis acquired from experts representing Sunni and Shia sects. I am still in the process of learning, and as time goes by, I am hoping that with the help of Allah and through the right sources, my understanding of Islam will continue its journey toward the absolute truth. My goal was to extract as much information as I could from all non-Shia sources. This was important, because I wanted to look at the whole scenario from the opposite side of the fence. My approach started to crystallize the facts once the overwhelming burden of sorting data and information from thousands and thousands of pages of dedicated work from experts was subjected to this filtration process.

Syed Abbas Rizvi

EXORDIUM

The bright red of the sun shone down on the burning desert sands of Karbala. Waves of heat rose from the burning sand, creating a frosted-glass effect, each grain shifting about with the warm breezes and being lifted off the ground for a much-welcomed vacation into the air, only to land again on the scorching ground in disappointment. One grain flew not more than a few feet from its original home and landed under the shade of a human body. Hundreds of thin crimson streams like thread from a needle formed warm puddles underneath them that coagulated from the immense level of heat and mixed into the sand. The man was barely able to keep himself propped up on his elbows; a vast multitude of arrows dotted his back and chest. His arms moved in staggered thrusts to push a mound of sand in front of his head; he was barely able to prop himself up and move the sand at the same time. When the small mound was completed, he dropped his head upon it as softly as he could. "Today, Hussain has completed the task you bestowed upon him, oh lord of the universe. Ya Allah, Hussain has sacrificed all for you and is ready to leave this earth." The mound began to melt away underneath the blood gushing from his head. This was Hussain ibne Ali ibne Abu Talib, the Hashemite prince and grandson of the Prophet of Islam, Muhammad. Hussain continued his prayer as he heard the crunching of footsteps coming near him. A man stood next to Hussain and lifted his sword, its tip sadistically sparkling from the intense sunrays. Suddenly, the sword fell, and the grain of sand was washed away by the fast-running river of blood. The sword fell, and with that a new revolution was born, and an example was established for all of eternity.

I grew up living my life as two completely different people. When I was in school or with friends, I was an American, completely oblivious to race and religion. At home or in the mosque, I was a Muslim, and I would take part in all activities that were required by a Muslim. I would spend the day playing with the other kids in school, laughing and having fun, and later that night at the mosque, I would be crying and mourning the death of Hussain ibne Ali. For me, this was normal. The only time religion would come into play in my other life was during Islamic holidays. I never questioned the faith I had chosen, because for me, my parents saying that this was what I should follow was enough. My dad would tell me to go and research Islam, but I never did, because I was complacent regarding what my life and my religion, or at least what I knew of them, were.

9/11, 2001. The world changed, and with it my microcosm of a life changed as well. For the first time in my life, my religion was being brought up every day, mostly along with insults and hate. I was incredibly frustrated at my lack of knowledge of Islam and my inability to defend myself. I remember returning home from school and going online to research what Islam had to say about terrorism, al-Qaeda, and the murder of innocent civilians, and I began to actually have discussions about my religion in the classroom with my peers. For the first time, Islam had entered the entirety of my life, and I was engrossed by what it had to say. I found myself spending hours researching aspects of the religion and asking my parents hundreds of questions about it. The fact that these terrorists had quoted the Quran to justify their actions nearly drove me away from Islam, but I then began to research these quotes and saw the realities behind them, as well as the extreme level of misinterpretation that was taking place. A text that called for unity, peace, love, respect, and justice was being used instead to justify some of the darkest crimes in human

history, and I vowed that I could not let them get away with it. I entered debates in school almost daily to demonstrate that Islam was not a religion of hate and intolerance, and I gave the examples I knew best of Hussain ibne Ali's struggles for justice, peace, and equality. The shift that took place in my life after that fateful day was immense and swift, and I knew I was ready for it. I had now officially become defined as an American Muslim rather than just an American and a Muslim.

3/19/2003. The Iraq War began, and shortly thereafter, a massive and bloody conflict took place between the Shi'a and the Sunnis. I had known there were two separate schools of thought in Islam, but I had not even begun to comprehend the differences or the misconceptions between these two faiths. I began my journey through books, reading Sunni histories, comparing them to Shia documentation, and learning more about the differences between the two online. The information was vast, and most was ridiculously biased with a level of hatred I had not seen before. After years of research and debate, I began arguing the case of why there should never have been a split in the first place. After my freshman year in college, I felt I had learned all there was to know. Then my father arrived from Saudi Arabia and told me the heart-wrenching tale of the vindictively vicious treatment by the House of Saud against the most revered shrines of the Prophet Muhammad's immediate family (his children, their children, etc., and Fatima binte Muhammad most of all). He approached me with an opportunity to write a groundbreaking book on the case of Fadak and the mistreatment of the family of Muhammad. I immediately accepted, thinking that I had a great deal of information that I could lend to this book. Quickly, though, I realized that there was far more to it than I could have ever imagined. We changed the scheme of the book at my behest to correlate the events of Fadak and the falling out thereafter

with the conflicts and political movements of modernity, leading to one of the most thought-provoking and taxing undertakings I have ever been involved in. For my father, his experience in Saudi Arabia was the deciding factor in his life that led him to create this book. For me, it was 9/11, the Iraq War, and the immense impact on me of the events in Karbala. The combination of our personalities and different viewpoints lead to an unbelievably diverse book, covering the spectra of our own personal views and the definitive collection of information we gathered. For me, this book was a chance of a lifetime and the first time I had defined myself specifically as an American Shia Muslim, a transition of one word that created a massive change in who I was and what I was to become. This was my argument of faith, my prologue to a brand new life, and my tribute to the most defining events that shaped who I have now become. My hope is that what these events did to shift who I was in my life, this book will do for those who read it, allowing them to define themselves not by the color of their skin or their culture, but by who they really are.

The sun set on Karbala, and with that, a revolution was born. Millions of people across the kingdom of Yazid Ibn Muawiah began to revolt, waking their senses to the deplorable conditions they were living in and the cruel placidity of their leader toward one of humanity's most tragic chapters. A wind of change lifted the sands of Karbala and knocked at the door of Yazid with a call for hope and justice. When Yazid was removed, the people of his kingdom said "never again" and vowed to always hold the gallant example of Hussain in their hearts. Just as fast as those winds of change had lifted and altered the status of mankind, so were they forgotten. No sooner had Yazid died than a new vicious dictatorial regime began spreading its dark and stifling tentacles over the populace. The family of Hussain that had

become so revered was now facing oppression and hate from these rulers without a single cry for change. A second Hussain never came, and the same level of malevolent placidity covered the land with its shadow, closing the eyes of those who had once been jolted awake. Hundreds of years after Hussain, kings still rule over their people with iron fists, dictators still kill innocent droves to assert their power, and men who fight for justice still are murdered without a single tear shed in their honour.

My dream is that this book will provide a jolt to those who read it that will allow them to awake again and stand tall with hope and flaunt it in the faces of those whose weapon is despair. We do not need another Hussain; we simply need to remember for the sake of the hundreds of generations to come.

Khasim Rizvi

TABLE OF CONTENTS

INTRODUCTION

"We have revealed the book to you with the truth that you may judge between people by means of that which Allah has taught you" (Quran 4:105; translator, Yousuf Ali).

إِنَّا أنزَلْنَا إِلَيْكَ الكِتَابَ بِالحَقِّ لِتَحْكُمَ بَيْنَ النَّاس بِمَا أرَاكَ اللّهُ
وَلاَ تَكُن لِّلْخَائِنِينَ خَصِيمًا

A voice suddenly rose that ripped the shackles of pain and endurance and smashed the dark clouds of despair that had been asphyxiating the rights of women and human dignity. This voice struck like a bolt of lightning, shattering the barriers that had undermined women since the beginnings of mankind. The inceptions of gender equality and the empowerment of women were set into motion. Women's rights saw new hope and vision for the first time in history. Human rights vaulted to levels that had been unattainable in the past.

It was the voice of the first woman in mankind to demand her rights in a male dominated world. This was a voice personifying Islam and the Quran. This was the voice of a pure, innocent teenage girl—a devoted daughter, mother, and wife. It was the voice of a fragile girl intellectually gifted with exceptional oratory powers able to stagger even the strongest of opponents. Even the harsh social environment of the time could not deter her. It continued to invoke, motivate, and provoke all aspects of human rights. This voice belonged to Fatima and only Fatima, daughter of Muhammad, the last messenger of Allah. The Quran, traditions, and history described her as an unblemished

sculpture of womanhood, an icon enriched with Islamic morals and virtues.

This was the first time in the history of Islam that women's rights were put to the test. The pennant of egalitarianism was hoisted for the first time, providing full protection of women's rights established under the Quranic tenets. Allah, through the Quran, had emphatically guaranteed the rights of women, making it part of the Islamic legal rights. Muhammad's treatment of women with respect, honor, and love was not only an assignment, but also an essential part of his personal and public life. The manifestation of human rights and women's rights gyrated between lows and highs during the last fourteen centuries. Even today, the advocates of human rights and women's rights are caught in a posture of contravention.[1] It is interesting to note that in current times, the only things that have changed have been in respect to terminology and nomenclature.

Women's rights in the last 1,400 years have made very little to no progress in the Muslim world. It should be borne in mind that Islam clearly denounced the mistreatment of women. The blame of allowing the mistreatment of females in Islam is unfair. Human rights and women's rights in Islam have been hot topics of discussion by a great many scholars, and scores of books have been written on them. These expert opinions, discussions, and references have been presented later in the book to show that it was Fatima who initiated the process 1,400 years back with a powerful attack against ill-fated un-Islamic policies. She blazed the trail of women's rights in the mosaic of an uncultured, unsophisticated, and primitive world where unsavvy, brutal politics ruled.

Fatima's troubles started with the brief illness of Muhammad. This period before Muhammad's death is of special significance in the history of Islam. Fatima was with him before and at the

time of his death and was passively involved in all the events that were beginning to shape the future. With the paragon of peace and justice gone, Fatima and her family were thrown reeling into a state of shock and intense grief. Conditions abruptly changed. Politicians seized the opportunity to gain control while Muhammad's body was deliberately left behind.[2]

Muhammad's sudden death had left a leadership vacuum. This traumatizing shock created an opportunity for politicians to mobilize public emotions to create an atmosphere conducive of the impression that Muhammad had left a void to be filled in by the community. It is difficult to believe that a visionary leader like Muhammad would ignore securing the future of his mission. An effective propaganda campaign was launched to convince the public that the selection of a khalif (successor) by a small selected group was acceptable under dire circumstances. The few who opposed this were silenced by guarantees in the power-sharing scheme. Religious principles were impaired in the process. Thus, a non-paradigm shift was adopted to take over *Khilafath* (vicegerency) by initiating the conditions favoring a state uncoupled from religion.

The dilemma of separation of state and religion is not an Islamic phenomenon. Muhammad had demonstrated that state and religion were inseparable. Muhammad's life was a reflection of the Quran; his actions, policies, and techniques of management superimposed the Quranic revelations. Muhammad had demonstrated that religion and state are to be blended in a unique set of conditions to address the needs of the community at large with honesty, justice, love, and mercy. Justice accordingly can only be served by a standard set of rules that are even handed with no room for flexibility. The idea of equilibrium between state and religion was established such that equality

was efficiently exercised irrespective of class, color, creed, race, or religion. It was after his death that deviation from the policy of Muhammad errantly shaped the future of Islam. It was the selection of the first khalif and the associated political maneuvering that constituted the initiation of the separation of state and religion. Incredible amounts of literature by Muslims and non-Muslims relating to this topic have emerged in the past few centuries. The discussions that are relevant to this book have been deferred to later chapters. Muhammad's death and the environment surrounding it provided opportunity for an aversive takeover along with aggressive measures put in place to fend off any possible threats to the newly formed regime. Conditions after Muhammad's death brought hidden agendas to the surface through an aggressive move toward a coup that spun the community into a frenzy, creating difficulties for the family of Muhammad. Although Fatima and Ali were in a state of shock from the loss, the emerging leadership was fearful that the worthy and deserving were certain to become a formidable threat to them. Hence, a forceful approach was implemented to weaken Muhammad's family in any way possible.

Thus, soon after Muhammad's death, the quick sands of horror and pain suddenly engulfed Fatima. Her rights were nabbed. Fadak, a property left for Fatima as an inheritance from her father, was confiscated by the new regime. The confiscation of Fadak was a political move geared to financially deprive her and Ali from posing any political challenge to the legitimacy of their claim to Khilafath. She was determined to claim her Islamic rights and challenge the novice regime. This was a flash point that charged the ideological war between the family of Muhammad and others. Fatima's famous claim of Fadak reverberates as an admonition to humanity.

"Those who unjustly eat up the property of
orphans eat up a Fire into their own bodies:
They will soon be enduring a Blazing Fire!"
(Quran:4:10; translator, Yousuf Ali)

إِنَّ الَّذِينَ يَأْكُلُونَ أَمْوَالَ الْيَتَامَى ظُلْمًا إِنَّمَا يَأْكُلُونَ فِي
بُطُونِهِمْ نَارًا وَسَيَصْلَوْنَ سَعِيرًا

Fatima's exposé of the unfair, unjust, and un-Islamic sequence
of actions leading to Khilafath and its consequential impact on
the future of Islam were the highlights of her speech. She was
claiming her rights to Fadak in a mosque before the new khalifa
and his supporters, challenging the judicial system the new regime
was creating. Her speech was designed to penetrate the past and
provoke the present. The changes that her father had brought
about in a land stricken with anarchy, rule of savagery, brutality,
and immorality were specifically referenced as a reminder of their
past. Her address was brilliantly configured to acknowledge the
absolute authority of Allah; the supreme authority of Muhammad;
Muhammad's contributions to Islam and Muslims; the unique
place of her family and her husband, Ali; and the obligations
of the Muslim community in accordance with the Quran and
Allah toward Muhammad and his progeny. The objective of her
speech was to apotheosize true Islam, rejuvenate the concept of
vicegerency, and invoke women's rights specific to inheritance
and the criteria for the appointment of a khalif as laid out within
the Quran and by Muhammad.

The theme of this book is to shed light on the complex
series of events that led to the political fallout after the death
of Muhammad, to examine its impact on the course of Islam,
and to objectively argue the plight of Fatima. This book is an

attempt to appeal to a conscientious mind to analyze the facts and deploy methods to decipher the information from a matrix of hundreds of thousands of pages compiled or written by *Muhadiseen* (collectors of ahadith—explained in reference),[3], historians, intellectuals, and scholars with established credibility. Truth-seeking scholars and sources have been carefully selected for their impartial evaluation of facts. The primary objective is to set ground rules and reconstruct the political conditions implemented to deny Fatima's rights to Fadak and Ali's rights to Khilafath as originally designated to him by Muhammad. The pitfalls and possible solutions to various aspects of these controversies have been systematically presented to help the reader obtain a birds-eye view of all possible scenarios that differentiate facts from falsities. A discourse concerning these scenarios is constructed to adjudicate paradoxes. Over the past 1,400 years, these differences have spiraled out of control whenever the Shia have risen and threatened old discriminatory policies, as in the case of Iraq, where every effort has been enacted by the 9/11 insurgents to remove the Shia from a stronger position in the reconstruction of the country. It is obvious that the stimulus provided by these outside agencies is based on some serious religious issues originating more than a millennium ago. Experts claim that there is no connection between Saddam and Al-Qaeda. Now the landscape of Iraq has become a joint venture of the external terrorist groups and national agencies and the agencies within Iraq itself. These are the forces providing the stimulus and assistance needed for power-scheming murders and fear-inspiring bombings across the nation. One has to keep in mind that Al Qaeda is an organization with its origins tracing back to the fabricated ahadith and misinterpretations of the Quran that are, according to most theologians and scholars, completely out of balance with the intended message of the text.

Interestingly, the inconsistencies and the conflicting information in ahadith and histories relating to the Quran can be envisioned as realities of a diverse human psyche, inducing internal political wars fueled by group loyalties, differences in political philosophies, and more importantly, commitment to tribal patronage. The influence of this on the recorders of ahadith and histories has been profound. These substantial differences in religious-political philosophies have been hashed out through a systematic process of establishing guidelines acceptable to common sense. Analytical methods to examine constituent parts of the Quran, ahadith,[4] Sunnah,[5] and history within the domains of set ground rules have been instituted to unequivocally expose the facts. The Quran obviously has been the natural choice and the primary source in generating the ground rules.

The three constituents that establish the ground rules are as follows:

First and foremost is the Quran. The Quran is a manual to train, discipline, and condition the mind toward perfection while laying heavy emphasis on knowledge and justice as fundamental requirements. These components tie uniquely into the spirituality that is embodied in the five pillars of Islam known as *Usul-e-deen* that form the basis of the intrinsic spiritual component of the religion. These are the requirements that shape a human mind to experience peace and love representing an ideally complete way of life.

The Quran is a primary source of reference to gauge one's actions and convictions. Islam is a combination of beliefs projecting the will of Allah through the Quran and the life of Muhammad as an example to structure our own lives around. Muhammad's life revolved around the Quran and is a mirror reflection of it.

The power of the Quran and Islam is based, in essence, on one of its most essential components, "the absolute justice." This concept of universal justice is unique only to Islam and is a fundamental requirement of a practicing Muslim. Any deviation from this principle is automatically considered contemptible and un-Islamic. The Quran does not tolerate any kind of injustice against any non-Muslim or Muslim. In fact, strong warnings are present throughout the Quran, and severe punishment protocols are imposed in the Islamic legislation.

The Quran's interpretation, however, has been a challenge. These interpretations have opened up a slew of inconclusive debates that have been raging for almost 1,400 years. Exegeses and hermeneutic results emerging out of it relating to the Quran and the modern views about its intent and expectations have been intensely debated by academicians of present times, such as Amina Hudud[6] and Asma Barlas[7]. Care has been exercised to present only those selected verses of the Quran that have universally acceptable interpretations.

The second component is a combination of ahadith and Sunnah explained in later chapters. Hadith and the science relating to it are inevitably complex and subjective. To add to this already existing problem, the collection and compilation processes of ahadith did not start until more than two hundred years after Muhammad's death. Coincidentally, this happens to be a period of notorious regimes known for heavy-handedness on atrocities, suppression, intimidation, and coercion. During this period, thousands of ahadith were fabricated to please the khalifs. Effort has been made to select only those ahadith that do not conflict with the Quran.

The third element is the history of Islam. Islamic histories and their development processes, similarly to hadith, did not become

systematic until one hundred years after the death of Muhammad. A historian's dependence on the process of reporting verifiable information, validating the transmission of information through various sources, and bypassing and ignoring any pressures from their employer-masters and dictatorial regimes is in itself a great challenge. The development of the *Sira* (biography) of Muhammad also suffered a similar adverse outcome.

The good news is that even with all the complexities outlined so far, a person with an open mind who is determined to seek the truth will be able to read between the lines and analyze all of the information available. The emerging conclusions will undoubtedly be enlightening as one begins to peel off each layer from the stratified structure of historic events that have been shrouded with skillfully designed malice against Fatima, Ali, and their family. The conditions and circumstances connected to each event are assured to lead to the straight facts.

The first chapter is unique. It is intended to take the reader through a historically important phase leading toward an intensely horrific chain of events. It provides a riveting outline of facts often downplayed and intentionally overlooked because of its impact on the early development of the history. However, it forms a good basis for the formulation of ground rules, effectively making the connections between the following chapters almost seamless. The development of ground rules and a brief history of early Islam, Muhammad's message, events before and after his death, and his death's impact on current developments are presented in a chronological order. Current issues dealing with human rights and women's rights—in particular the issues of slavery, mistreatment of one's spouse (wife), and the inheritance of women in Islam—have been discussed in Chapter 8.

The most important aspect, without which this effort would be incomplete, is the role of Fatima and Ali. Without any doubt, her famous Fadak speech was the turning event in the history of Islam that revolutionized its course and revitalized the forgotten message of the Quran and Islam. Fadak remains an emotional scar on the history of Islam. The hadith that "Allah's Apostle said, 'Our property will not be inherited, whatever we [i.e., prophets] leave is Sadaqah [to be used for charity],'" has to be reassessed in light of the Quran. A detailed discussion on this subject has been presented. The final phase of the book has been purposely devoted to the incredibly vital speech of Fatima, which serves as a pulsating nerve responsible for keeping the heart of Islam beating in synchrony with the Quran. This is followed by discussions about reformists, modernists, and current issues along with how freedom, democracy, and education fit into Islam. The conclusions and reflections in the last phase are intended to help draw a firm understanding based on the material provided under different phases of Islamic history as the events unfolded from right after Muhammad's death to the current times.

CHAPTER 1

Under Siege

"And (as for) those who strive hard for us, we will most certainly guide them in our ways" (Quran 29:69).

وَالَّذِينَ جَاهَدُوا فِينَا لَنَهْدِيَنَّهُمْ سُبُلَنَا وَإِنَّ اللَّهَ لَمَعَ الْمُحْسِنِينَ

Fatima, the only daughter of Muhammad-e-Mustafa, when eighteen,[1] was struck by an unremitting chain of tragedies and atrocities. Gloom, horror, and intensely profound fear enveloped Fatima with a tenacious vengeance. Muhammad, the messenger of Allah, had just died.[2] He left the world in disappointment and anger because of the sudden change in the behavior of his companions, who acted to undermine him just before his death.[3] He was betrayed by the people whom he had entrusted to display love, compassion, and above all, justice. Fatima was without her father. Her husband, Ali, had lost his cousin, father-in-law, and mentor. Her children—Hassan, Husain, Zainab, and Kulthum— had lost a grandfather who adored and loved them and considered them an essential part of his life.[4] Muhammad's distinguished followers had lost a personality that infused their lives with richness of love, peace, respect, and justice. Fatima's family was in intense pain from a huge loss. Fatima and Muhammad had been inseparable. She was tired and exhausted from the complexities of the calamities she had undergone during her pregnancy.

Grief stricken, Fatima was further catapulted into relentless harassment from those whom her father had once called his companions. Her home was attacked and threatened to be burnt by the newly self-appointed khalif Abu Bakr and his supporters.[5] Abu Bakr was selected by a small group of supporters, not by Muhammad, and he was entrusted by these people to enforce justice and peace. History, however, tells a different story. The door of Fatima's home was hacked and forced open by Umar.[6] She became the victim to a crushing blow that gashed her ribs and made her fall in a pool of her own blood. Fatima's husband, Ali, was dragged out of their home, shackled, and threatened to face death if he did not accept the self-proclaimed Khilafath.[7] Fatima was physically hurt and was barely able to move.[8] She made a feeble attempt to end the violence but was shunned and shoved aside. Distinguished followers of Muhammad, such as Salman-e-farsi, Abu Dharr Ghafari, Ammar-eYasir, Abbas ibne Mutallib, Talha, Zubair, and many others who were with Ali and Fatima, could not tolerate any further torture and demanded an end to the brutality. Abu Bakr, realizing the ramifications of this act and the possible political carnage that would occur to his new leadership, was forced to back off from further harassment. The group left. Fatima, Ali, her family, and the followers of Muhammad were left to lament after a shocking barrage of hostilities.

The family of Fatima was crushed by the politically savvy mercenaries waiting for an opportunity to strike at the first chance. The death of Muhammad became a moment for the opportunists to grab power, implement and modify regulations, and reintroduce old traditions and practices tailored to fit their needs. The ideal Islam of Muhammad was under siege, and it threatened to fall back into the hands of the enemies of Islam, who had encountered an unending trail of defeats that had turned them powerless and ineffective.[9] The enemies of Islam

(Abu Sufyan and his supporters) were finally regrouping and showing their true colors after a long dormant period during which they enacted a self-imposed policy to accept Islam to protect themselves from harm. These infiltrators and hypocrites were now in the fold of Islam; they were full of vengeance and hatred that would bloom into dictatorship in the period of Bani Ummayah and Bani Abbas.[10] Nothing could stop them now. With Muhammad gone, the ideal Islamic leadership appeared to have dissolved into the centuries-old paganistic undercurrents, finally cracking the barriers of a vibrant but still juvenile socio-Islamic culture.[11] Thus an imposter establishment had trapped a just social environment of peace, harmony, and mutual respect that had previously shown impeccable records in the system of justice. Within hours of Muhammad's death, all the fundamental doctrines of Islam were beginning to disintegrate.[12] Deceitful political strategies undermining the basics of Islam had begun to cause doubt to be cast upon the legitimacy of Khilafath. Retributions from past defeats were beginning to shape the future under the patronage of a politically driven hybrid Islam. In short, Islam was under attack by the internal forces stationed in ambush.

Muhammad's forty or more years of revolutionary mandate to form a divine socioeconomic and sociohumanistic structure designed to create love, order, and respect across the world was changing hands.[13] The monumental task accomplished by Muhammad was suddenly under the threat of being dismantled. Muhammad's place had to be filled in by someone of equal stature and charisma. Fatima, who enjoyed a unique place in the life of Muhammad and in the early life of Islam along with Khatija and Ali, felt the necessity to resurrect a still juvenile Islamic community to its original state of affairs. Her love for and commitment to the principles of Islam of Muhammad were incredibly solid. This

was a driving force positioned to prevent the destruction of an exceedingly solid socioreligious structure of life. This was a time when all anti-Islamic forces were operating in sync against the precepts of Muhammad's Islam.

Fatima was ready for a showdown. The Muslim community was aware that she was the only person whom Muhammad would rise up to greet. Muhammad introduced Fatima as a component of him to the Muslim world, and that whoever hurt her was considered to have hurt Muhammad and Allah simultaneously.[14] Fatima was a daughter that shared difficulties, successes, and victories with Muhammad. Muhammad's recapture of Mecca was a victory that shattered the old, paganistic pride. She was there to share his success. Fatima was elevated to new heights as the new community recognized the special respect and honor bestowed upon her as she entered Mecca. This was the daughter of a man who had changed the entire region into a practicing Islamic community. Undoubtedly, Fatima was the joy and love of Muhammad.[15]

Still not fully recovered from her injuries and having just faced the loss of a child in premature stillbirth from the violent attack on her, Fatima was weighing her options in executing her task. She had two choices: endure pain and accept injustice, or rise up and stand for her rights. After taking punishing blows from an unjust regime, any other women would have conceded and reluctantly accepted the demolition of Muhammad's and Khatija's intense sacrifices.

The task before Fatima was monumental. Her resources were limited, but her determination was as strong as that of Muhammad when he had first delivered the message of Islam to the nomads of Mecca. Quranic justice was her driving force.

Fadak, a property Muhammad had given to her, was confiscated by the new regime.[16] Fadak was a springboard that Fatima used to launch a unique movement critically positioned to recharge public emotion and inform the future generations about the political violence against Islam's holistic image.

Fatima was shocked by a multitude of tragedies. The death of Muhammad, the confiscation of Fadak, and the coup for Khilafath all took place within a matter of days. Fatima was unyielding and determined to demand justice from her enemies with unflinching fortitude. Just ten days after her father's death, she decided that it was time for her to stand up and claim what rightfully belonged to her. Fadak, which had belonged to her father, was technically and Islamically her property.[17] Fatima was setting precedence for the suppressed to stand up for their rights regardless of the outcome. After all, Islam's fundamental reform to recognize womens rights was one of the major upsets of past pagan practices. The task was difficult and the results were predictable, but Fatima was strong and confident, and she shook the will of the leadership by presenting her case with unwavering resolve. She was as strong and determined as Muhammad had been at his first call to Islam in Zulasheera[18] to his last sermon in Ghadir-e-Khumm.[19] Her case was solid; it was backed by the Quran and the Sunnah of Muhammad. She was ingrained with training, knowledge, wisdom, and charisma from her upbringing. Above all, she was a gift from Allah to Muhammad for carrying out a specific task, and there was no way she would have compromised for anything less.

Fatima had to think, act, and transform into Muhammad. She took a group of women supporters with close ties to Muhammad and walked toward the masjid that her father had built, managed, and directed. This was the place where her father delivered sermons, spread the word of Allah, and preached justice, love,

compassion, and peace on a daily basis. She was familiar with the old-time, friendly atmosphere of the place. She was also aware that the people who had once shown affection and love toward her father were now her bitter enemies who had unleashed terror to hold onto their leadership. As she walked toward the masjid, her mind perhaps started to unwind the respect and special treatment she and her family had received when her father was alive. A passionate past must have infused her with formidable strength to reach the mosque. This dramatic entrance of Fatima into the Mosque must have dwarfed the leadership. They were perhaps surprised and overshadowed by this unexpected visitor. She was Islam in its full grandeur. The Quran was her home language. Her home was the home in which Islam and the Quran had been nurturers. All of the key personalities of Islam that were connected intricately through blood ties lived in her home. Fatima was the point of convergence.

Emboldened by her firm belief in Allah, she delivered a speech that injected a concentrated dose of reality that was intended to augment the passions of the listeners as she summarized the past and predicted the future of Islam. Her oratory was flawlessly balanced. Her intellectual prowess regarding her command of the Quran, language, juristic reasoning, and logic derived from the principles so dear to her had become unchallengeable. Amid all the chaos, Fatima demanded the release of her confiscated property, Fadak, from the newly self-proclaimed Khalifa and his supporters. The leadership began to display signs of weakness and confusion. Unable to react to this challenge with reason, the leadership attempted to defuse the challenge by presenting weak and unsubstantiated arguments. Fatima was unflinching in her responses. Abu Bakr was initially unwilling to accept or negotiate her claim to Fadak, but was perhaps overcome by his guilt and the unfair handling of her claims. Abu Bakr started to show signs

of wavering. Unable to technically and Quranically outmaneuver her skillful defense, he realized that his leadership, as well as the fundamental principles of Islamic justice, would be at stake and he reluctantly accepted her claim and wrote a decree assigning Fadak in her favor.

Abu Bakr said to Fatima, "Surely Allah and His Apostle are truthful, and so has his [the Prophet's] daughter told the truth. Surely you are the source of wisdom, the element of faith, and the sole authority. May Allah not refute your righteous argument, nor invalidate your decisive speech. But these are the Muslims between us who have entrusted me with leadership, and it was according to their satisfaction that I received what I have. I am not being arrogant, autocratic, or selfish, and they are my witnesses."

Abu Bakr wrote a decree releasing Fadak in Fatima's favor, but Umar intervened.

Umar said to Abu Bakr, "What is it that you hold in your hand?"

Abu Bakr said, "A decree I have written for Fatima, in which I assigned Fadak, her father's inheritance to her."

Umar responded by saying, "What will you spend on the Muslims if the Arabs decide to fight you?!"

Umar then seized the decree and tore it up!

Fatima was stunned by this act. Disappointed and angry, she left the masjid saying, "You have hurt me and have made me unhappy. Allah is my witness and you will pay for your actions on the Day of Judgment. Be aware that Allah and Muhammad are witness to your actions."

A second version from *Bukhari* is as follows:

Abu Bakr and Umar visited Fatima.

Fatima "If I narrate to you a *hadith* from the prophet will you acknowledge it and act on it?"

They said: "Yes."

She said: " I adjure you by Allah. Did you hear the prophet saying; ' Fatima's contentment is my contentment and her discontentment is my discontentment. Whoever loved Fatima loved me, whoever pleased her pleased me, and whoever displeased her displeased me."

They said: "Yes."

She said: " I call Allah and his angels to witness that you have displeased me and have never pleased me. That, when I meet the prophet, I will complain of both of you to him."[20]

Fatima's place in Islam and in the history of Islam was extraordinarily special. Barbara Stowasser sums it up as follows:[21]

> "A number of traditions on the authority of
> the Prophet establish that Asya (Pharaoh's wife)
> and Mary (Mother of Jesus), Muhammad's
> wife Khadija bint Khuwaylid and Muhammad's
> daughter Fatima are ' the best women of the
> world' and also the ruling females in heaven."

It is important to quote Muhammad's famous, universally accepted hadith: "Fatima is from me and I am from Fatima, who

ever hurts Fatima has hurt me and whoever has hurt me has hurt Allah" and "Fatima is a part of me [Muhammad]."[22]

These dramatic series of events before and after the confiscation of Fadak are to be evaluated under set guidelines in the following chapter. Fadak goes much deeper than the question of the legal rights to a property owned by Muhammad. It opens up a large number of questions not just relating to its ownership, but to a violent breakdown of the entire system on which stood the structure of Islam. A complete analysis of the conditions, political implications, violations of laws, abuse of property rights, abuse of human rights, abuse of women's rights, the validity of ahadith relating to and against it, and most importantly, the desecration of the laws of Islam and Quran are focused on with a truth-seeking mandate.

CHAPTER 2

Ground rules

*"And cover not Truth with falsehood, nor conceal
the Truth when ye know what it is"* (Quran 2:42;
translation, Yousuf Ali).

وَلَا تَلْبِسُوا الْحَقَّ بِالْبَاطِلِ وَتَكْتُمُوا الْحَقَّ وَأَنتُمْ تَعْلَمُونَ

1,400 years of Islamic law and order, discipline, respect for human life, enforcement of women's rights, and restitution of the dignity of women, as well as about 250 years of the enactment of constitutionality and the promotion of democratization and more than 50 years of an international organization with a mandate to maintain peace (United Nations) have sadly regressed.

Dictatorial regimes still exist, monarchy in some areas is healthy and well fed, genocide is in tune, cultural and religious clashes are on the rise, the rise and fall of communism still has live tentacles, economic and social wars are continuously on the horizon, the so-called world order is in a disarray, and the suppression of minorities and weak governments is the story of every nation. Law and order through the UN is a miscalculation, and it stands as an imbalance of the equation between international peace and justice. Its establishment—though not in a democratic sense fair, or its charter free of flaws—still has most of the world looking upon it as a system with laws and authority to enforce justice and

peace, forgetting that it is only those nations themselves that can make the United Nations act in the interest of the world. Unlike the European Union, the United Nations has been established as a weak governing body that can only act when the nations within it decide that action must be undertaken. In the case of Israel vs. Palestine, President Jimmy Carter, in his book *Palestine: Peace not Apartheid,* noted that several United Nations resolutions were enacted against the state of Israel, none of which any UN members decided to act upon. Palestine, on the other hand, has not had a single UN resolution passed against it to date, and though Israel has ignored all of these resolutions, no nation in the UN decided to stand against Israel, therefore effectively preventing the loose fabric of the UN council from acting at all to prevent such military action.[1] This is not to say that Israel is to be criticized or is the discussion of this book, but rather to demonstrate the complete lack of strength the UN holds.

Its programs for human rights, particularly women's rights, have yet to be employed with any level of certainty. The structure of the UN, as noted before, does not even have the authority to implement just laws, set tribunals, and rules because of the special powers it grants to a few who can easily manipulate it in their favor and effectively prevent a UN resolution from passing, and if a resolution were to pass, it would still not hold any strength or validity unless its member nations decided to act upon it.

Constitutions are developed to run governments or international organizations effectively and fairly through synthesized laws that facilitate a controlled environment for freedom under protection. Laws and rules govern the direction of justice. Justice protects human rights. Laws deliver security, creating an environment conducive to peace and a guarantee of individual rights at national and international levels. Laws provide

guidelines to distinguish right and wrong. The case of Fadak is unique in Islam in that it demonstrates the successive stages of events after Muhammad's death that brings to life the violations of the laws of Islam. The ground rules enumerated below act as a lens used to focus on the deep-rooted social and political maneuvering that undermined an idealistically pure and just version of Islam.

The development of ground rules is essential to the process of exploring the historic perspective of Muhammad's character and his Islamic ideals. To understand the underlying events that made Islam a formidable force that changed the course of human destiny, one has to examine the source—Muhammad. From his birth until his proclamation as the last divine messenger of Allah, he presented a character that was an example of perfection. For forty years prior to that proclamation, he lived among the people and interactively carved an image that made his message irresistible even to his staunch enemies. From his first invitation to Islam until his death—a span of twenty-three years—Muhammad was responsible for a staggering number of conversions. His impeccable record on implementing justice provided a magnetic appeal to the message for which he was created. The quotation from Quran that summarizes the impeccability of Muhammad's character is in the following verse:

> And thou (standest) on an exalted standard of
> character. (Quran 68:4; translator, Yousuf Ali)

$$وَإِنَّكَ لَعَلَى خُلُقٍ عَظِيمٍ$$

The word *Azeem* in the above verse is an attribute not easily describable. The vastness of its definability is synonymous to exquisite, immaculate, faultless, flawless, and unmatchable. In this

verse, the word *character* in the broad sense refers to Muhammad's greatness as a man with high-profile mannerisms impregnated with respect and love for fellow human beings. His message continues to transform mankind into his own image. He has left an indelible imprint on thinkers, philosophers, statesmen, scholars, and visionaries. His immediate family of Khatija, Fatima, Ali, Hasan, Husain, Zainab, and Kulsum were cast into his mold. Muslim history and the Quran have introduced his *Ahlul bayth* as role models for mankind. Statesmen, scholars, and peace activists have similarly recognized them for centuries. Anita Rai has compiled an impressive collection of these in her book titled *An Affair of the Heart.*[2]

Submission and surrender to the will of Allah is the basic requirement of accepting Islam. The power of the rules of Islam derived from the Quran in purifying oneself to attain ultimate peace and salvation through the practice of compassion, love, mercy, and respect toward fellow human beings is essential to Islam. Muhammad illustrated that these attributes can be acquired only through uncompromising submission to Allah.

> Whoever submits his whole self to Allah, and
> is a doer of good, has grasped indeed the most
> trustworthy hand-hold: and with Allah rests the
> End and Decision of (all) affairs. (Quran 31:22;
> translator, Yousuf Ali)

وَمَن يُسْلِمْ وَجْهَهُ إِلَى اللَّهِ وَهُوَ مُحْسِنٌ فَقَدِ اسْتَمْسَكَ بِالْعُرْوَةِ الْوُثْقَى وَإِلَى اللَّهِ عَاقِبَةُ الْأُمُورِ

As we begin to lay down the rules, we need to keep in mind that these basic requirements are an important and integral part of our discussions as we begin to extract information to illustrate

our point about the important events directly affecting the Islamic community and its history. The following rules have been carefully prepared to maintain simplicity and comprehensibility as delineated in the Quran:

> O ye who believe! stand out firmly for Allah, as
> witnesses to fair dealing, and let not the hatred
> of others to you make you swerve to wrong and
> depart from justice. Be just: that is next to piety:
> and fear Allah. For Allah is well-acquainted with
> all that ye do. (Quran 5:8; translator, Yousuf Ali)

يَا أَيُّهَا الَّذِينَ آمَنُوا كُونُوا قَوَّامِينَ لِلّهِ شُهَدَاء بِالْقِسْطِ وَلاَ يَجْرِمَنَّكُمْ شَنَآنُ قَوْمٍ عَلَى أَلاَّ تَعْدِلُوا اعْدِلُوا هُوَ أَقْرَبُ لِلتَّقْوَى وَاتَّقُوا اللّهَ إِنَّ اللّهَ خَبِيرٌ بِمَا تَعْمَلُونَ

Firmness in belief and commitment to the Quran is the first step as a Muslim in understanding the profundity of the message and its underlying philosophy. The entire faith is condensed into this fundamental feature that expands into an infinite world of Islam.

Rule 1. Muhammad does not act or speak without revelation from Allah.

Muhammad, according to the Quran, does not say anything on his own except what Allah desires. This implies that every action, statement, and order given by him is based on the revelation from Allah. The Quranic verses that support this statement are:

He (Muhammad) does not speak from his desires,
it is nothing but a revelation revealed to him.
(Quran 53:3; translator, Mir Ahmed Ali)

Nor does he say (aught) of (his own) Desire.
(Quran 53:3; translator, Yousuf Ali)

وَمَا يَنطِقُ عَنِ الْهَوَى

This verse sets the tone of the direction of the ground rules
that are to follow, emphasizing once again their stringent nature.
Muhammad's honesty, fairness, and adherence to the Quran are
established.

He who obeys the Messenger, obeys Allah. But
if any turn away, We have not sent thee to watch
over their (evil deeds). (Quran 4:80; translator,
Yousuf Ali)

مَّنْ يُطِعِ الرَّسُولَ فَقَدْ أَطَاعَ اللَّهَ وَمَن تَوَلَّى فَمَا أَرْسَلْنَاكَ
عَلَيْهِمْ حَفِيظًا

Verily those who plight their fealty to thee do no
less than plight their fealty to Allah. The Hand
of Allah is over their hands: then any one who
violates his oath, does so to the harm of his
own soul, and any one who fulfils what he has
covenanted with Allah,- Allah will soon grant him
a great Reward. (Quran 48:10; translator, Yousuf
Ali)

إِنَّ الَّذِينَ يُبَايِعُونَكَ إِنَّمَا يُبَايِعُونَ اللَّهَ يَدُ اللَّهِ فَوْقَ أَيْدِيهِمْ فَمَن نَّكَثَ فَإِنَّمَا يَنكُثُ عَلَى نَفْسِهِ وَمَنْ أَوْفَى بِمَا عَاهَدَ عَلَيْهُ اللَّهَ فَسَيُؤْتِيهِ أَجْرًا عَظِيمًا

These verses from the Quran form the basis of the first rule. These verses, no matter how one interprets them, lead to one conclusion: that Muhammad's sayings have the same significance as the Quran. The following hadith is a universally accepted hadith; it does not conflict with the Quran and is hence valid:

Muhammad said, "If you hear any hadith that agrees with Quran then accept it; otherwise reject it".[3]

Rule 2. Obedience to Allah is the crux of Islam.

Any action, behavior, historic or political event, episode, legislation, or jurisprudential ruling in conflict with the word of Allah in the Quran or as outlined in Islam would be considered objectionable to Islam and hence un-Islamic.

> Were it to obey and say what is just, and when
> a matter is resolved on, it were best for them if
> they were true to Allah." (Quran 47:21; translator,
> Yousuf Ali)

طَاعَةٌ وَقَوْلٌ مَّعْرُوفٌ فَإِذَا عَزَمَ الْأَمْرُ فَلَوْ صَدَقُوا اللَّهَ لَكَانَ خَيْرًا لَّهُمْ

If any, after this, invent a lie and attribute it to
Allah, they are indeed unjust wrong-doers. (Quran
3:94, translator, Yousuf Ali)

فَمَنِ افْتَرَىٰ عَلَى اللَّهِ الْكَذِبَ مِن بَعْدِ ذَٰلِكَ فَأُوْلَـٰئِكَ هُمُ
الظَّالِمُونَ

Whoever submits his whole self to Allah, and
is a doer of good, has grasped indeed the most
trustworthy hand-hold: and with Allah rests the
End and Decision of (all) affairs. (Quran 31:22;
translator, Yousuf Ali)

وَمَن يُسْلِمْ وَجْهَهُ إِلَى اللَّهِ وَهُوَ مُحْسِنٌ فَقَدِ اسْتَمْسَكَ بِالْعُرْوَةِ
الْوُثْقَىٰ وَإِلَى اللَّهِ عَاقِبَةُ الْأُمُورِ

Disobedience to Allah is considered suicide of one's belief in
the religion. Any action of an individual, whether he or she is in
a responsible leadership position or not, will be judged by these
rules. The primary objective of an administrator and implementer
of the laws extracted from the Quran is his ability to maintain these
laws effectively and diligently. His methods of implementation of
these laws as an administrator will serve as a determining factor
of his skills as a supreme commander dedicated to manage the
welfare of the *Umma* (community) honorably and justly.

Rule 3. Only ahadith and sunnah consistent with the Quran
can be accepted.

A hadith, narrated by Imam Fakhru'd-Din Razi in his *Tafsir
Kabir* reports that the Prophet said, "When a hadith from me is

reported to you, put it before the Book of Allah. If it agrees with the Holy Qur'an, accept it. Otherwise, reject it."[4]

All ahadith that are in conflict with the Quran are to be automatically discarded as unreliable, irrespective of whom the narrator was. The science of hadith has unfortunately created havoc in the religious and legislative processes of Muslim communities for centuries. Heads of state have abused the laws of Islam in the name of Khilafath through manipulation of ahadith to serve their interests. As a result, the history of Khilafath is overwhelmingly burdened with conflicts between itself and the Quran and Islam. Unfortunately, "history of Khilafath" has inappropriately acquired the name of "history of the Islam."

The application of this rule leads toward the historic events and episodes recorded that are subject to human error, recorder's idiosyncrasies, and prejudices. Any action of Muhammad recorded in histories in conflict with the Quran would automatically become null and void for the reason that Muhammad is created in the image of Quran and that his words and actions are synchronous with the Quran. Muhammad and his Ahlul Bayth have a special place in the Quran and Islam. Developments of histories on numerous occasions have demonstrated malice toward them under strategic orders of the ruling parties. But the charisma of their characters has never failed to outshine their enemies.

A further complication has emerged since the advent of Islam, in that the terms *history of Islam* and *Muslim history* have been intermittently and wrongly used to suggest that the words Islam and Muslim are interchangeable. This view is false and misleading. The history of Islam and the histories of Muslim rulers/histories of Khilafath follow completely opposite paths. The first one represents the path of the divine will, while the latter is bound by the will of a monarch, dictator, or ruler with

his or her own agenda. Islam does not tolerate its followers to deviate from its principles and still remain Muslim. It is outrageous that the name of Islam has been desecrated throughout history by Muslim dictators and tyrants while the genuine religious authorities have invariably found themselves at the receiving end of the deal. Islam is a religion of peace and harmony. Aggression, suppression, and repression are not acceptable alternatives under any circumstances. The Quran clearly dictates that religion is optional and cannot be imposed or forced upon anyone. It is by free will and not by force that a person accepts Islam, and it is the duty of a religious leader to represent the community with exemplary Islamic moral values set by the Quran.

> Let there be no compulsion in religion: Truth stands out clear from Error: whoever rejects evil and believes in Allah hath grasped the most trustworthy hand-hold, that never breaks. And Allah heareth and knoweth all things. (Quran 2:256; translator, Yousuf Ali)

لَا إِكْرَاهَ فِي الدِّينِ قَد تَّبَيَّنَ الرُّشْدُ مِنَ الْغَيِّ فَمَنْ يَكْفُرْ بِالطَّاغُوتِ وَيُؤْمِن بِاللَّهِ فَقَدِ اسْتَمْسَكَ بِالْعُرْوَةِ الْوُثْقَىٰ لَا انفِصَامَ لَهَا وَاللَّهُ سَمِيعٌ عَلِيمٌ

Let us not forget that the freedom and openness proudly heralded as the most essential part of the process of democratization was put forth into law by Islam some 1,400 years ago and that the Muslim monarchs were the first to undermine this principle of their faith. Selected events recorded in the histories of Muslim rulers and early Khilafath play an important

role in shedding light on this aspect and its impact on the course of Islam.

Muhammad was a paradigm of leadership. As a Muslim with supreme authority, he carried out the tasks assigned to him by Allah to perfection. He was a miracle of the Quran, as stated below.

> And thou (Muhammad, standest) on an exalted standard of character. (Quran 68:4; translator, Yousuf Ali)

وَإِنَّكَ لَعَلَى خُلُقٍ عَظِيمٍ

The character of a Muslim is of utmost importance in Islam. Allah's judgment is dependent upon whether a person as an ordinary Muslim or as a khalif has maintained his or her moral ethical standards of Islam.

> Verily, We create man in the best conformation. (Quran 95:4; translator, Yousuf Ali)

لَقَدْ خَلَقْنَا الْإِنسَانَ فِي أَحْسَنِ تَقْوِيمٍ

A human being is an awesome creation. He is equipped with extraordinary abilities impossible to duplicate. His amazing makeup remains a mystery. His marvelous body is a physiological miracle. The intricately connected components making up a human structure are synchronized to allow coordination

between body and mind in a uniquely designed configuration. Physicians and scientists alike have spent their entire lives trying to understand the complexities of a simple thing, such as the functions of uniquely designed cell structures. Every discovery is punctuated by a new challenge. This process presents itself in every aspect of a human being, with brain and mind being the ultimate challenge. The human mind is specifically outfitted with exceptional powers of reason and judgment. These qualities are incorporated so that justice is served proficiently.

One of the attributes that a human brings into this world is his inner self. This built-in attribute has been embedded in the conscience and provides distinction between wrong and right. Moral faculty, hence, serves as a judge of one's actions. This quality installed in one's conscience is programmed to allow freedom of choice between good, bad, wrong, and right. This characteristic is subconsciously ingrained in the conscience and is a resulting attribute that a human acquires from training as well as from interactive learning experiences as one blends into society. The cause and effect through experimentation and observation are designed to teach various natural responses to activities one is involved with. The net result is that no matter how one develops his or her character, one is aware of the effects he or she is responsible for.

A true representative of Islam receives the honor of managing the Islamic society according to the will of Allah by suppressing his personal desires. The development of Islamic history is significantly dependent on the character and moral fiber of the khalifas, Muhadetheen (hadith collectors), and historians.

> It is not fitting for a Believer, man or woman,
> when a matter has been decided by Allah and
> His Messenger to have any option about their

decision: if anyone disobeys Allah and His
Messenger, he is indeed on a clearly wrong Path.
(Quran 33:36; translator, Yousuf Ali)

وَمَا كَانَ لِمُؤْمِنٍ وَلَا مُؤْمِنَةٍ إِذَا قَضَى اللَّهُ وَرَسُولُهُ أَمْرًا أَن
يَكُونَ لَهُمُ الْخِيَرَةُ مِنْ أَمْرِهِمْ وَمَن يَعْصِ اللَّهَ وَرَسُولَهُ فَقَدْ
ضَلَّ ضَلَالًا مُّبِينًا

They say, "We believe in Allah and in the apostle,
and we obey": but even after that, some of them
turn away: they are not (really) Believers. (Quran
24:47; translator, Yousuf Ali)

وَيَقُولُونَ آمَنَّا بِاللَّهِ وَبِالرَّسُولِ وَأَطَعْنَا ثُمَّ يَتَوَلَّى فَرِيقٌ مِّنْهُم
مِّن بَعْدِ ذَلِكَ وَمَا أُوْلَئِكَ بِالْمُؤْمِنِينَ

When they are summoned to Allah and His
apostle, in order that He may judge between
them, behold some of them decline (to come).
(Quran 24:48; translator, Yousuf Ali).

وَإِذَا دُعُوا إِلَى اللَّهِ وَرَسُولِهِ لِيَحْكُمَ بَيْنَهُمْ إِذَا فَرِيقٌ مِّنْهُم
مُّعْرِضُونَ

The answer of the Believers, when summoned to
Allah and His Messenger, in order that He may
judge between them, is no other than this: they
say, "We hear and we obey": it is such as these
that will attain felicity. (Quran 24:51; translator,
Yousuf Ali)

إِنَّمَا كَانَ قَوْلَ الْمُؤْمِنِينَ إِذَا دُعُوا إِلَى اللَّهِ وَرَسُولِهِ لِيَحْكُمَ
بَيْنَهُمْ أَن يَقُولُوا سَمِعْنَا وَأَطَعْنَا وَأُوْلَئِكَ هُمُ الْمُفْلِحُونَ

From the above verses of the Quran, one can deduce the prescribed qualities in every Muslim, particularly in those who have taken charge of administration and are responsible for the legislation of the laws of Islam, especially those laws that implement equality and justice. Just laws of Islam have a single standard across the board, and the responsibility of the administrator is to govern with equality irrespective of race, creed, class, clan support, friendship, and relationships. Simplistically, any deviation from these rules would be categorized as failure to the will of Allah, Muhammad, and the Quran.

The criteria for the appointment of a vicegerent (Khilafath) are based on three factors: Knowledge, ability and strength to defend and protect Islam, and the capacity to be a just authority under all circumstances. The responsibilities of a Khalif, as outlined in the Quran, are clearly mentioned in the following verse:

> O David! We did indeed make thee a vicegerent
> on earth: so judge thou between men in truth
> (and justice): Nor follow thou the lusts (of thy
> heart), for they will mislead thee from the Path
> of Allah. For those who wander astray from the
> Path of Allah, is a Penalty Grievous, for that
> they forget the Day of Account. (Quran 38:26;
> translator Yousuf Ali)

يَا دَاوُودُ إِنَّا جَعَلْنَاكَ خَلِيفَةً فِي الْأَرْضِ فَاحْكُم بَيْنَ النَّاس
بِالْحَقِّ وَلَا تَتَّبِع الْهَوَى فَيُضِلَّكَ عَن سَبِيلِ اللَّهِ إِنَّ الَّذِينَ
يَضِلُّونَ عَن سَبِيلِ اللَّهِ لَهُمْ عَذَابٌ شَدِيدٌ بِمَا نَسُوا يَوْمَ
الْحِسَابِ

The above verse sets the criteria for the required characteristics of a Khalifa. Justice appears to be the primary required commitment of a Khalifa of Allah to carry out his duties. Jacob is informed of this very special and essential component of becoming a representative of Islam and thus Allah, the other characteristics being a strong command of the Quran, *Shariah* (see note 1 for more details), the principles of the religion of Islam, and the ability to be a physically strong leader who can represent the community with courage and fearlessness. The three ground rules set forth above have to be applied in every case to evaluate the events, actions, and the determination of one's will as a leader in Islam. Any deviation from these ground rules would deem that action and an event as contemptible in view of the Quran. Again, the focus is on honesty, fairness and justice, and a reminder that in the end there will be accountability for your deeds in this world.

CHAPTER 3

The Foundations and Establishment

"Know they not that for those who oppose Allah and His Messenger, is the Fire of Hell?- wherein they shall dwell. That is the supreme disgrace" (Quran 9:63; translator, Yousuf Ali).

أَلَمْ يَعْلَمُواْ أَنَّهُ مَن يُحَادِدِ اللّهَ وَرَسُولَهُ فَأَنَّ لَهُ نَارَ جَهَنَّمَ خَالِدًا فِيهَا ذَلِكَ الْخِزْيُ الْعَظِيمُ

Muhammad, from birth to the announcement of Islam, had built an unmatched reputation of honesty, trust, and respect. Forty years prior to the introduction of Islam, Muhammad had been preaching Islam indirectly and interactively. From his creation up until his formal introduction of Islam, he had been presenting to his fellow humans an exemplary Islamic character that was irresistible to ignore in a society deprived of human values, such as respect, honor, mercy, fair play, and love. Muhammad was preparing the path and gathering resources to build a divine empire from where the Almighty would lift mankind to its highest level of perfection. Muhammad and Khadija had shared the same ancestors. Muhammad, a distant cousin of Khadija, had turned into a successful partner. She was a woman of high profile in the world of business in an area and time where women were considered a disgrace and a liability to the family, a trend

characteristic of the society of Jahiliah. Muhammad and Khadija had started out in a business relationship that later culminated in a wedlock. They were amalgamated and synchronized to develop a nation—a complete system of life. They were given a daughter, Fatima, who was enviably positioned to be wedded with Ali Ibn Abi Talib. Fatima was seen by Muslims as being specifically saved by Allah to allow Muhammad's progeny to continue indefinitely. The explosive growth of Islam from a handful of people in 620 AD to more than a billion today is to be shared between Muhammad and Khadija. Khadija's sacrifices unquestionably energized the spread of Islam under Muhammad's leadership. Khadija's dose of energy that was comprised of all her wealth, as well as her social and spiritual life, was given away for the future of Islam. Khadija's only husband was Muhammad. Khadija's place in Islam and her stature in the life of Muhammad were unrivaled. Muhammad's love for Khadija was exclusive and unparalleled. Khadija had the distinction of being the first to accept Islam and also of raising Fatima and Ali, two matchless personalities of Islam that Muhammad himself exquisitely raised to advance Islam.

Khadija and Ali were already exposed to this revolutionary belief of a monolithic philosophy. Ali was brought up and trained by Muhammad and was a witness to all the revelations from the beginning. When Muhammad recognized that the time had come for him to introduce Allah's message to the world, he called for help and support of Khadija, Ali, and Abu Talib (Ali's father and Muhammad's paternal uncle), who had provided him shelter from the time that he was only five years old. Ali and Abu Talib convened the gathering for Muhammad to present Islam to the sons and relatives of Abdu'l Muttalib. The main helpers were Ali and Khadija. Among those who were invited were representatives of Quraysh clans Abbas, Hamza, Abu Laheb, and others.[1]

Predictably, Muhammad's first call to Islam turned into a
devastating blow to the people whose centuries-old beliefs were
not only being challenged, but were also being denounced.
Confused and humiliated, all those who were invited turned down
the message of Islam.[1] Ali, then a nine (or ten) year old, stood up
and pledged his commitment to Islam. This process was repeated
for the following two days, and each day only the nine year old
stood up to pledge his allegiance to Muhammad and Islam. Upon
hearing this from Ali, Muhammad said "This is my brother, my
executor, and my successor among you. Harken to him and obey
him."[2] Obviously, Khadija was the first to accept Islam, with
Ali being the second. It is interesting to note that among those
who not only refused to accept Islam but also threatened to kill
Muhammad were Abu Lahab and Abu Jahal.[3] Abu Sufyan, the
leader representing the clan of Bani Umayyah, later joined Abu
Lahab to pursue Muhammad. The following is a translation from
Ahmad Bin Hanbal masnad:

> The Prophet stood up among them and said: "O
> descendants of Abdu'l-Muttalib! Allah Almighty
> has sent me as a messenger to the whole of
> creation in general and to you in particular.
> I invite you to make two statements that are
> light and easy for the tongue, but on the scale
> of action they are heavy. If you make the two
> statements, you will be masters of the lands of
> the Arabs and the non-Arabs. Through them you
> will go to Paradise and will obtain immunity from
> Hell. These two expressions are: first, to bear
> witness to Allah's Oneness, and second, to bear
> witness to my prophethood. The one who first
> of all acknowledges my call and helps me in my

mission is my brother, my helper, my heir, and my
successor after me."

The Prophet repeated the last sentence three
times, and each time none except Ali responded
to him, saying, "I will aid and help you, O
Prophet of Allah!" So the Prophet declared:
"This Ali is my brother, and he is my successor
and Caliph among you."[4]

Zayd bin Haritha was the second male to accept Islam. The
disbelievers were angry about this new faith and had already
initiated a campaign to stop this radical movement that was about
to storm the Arab world. With support and protection from his
paternal uncle Abu Talib and his cousin Ali, Muhammad started
to make headway in spreading the word of Allah. Muhammad's
aggressive movement was experiencing resistance and setbacks.
Difficulties during his preachings in Mecca, his migration to
Madina, the siege of Muhammad's family, and the deaths of
Abu Talib and Khadija had put Muhammad and his family
through a vortex of agony. However, the glamour and allure of
this message was slowly gripping the community's think tanks,
and new converts were falling into the folds of Islam. The Bani
Ummayah's representative Abu Sufyan, as well as Abu Lahab,
who was representing the Quresh, created the two strongest
opponents of this new movement. The first clash between the
combined forces of Abu Sufyan and Abu Lahab and the relatively
weak force of Muhammad took place at the battle of Badar.[6]

Among the elite who brought victory were Ali (the young
cousin of Muhammad), Muhammad's uncle Hamza, and Ubayda
b. Harith. They were the spotlight in the heated action of the
war. Ali had killed a great majority of the enemies, and among
those killed were many members of Abu Sufyan's family. Abu

Sufyan had lost many of his relatives in this war. Hamza had the second-highest number of enemies to his credit. Others who were present in this war were Abu Bakr and Umar, and also there was Uthman, who preferred to stay on the sidelines for the most of the heated battle.[7]

The Battle of Uhad (second major battle) brought some of these hidden personalities, infiltrators, and hypocrites into the open. The battle, which had been being won by the Muslims, turned into a loss. The group that was supposed to stay in place in a strategically defensive position on a mount had left to collect booty against the orders of Muhammad. Muhammad was injured, and the enemy circulated a rumor that Muhammad had died, which created chaos and confusion. Ali and Fatima were with him, but a large group of his army defected from the war. Among those who ran for cover were Abu Bakr , Umar, and Uthman.[8]

Bukhari:

Volume 4, Book 51, Number 28: [9]

The Prophet said, "Avoid the seven great
destructive sins." The people enquire, "O Allah's
Apostle! What are they? "He said, "To join others
in worship along with Allah, to practice sorcery,
to kill the life which Allah has forbidden except
for a just cause, (according to Islamic law), to eat
up Riba (usury), to eat up an orphan's wealth,
to give back to the enemy and fleeing from the
battlefield at the time of fighting, and to accuse,
chaste women, who never even think of anything
touching chastity and are good believers.

Hamza, Muhammad's uncle, was killed. The Quresh, represented by Abu Sufyan, mutilated the bodies of Muslims who had sacrificed their lives for Islam. Hinda, the wife of Abu Sufyan and mother of Muawiah ibn Abu Sufyan who was famous for her promiscuity and barbaric voracity, chewed the liver of Humza in the battlefield.[10] Ironically, the son of Hinda, Muawiah, became a Khalif later. Ali had once again played a central role in this battle.

The Battle of Khandaq is especially important, because it was initially single-handedly won by Ali, as he set the tone for the rest of the battle to come during his opening clash with Amr Ibn Abduwad. This is the battle in which the newly founded Muslims faced the coalesced forces of Quresh, the Jews, and the Christians. The Muslims had dug a trench, as recommended by Salman-e-Farsi, to fend off the attack by the coalition forces. Amr ibn Abduwad, a legendary warrior of the time, managed to cross the trench and challenged Muhammad to send a soldier to fight him. Each time Muhammad asked his elite soldiers if there was anyone who would stand up against Amr's challenge, only Ali stood up. Among those present were Abu Bakr, Umar, Uthman, Abbas, and others. Ali took the challenge and offered Amr the option to accept Islam or to return. When he declined, Ali vanquished him after an aggressive exchange of strokes.[11] This was yet another victory of Ali that brought success to the Muslims and Islam.

The battle of Khayber is a eulogy in praise of Ali. The Jews had barricaded themselves inside the fort of Khayber, and the Muslims were facing great difficulty breaking the entry door that normally required more than ten, or by some reports forty, men to open it. Muhammad first sent Abu Bakr, who fought and came back after heavy losses. The next day he sent Umar, only to see him

meet with the same dismal results. On that same day, Muhammad said, "By Allah tomorrow I shall give the opportunity to the one who loves Allah and His Messenger, and whom Allah and His Messenger love , and who will take it in humble obedience."[12] The following day, he called Ali and gave the flag of Islam and command to him. Ali captured Khayber. A very interesting account of the details of this fierce battle led successfully by Ali is given in Tabari, as well as in Ibn Ishaq's *Sirath Rasul Allah*.[13] An important aspect of this war is its connection to the issue of Fadak. The Jews realized their inability to defend against the forces of Muhammad and decided to give Fadak without contest as a gift to him. Fadak thus became Muhammad's personal property given to him by the Jews.[14]

The following verse was stated on this occasion:

> Your Lord is He that maketh the Ship go
> smoothly for you through the sea, in order that ye
> may seek of his Bounty. For he is unto you most
> Merciful. (Quran 17:66)

رَّبُّكُمُ الَّذِي يُزْجِي لَكُمُ الْفُلْكَ فِي الْبَحْرِ لِتَبْتَغُوا مِن فَضْلِهِ إِنَّهُ كَانَ بِكُمْ رَحِيمًا

We shall come back to this when we begin our deliberations on Fadak.

"Sura Tawbah – Sura Barah" incites a strong sense of merit-based preferences between Muhammad's companions. The verses, which relate to the prohibition of the idolaters from entering Kaaba (house of Allah), circumambulating Kaaba without clothes, and dishonoring their pact (suleh Hudaibiyah) with Muslims, were initially given to Abu Bakr from Surah

Tawbah for public announcement. He was on his way to Kaaba to announce these verses when Muhammad received a revelation from Allah ordering him that these verses be read either by him (Muhammad) or someone from him (someone of his stature). Muhammad called Ali and explained to him the new development and ordered him to stop Abu Bakr and take over the responsibility of reciting the verses of Sura Tawbah. Ali took over the task from Abu Bakr and delivered the verses at Kaabah among the enemies of Islam. A disappointed Abu Bakr approached Muhammad and asked him what had brought about this change. Muhammad repeated the revelation he received from Allah ordering the change in assignment of the mission to be completed only by him (Muhammad) <u>or someone like him</u> (of Muhammad's status).[15]

Muhammad's final pilgrimage carried a mandate that he had to fulfill under the revelation from Allah that was guaranteed to keep the Muslims from going astray after him. His sermons throughout this pilgrimage bore significant importance. The final sermon at Ghadir-e-Khumm was meant to bear an everlasting impression on the Umma, as Allah was planning to confer vicegerency on Ali, similar to the way he conferred Moses's successorship to his brother Aaron.

Ghadir-e-Khumm was demographically a strategic place; it was a point of divergence from which the pilgrims usually split in different directions. The stage was set by Allah to assign the mission of carrying the weight of vicegerency to Ali ibn Abi Talib. Details of this important event in the history of Islam have been presented in many books.[16] Interestingly, Umar and Abu Bakr were among the first few who congratulated Ali for his succession[17]. Muhammad completed his obligation by announcing before a gathering of more than a hundred thousand pilgrims (according to some sources), "Of whomsoever I am the Maula,

(master) this Ali is his Maula." After this he raised his hand and prayed to Allah. "O Allah, be you a friend to him who is a friend to him (that is, Ali) and be an enemy to him who is an enemy to him (Ali). Help him who helps Ali and forsake him who forsakes Ali."[18] The famous historian of the fourth century, Hijri Abu Ja'far Muhammad Bin Jarir Tabari (died 310 A.H.), gives complete details of the hadith of Ghadir in his book *Kitabu'l-Wilaya* and has narrated it through a chain of seventy-five transmitters.[19]

The following verse was revealed upon completion of the above assignment.

> This day have I perfected your religion for you,
> completed my favour upon you, and have chosen
> for you Islam as your religion. But if any is forced
> by hunger, with no inclination to transgression,
> Allah is indeed Oft-forgiving, Most Merciful."
> (Quran 5:3; translator, Yousuf Ali)

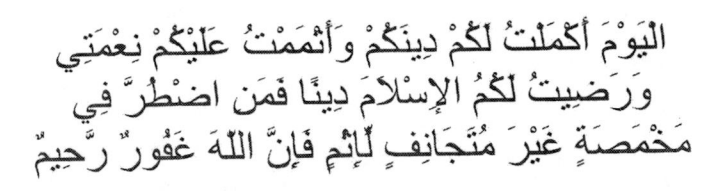

اليَوْمَ أَكْمَلْتُ لَكُمْ دِينَكُمْ وَأَتْمَمْتُ عَلَيْكُمْ نِعْمَتِي وَرَضِيتُ لَكُمُ الْإِسْلَامَ دِينًا فَمَنِ اضْطُرَّ فِي مَخْمَصَةٍ غَيْرَ مُتَجَانِفٍ لِإِثْمٍ فَإِنَّ اللَّهَ غَفُورٌ رَّحِيمٌ

This event has been labeled as highly controversial for political sectarian reasons. The fact of the matter is that this event was real and has been shoved under tons of pages written in its denial. After this ceremony, Umar was the first one who said to Ali "May this position be pleasing to you, for now you are my master and the master of all the believers."[20] Bahrani has cited eighty-nine Sunni and seven Shia sources.[21]

Let there arise out of you a band of people
inviting to all that is good, enjoining what is right,
and forbidding what is wrong: They are the ones
to attain felicity. Be not like those who are divided
among themselves and fall into disputations after
receiving Clear Signs: For them is a dreadful
penalty." (Quran 3:104–5; translator, Yousuf Ali)

وَلْتَكُن مِّنكُمْ أُمَّةٌ يَدْعُونَ إِلَى الْخَيْرِ وَيَأْمُرُونَ
بِالْمَعْرُوفِ وَيَنْهَوْنَ عَنِ الْمُنكَرِ وَأُوْلَـئِكَ هُمُ
الْمُفْلِحُونَ
وَلاَ تَكُونُواْ كَالَّذِينَ تَفَرَّقُواْ وَاخْتَلَفُواْ مِن بَعْدِ مَا
جَاءهُمُ الْبَيِّنَاتُ وَأُوْلَـئِكَ لَهُمْ عَذَابٌ عَظِيمٌ

Muhammad had delivered his last message. He knew that
his task had come to a conclusion; that his time on earth was
to be drawn short soon. His last days were nearing, and the
environment around him was growing hostile. Underhanded
political maneuvering had already begun, and his final orders and
requests were to be denied by those he had treated as close friends.
The episode that needs special attention is the refusal to provide
paper and pen to Muhammad upon request before his death. To
recapitulate the events briefly, let us look at Umar's words: "(The)
Prophet of Allah is hallucinating, the book of Allah is enough
for us." Some have also noted the following statement from
Umar: "What is the matter with him? Is he talking nonsense?"
Was this reaction of Umar to Muhammad's orders for a pen and
paper to execute Allah's will and advice to the Umma acceptable?
Muhammad was very furious at this response. He angrily shunned
them (Umar and others).[22] (See note 1.)

The blame is only against those who oppress
men and wrong-doing and insolently transgress

beyond bounds through the land, defying right
and justice: for such there will be a penalty
grievous. (Quran 42:42; translator, Yousuf Ali)

إِنَّمَا السَّبِيلُ عَلَى الَّذِينَ يَظْلِمُونَ النَّاسَ وَيَبْغُونَ فِي
الْأَرْضِ بِغَيْرِ الْحَقِّ أُوْلَئِكَ لَهُم عَذَابٌ أَلِيمٌ

This direct denial of paper and pen to the Prophet has serious
political, ethical, and moral implications. This behavior at best
can be described as disobedience to Muhammad, unwillingness
to trust the words of the Quran (in which Muhammad is stated
to be a direct speaker under Allah's will), and the denial of the
will of Allah to the followers of Islam.[23] The following verses
characterize the response of the Quran in reference to this
episode:

> He (Muhammad) does not speak from his desires,
> it is nothing but a revelation revealed to him.
> (Quran 53:3)

وَمَا يَنطِقُ عَنِ الْهَوَى

The statement about Muhammad hallucinating is insulting.
It undermines the Quran and in turn draws into question their
validity as Muslims, and it also shows that they fail to live up to
the fundamental expectations of a Muslim. The person (Umar)
who said that the Book (the Quran) was enough was breaking his
own tenet.

Those who annoy Allah and His Messenger -
Allah has cursed them in this World and in the
Hereafter, and has prepared for them a humiliating
Punishment. (33:57; translator, Yousuf Ali)

إِنَّ الَّذِينَ يُؤْذُونَ اللَّهَ وَرَسُولَهُ لَعَنَهُمُ اللَّهُ فِي الدُّنْيَا
وَالْآخِرَةِ وَأَعَدَّ لَهُمْ عَذَابًا مُّهِينًا

Muhammad was so angry at the behavior of Umar that he
ordered the group to be removed from his sight.[24]

And this is a Book which we have revealed as a
blessing: so follow it and be righteous, that ye may
receive mercy. (Quran 6:155; translator, Yousuf
Ali)

وَهَـٰذَا كِتَابٌ أَنزَلْنَاهُ مُبَارَكٌ فَاتَّبِعُوهُ وَاتَّقُوا لَعَلَّكُمْ
تُرْحَمُونَ

A True follower of Islam who is aware of this episode is
compelled to either believe the Quran as the ultimate word of
Allah or agree with Umar's response and ignore the Quran. These
tragic sequences of actions clearly demonstrate the violation of
every rule we put forth in the last chapter.

Muhammad is no more than an apostle: many
Were the apostle that passed away before him.
If he died or were slain, will ye then Turn back
on your heels? If any did turn back on his heels,
not the least harm will he do to Allah. but Allah

(on the other hand) will swiftly reward those
who (serve Him) with gratitude. (Quran 3:144;
translator, Yousuf Ali)

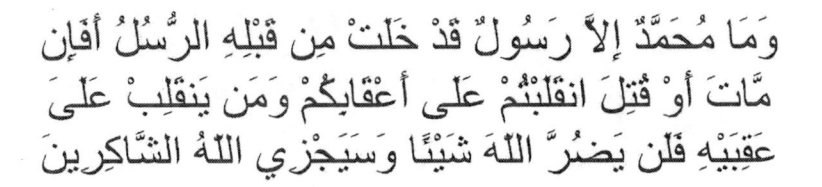

وَمَا مُحَمَّدٌ إِلاَّ رَسُولٌ قَدْ خَلَتْ مِن قَبْلِهِ الرُّسُلُ أَفَإِن
مَّاتَ أَوْ قُتِلَ انقَلَبْتُمْ عَلَى أَعْقَابِكُمْ وَمَن يَنقَلِبْ عَلَىَ
عَقِبَيْهِ فَلَن يَضُرَّ اللّهَ شَيْئًا وَسَيَجْزِي اللّهُ الشَّاكِرِينَ

Sadly, dissention, disobedience, contentious quarreling, and disregard for Muhammad's orders plagued the last few days of Muhammad's life. This made him furious. There were two distinct groups emerging out of this chaos. Those who loved and were concerned about Muhammad and his well-being and those who were looking out for their own interests should any thing happen to Muhammad. The environment was highly polarized. Aisha (Abu Bakr's daughter) and Hafsa (Umar's daughter) were working from inside to make the best out of this in the interest of their parents at the time Muhammad was nearing death.

Ibn Abbas said, " The Messanger of Allah asked for Ali." But Aisha said, "I wished you had asked for Abu Bakr!" And Hafsa said, " I wish you had asked for Umar."[25] The accounts of these are well documented in several books.[26] Muhammad obviously was asking for Ali to make sure that his mission was transferred into the hands of Ali and that his will was conveyed to the community in accordance with the command of Allah. It is obvious that Muhammad was not comfortable among Aisha and Hafza. Their response indicates that the developments taking place around Muhammad at a critical juncture of his life were against his will. This was also the point where two different schools of thought with opposite motives, beliefs, and agendas were sprouting.

CHAPTER 4

The Coup at Saquifa

"If anyone contends with the Messenger even after guidance has been plainly conveyed to him, and follows a path other than that becoming to men of Faith, We shall leave him in the path he has chosen, and land him in Hell,- what an evil refuge!" (Quran 4:115; translator, Yousuf Ali).

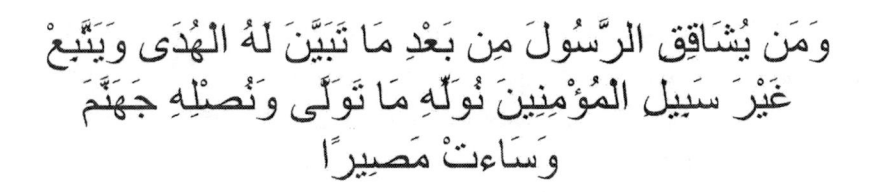

The messiah of reform, innovation, peace and love sent to humanity had completed his task. The only message Allah was adamant to deliver to the Umma was conveyed at Ghadir-e-Khumm.[1] See Appendix 1.

O Messenger. proclaim the (message) which hath been sent to thee from thy Lord. If thou didst not, thou wouldst not have fulfilled and proclaimed His mission. And Allah will defend thee from men (who mean mischief). For Allah guideth not those who reject Faith. (Quran 5:67; translator , Yousuf Ali)

يَا أَيُّهَا الرَّسُولُ بَلِّغْ مَا أُنزِلَ إِلَيْكَ مِن رَّبِّكَ وَإِن لَّمْ
تَفْعَلْ فَمَا بَلَّغْتَ رِسَالَتَهُ وَاللّهُ يَعْصِمُكَ مِنَ النَّاسِ إِنَّ
اللّهَ لاَ يَهْدِي الْقَوْمَ الْكَافِرِينَ

The above verse was the last element, a final word that was designed to set the direction intended for mankind by Allah. The strong warning to Muhammad about the task of declaring his successor connoted that if he did not carry out this mission from Allah, all his sacrifices and efforts would become futile. Muhammad had declared before a crowd of more than a 100,000 in Ghadir-e-khumm: "To whomsoever I am the master, Ali is his master." The verse of the Quran and the execution of the task associated with the Ghadir event have been debated for centuries and have been discussed in detail in many books, and this is not the intent of this book.[2] On numerous occasions, Muhammad made statements that Ali was his *wasi* (legatee), and none had disputed this fact. The following part of the verse was a follow up after the completion of the task of declaring his successor:

> This day have I perfected your religion for
> you, completed My favour upon you, and have
> chosen for you Islam as your religion. (Quran 5:3;
> translator, Yousuf Ali)

الْيَوْمَ أَكْمَلْتُ لَكُمْ دِينَكُمْ وَأَتْمَمْتُ عَلَيْكُمْ نِعْمَتِي
وَرَضِيتُ لَكُمُ الإِسْلاَمَ دِينًا

Muhammad, who was considered to have uplifted and dignified the status of man to perfection as stated in the Quran, was gone. His family had lost an icon of love and support. Hurled

into grief and sorrow, the family was in a state of deep shock and trauma as they started his burial preparations. The paradigm of freedom, liberation, and justice no longer existed. The community was under emotional distress and sorrow. The man who infused new life into a society lacking discipline, honor, and morality had left the world. His charisma suddenly disappeared from the scene, and the vacuum created by his loss was being viewed as an opportunity to grab power by some.

In general, the public reaction at a loss of a leader of the status of Muhammad should have been overwhelmingly sympathetic, sorrowful, and full of grief, and people should have poured out in large numbers to provide support. Usually, the family of the deceased is overwhelmed by the sympathies of their well-wishers. This is a natural phenomenon that is a part of every culture, tribe, and clan. The community's response at the time of the death of Muhammad should have been overpowering, passionately sorrowful, and sad. His friends, supporters, and followers should have been by the side of his family, extending condolences and support by lending a hand in the burial ceremonies.

> He who desires might and glory [ought to
> know that] all might and glory belong to God
> [alone]. Unto Him ascend all good words, and
> the righteous deed does He exalt. But as for
> those who cunningly devise evil deeds - suffering
> severe awaits them; and all their devising is bound
> to come to nought. (Quran 35:10; translator,
> Muhammad Asad)

مَن كَانَ يُرِيدُ الْعِزَّةَ فَلِلَّهِ الْعِزَّةُ جَمِيعًا إِلَيْهِ يَصْعَدُ الْكَلِمُ الطَّيِّبُ وَالْعَمَلُ الصَّالِحُ يَرْفَعُهُ وَالَّذِينَ يَمْكُرُونَ السَّيِّئَاتِ لَهُمْ عَذَابٌ شَدِيدٌ وَمَكْرُ أُوْلَئِكَ هُوَ يَبُورُ

The conditions at the time of Muhammad's death, however, were drastically abnormal. The atmosphere was unfriendly and hostile. The people that were known to be his friends and supporters had turned against his progeny. History shows that Muhammad's body was deliberately left unattended in the hands of his immediate family. Fatima, Ali, and their friends were the only ones busy preparing for his burial. Some took advantage of the circumstances and rushed to Saqifa, where politicking for leadership was underway. Abu Bakr and Umar, upon being informed of Muhammad's death, raced to Saqifa to interject themselves in the leadership selection process.[3] Was this a normal response to the death of their leader? Does this conduct bear any accord to the compassion reiterated in the Quran?

This subversive event of early history appears to have been evolved out of age-old animosities and clan-based prejudices as the selection/election of a Khalifa began with an explosive burst of energy. The vicegerency (Khalifath) is a vital portfolio conferred on a person who has demonstrated a high level of *Taqwa*[4] and compassion with full commitment and devotion to implement justice under all circumstances by Allah. The first Khalifa was Adam. Abraham (Ibrahim) was also bestowed with this honorable status of Khilafath as well as Immamath,[5] and after progressively completing a series of important tests (including a test of his willingness to offer to sacrifice his son in the way of Allah), he became one of the five grand messiahs of Allah. Similarly, all other Apostles of Allah were granted this

title upon demonstration of the durability of their faith and commitment to Islam. The prerequisite to Khilafath is to provide unconditional commitment to justice, comprehensive knowledge of the Quran, the ability to implement laws derived from the Quran, and direct experience and knowledge of Muhammad's actions and sayings from the beginning to the last breath of his life, which included the legislative, political, social, spiritual, and philosophical rudiments of Islam.

> O David! We did indeed make thee a vicegerent
> on earth: so judge thou between men in truth
> (and justice): Nor follow thou the lusts (of thy
> heart), for they will mislead thee from the Path
> of Allah. For those who wander astray from the
> Path of Allah, is a Penalty Grievous, for that
> they forget the Day of Account. (Quran 38:26;
> translator, Yousuf Ali)

يَا دَاوُودُ إِنَّا جَعَلْنَاكَ خَلِيفَة فِي الْأَرْضِ فَاحْكُم بَيْنَ النَّاسِ بِالْحَقِّ وَلَا تَتَّبِعِ الْهَوَى فَيُضِلَّكَ عَن سَبِيلِ اللَّهِ إِنَّ الَّذِينَ يَضِلُّونَ عَن سَبِيلِ اللَّهِ لَهُمْ عَذَابٌ شَدِيدٌ بِمَا نَسُوا يَوْمَ الْحِسَابِ

The above verse reemphasizes the importance of justice as a lead attribute of a Khalifa. The wheeling and dealing that emerged out of Saquifa under any constitutional statute for selection of a successor to Muhammad by just means can at best be characterized as defective. To begin, the selection process at Saquifa was unlawful because Muhammad's consent was ignored, and there were several other important factors that were intentionally ignored to serve the interests of certain groups. The first basic rule that is missing is the proper representation of the

Umma at the time that this process was in progress. The Muslim community, which had grown to more than 120,000 followers, could not have been properly represented by a secretly formed group of about twenty-five or so. An obvious discrepancy in these proceedings was that there was no representation from the family of Muhammad, namely Ali, who had been raised, trained, and repeatedly introduced by Muhammad as his vicegerent and whose numerous contributions to Islam were considered unrivaled. The selection of a Khalifa without Ali's participation was, in all fairness, unjust, irresponsible, and unacceptable according to the rules of free selection. An Na'im challenges the legitimacy of the selection of the first and second Khalifas, and then he goes on to attack the complete breakdown of it with Muawiah and his successors.[6] The power brokering in Saquifa was first of all un-Islamic and unlawful according to any standard process that is supposed to be implemented in any true democratic procedure. In Islam, Khilafath is bestowed by Allah through Muhammad, not seized by manipulative methods (see the above verse of the Quran).

The usual explanation presented in this context for the appointment of the first Khalifa is that Muhammad did not pick a successor; that the community was assigned the task of selecting a successor through consultation is unfounded. This argument has serious defects under the scope of the Quran.

> [We sent all these] apostles as heralds of glad
> tidings and as warners, so that men might have
> no excuse before God after [the coming of]
> these apostles: and God is indeed almighty, wise.
> (Quran 4:165; translator, Yousuf Ali)

رُسُلاً مُبَشِّرِينَ وَمُنذِرِينَ لِئَلاَّ يَكُونَ لِلنَّاس عَلَى اللّهِ
حُجَّةٌ بَعْدَ الرُّسُلِ وَكَانَ اللّهُ عَزِيزًا حَكِيمًا

Is it possible that Allah and his apostle would leave the community without a leader? It is hard to believe a visionary like Muhammad would throw the community into chaos, knowing that there was a high probability of destabilization and that there would perhaps be a violent struggle for power. Historians and scholars of Islam who analyze the conditions on the basis of Islamic fairness will agree that Allah and Muhammad did appoint a vicegerent and created a system that was intended to have been continued in his footsteps so that it would remain unadulterated.

Muhammad, just before his death, ordered all his companions except Ali to go under the command of Osama ibn Zayd ibn Haritha for the expedition of Abil al-Zayt. Muhammad also demonstrated from this appointment that race, class, and clan are irrelevant, because Osama was not of Arab origin, but rather from Africa. A selected few of his companions, including Abu Bakr and Umar, refused. They knew that Muhammad must have sensed that there would be clashes and was planning to keep them out of the vicegerency or the takeover of Khilafath. Ayisha and Hafsa played major roles in keeping their parents (Abu Bakr and Umar) aware of the developments.[7] Analysis of the results from Saquifa and its aftermath clearly indicate that the process as demonstrated was in error. The person emerging victorious out of Saquifa, if selected according to just means, would have been a leader of the caliber and status of Muhammad. There was only one person with the knowledge, strength, and ability to implement justice under all circumstances, and that was Ali.

The Dilemma of Khilafath

Abu Bakr's inaugural address stated: "I have been put in charge of you although I am not the best of you. Help me if I do well, rectify me if I do wrong."[8] This suggests that he appeared shaky, lacked confidence in Islamic knowledge, and was not sure of his assignments and responsibilities. He had made numerous mistakes that he later regretted, and these are recorded in history. Some of these mistakes are presented in later chapters. A review of Abu Bakr's Khilafath reveals his inability to implement justice and fairness. When examined under the qualification doctrine of vicegerency, he lacks discipline, knowledge, and expertise on the Quran and in the jurisprudence required of a Khalifa.

> Say: "It is Allah Who gives guidance toward truth, is then He Who gives guidance to truth more worthy to be followed, or he who finds not guidance (himself) unless he is guided? what then is the matter with you? How judge ye?" (Quran 10:35; translator, Yousuf Ali)

قُل اللّهُ يَهْدِي لِلْحَقِّ أَفَمَن يَهْدِي إِلَى الْحَقِّ أَحَقُّ أَن يُتَّبَعَ أَمَّن لاَّ يَهِدِّيَ إِلاَّ أَن يُهْدَى فَمَا لَكُمْ كَيْفَ تَحْكُمُونَ

Khalid ibn Walid's (appointed to lead an expedition) brutal murder of Malik ibn Nuwayra (a revered Muslim) was an act punishable only by execution. Khalid's crime of killing Malik and taking Malik's wife to fulfill his lust on the night her husband was murdered was immoral, and he was Islamically liable to be punished for rape. Abu Bakr, however, decided to suspend his punishment and give him clemency. Umar was unhappy about

this ruling and removed Khalid from his position as commander when he became the Khalif. This Judgment of Abu Bakr was disgraceful and degrading.

Fadak was another issue that had grave implications on the execution of Islamic justice. Fadak's unlawful annexation was a direct violation of the Quranic law of inheritance, which will be addressed in greater detail in the eighth chapter.

The transfer of Khilafath to Umar, an expected outcome at the time of Abu Bakr's death, was basically a kickback. At Saquifa, Umar's dramatic pledge of allegiance to Abu Bakr was a politically driven move that was made with the understanding that the power would be transferred to Umar after Abu Bakr.[9] Taha Husayn of Egypt characterizes Umar's Khilafath as the period of The Great Fitna (The Great Sedition).[10] The issue that arises from this transfer of power genuinely challenges the theory of consultation, or *Shura,* as originally insinuated by Umar and Abu Bakr. The rules adopted during the appointment of the second Khilafa changed without any consultation or involvement of the Umma, as was allegedly required by the initial model put forward at Saquifa. Interestingly enough, Abu Bakr, who was sick and remained unconscious for a certain length of time before his death and yet is claimed to have regained his senses before his death, was given the opportunity and freedom to write his will without any interference in the appointment of Umar. But Muhammad—the founder, originator, and Messiah of Allah— was denied the right to write his will.[11] These inconsistencies and deviations from the principles and ethics of Islam show callous disregard to the Quran, Allah, and Muhammad by the planners of Saqifa's projected winners.

Khaled Abou El Fadl, in his book *Islam and the Challenge of Democracy,* while discussing Shura (see note 1) in the context

of the Quran (3:159 and 42:38), characterizes the selection of Abu Bakr, Umar, and Uthman as an approach that was against the intended purpose of consultative negotiations. Without the involvement of the Prophet's family in the consultative process at Saquifa, he suggests that this ostensibly created an oppressive and totalitarian mentality of the three periods of governance.[12]

Umar, during his last pilgrimage of his Khilafath, delivered a speech in which he admitted that the selection of Abu Bakr as Khalifa was unconstitutional (*falta*). The speech quoted below is a narration of Ibn Abbas in *Bukhari*:

> I have been informed that some of you have said that before 'Umar dies he would do ba'yat on the hands of someone. One should not be misled by the ba'yat-e Abu Sakr (i.e. vote of allegiance to Abu Bakr). It was unconstitutional (falta) and later on it was regularized. Yes, it was so. But God saved us from its evil consequences. Of you none is like Abu Bakr to whom people may submit. Whosoever receives ba'yat without consulting the Muslimeen should not be followed nor the person who did ba'yat with such a person, lest there be rift and fight among the Muslims.[13]

It is fair at this point to characterize Abu Bakr's selection as flawed; it was a politically driven anomaly that had no backing by Muhammad or the Quran and was intended to prevent Ali from becoming Khalif. The line of reasoning often presented is that Muhammad's companions from Quraysh were preferential for succession. This is overtly baseless. If this criterion of closeness to Muhammad was the assertion, then there was none closer to Muhammad than Ali. Ali was not only his cousin and son-in-law, but he was also a successful general, a victor in all the

major battles he had been, and one who was entrenched in the knowledge of Islam. He was believed to be the only witness to the revelation of every verse of the Quran; hence, he was deeply seated in epistemology, hermeneutics, and the intent of the Quranic text.[14]

Umar acknowledged Ali's abilities and intellectual dexterity when he made the following statements:

1. " I swear to God Ali was the most deserving of all the people to become Khalif."[15]

2. "If Ali was not there, Umar would perish."[16]

Muawiah, the son of Abu Sufyan, a staunch enemy of Islam, managed to take over Khilafath and later turned it into a dictatorial dynasty. Muawiah, when confronted with the question of his illegal accession to Khilafath, blamed Abu Bakr and Umar for orchestrating the plan to take Khilafath, which Muawiah claimed rightfully belonged to Ali. Muawiah wrote the following letter to Abu Bakr's son:

> We and your father (Abu Bakr) knew the virtues
> of Ibn Abu Talib (Ali Ibn Abu Talib) and his
> right that we had to regard and accept. When
> Allah chose His Prophet what he had, carried out
> His promise, spread his mission and cleared His
> mission and cleared His evidence then He raised
> his (The Prophet's) soul to the better world, your
> father and Umar were the first who extorted his
> (Ali's) right and opposed his claim. On that they
> agreed and became content. Then they asked him
> to pay homage to them but he did not respond

to them so they intended to force him to by any
means even the worst of it.[17]

Saquifa had become the point of no return of Islamic history.
What Muhammad had attempted to set up through Ali was a
lineage of Khalifas who would keep Khilafath as just that—
Khilafath. The coup at Saquifa had transformed that, making way
for huddled power giving and nepotic power-sharing schemes that
led to the creation of dynasties and dictatorial rule, far from the
original intent of Khilafath as declared in the Quran and by the
right of Muhammad. Abu Bakr's regime began an erosive process
that led to the values of Islam being set aside for puissance, lust,
and power building at the cost of blood, character, and the moral
right that was created for the title of Khalif. Islamic history was
not Islamic history from that point on; it became a continuous
downslide of further fractionalization and vicious bloodletting in
the way of scrounging power and ignoring the virtues of Islam
for anything other than the one thing they envisioned their help
in—holding total sway over the masses. The cruelty undertaken
at Saquifa was only the beginning, and the end to that cruelty has
yet to come, from Muawiah to the Taliban to Saddam and so on,
probably for the entirety of history.

CHAPTER 5

From Khilapath to Kingship

Saquifa laid the groundwork for the collapse of a lifetime of work done by Muhammad to create an awe-inspiring Muslim nation that promoted the key values, namely equality and beneficence. Upon the death of Muhammad, a new converse society was created under the rule of Abu Bakr that manipulated many of these principles for the sake of power building and the consolidation of force. Though the supporters of Ali and Muhammad saw Abu Bakr's rule as corrupt, the true shock arose at the moment Umar was ushered into office by Abu Bakr, and with this was ushered in a new era that sparked the collapse of one of the greatest governments erected in the Arab lands. Ali, when his time for Khilfath came, attempted to reconstitute the failed society that had been created by the past regime back to the original system under Muhammad, but his assassination demonstrated the true nature of violent upheaval via a precedent set by the Khalifas that administered before him. The authors of a recently published book titled *Terror Attacks–Brutal Acts Which Shocked and Horrified the World,* dedicated a section to the assassination of Ali Ibn Abi Talib (Ali), characterizing it as an act of terror of the early times.[1] The groundwork after Ali's time had been set for corruption and political consolidation, starting with Muawiah, as each leader strove to make a successor, claiming to follow the Sunnah of the previous Khalifa but diverting completely both on the initial selection process and later on issues that completely redefined the rulership of Arabia from one of an electable society

present under a just leadership of Ali to one led by tyrants and brutes who forced their hands to bring about their success at the cost of their populace. The decline had begun with Abu Bakr, and it continued on a strong downward spiral under Umar.

Umar was known in history as being short-tempered, easily irritable, and irrationally violent. His anger against Islam and Muhammad is best expressed in his threat to kill his sister and her husband when he found out that they had both accepted Islam.[2] Umar's violence against women was well known. He used to slap, beat, and threaten them without being reprimanded for these acts as required by the tenets of Islam. Fatima Mernissi, in her book *The Veil and the Male Elite,* presents these episodes to demonstrate that a responsible individual who claimed to be a Khalif, one who was supposed to adhere to Quran and Sunnah, was misogynic and yet held onto the Khilafath handed over to him by his predecessor, Abu Bakr.[3] In fact, he was one of few who behaved so irresponsibly, particularly against women.

His disbelief and misbehavior concerning Muhammad at the time of the treaty of Hudaibiyah demonstrated his utter disregard for the beliefs of the religion of Islam as a whole: "Today," Umar said to the Prophet of Islam, "I have more doubts about your prophet hood than I ever had before." Or, according to some historians, he said, "Are you (Muhammad) not the messenger of Allah?".[4] These statements, made by a person who claimed to be a Muslim, could be considered pejoratively dissenting with respect to the Quran.

> Know they not that for those who oppose Allah
> and His Messenger, is the Fire of Hell?- wherein
> they shall dwell. That is the supreme disgrace.
> (Quran 9:63; translator, Yousuf Ali)

أَلَمْ يَعْلَمُوا أَنَّهُ مَن يُحَادِدِ اللَّهَ وَرَسُولَهُ فَأَنَّ لَهُ نَارَ
جَهَنَّمَ خَالِدًا فِيهَا ذَلِكَ الْخِزْيُ الْعَظِيمُ

His indecorous behavior never seemed to cease. Muhammad, the torchbearer of Islam and the last of the grand Messiahs of Allah, asked for a pen and paper to write his will, and Umar's response was to say: "Muhammad is hallucinating; the Quran is enough for us." The denial to provide him a pen and paper is a clear indicator that Umar was afraid that Muhammad was going to appoint someone other than Umar or Abu Bakr as his successor.[5]

Umar's rage episodes are demonstrated throughout history. His uncontrollable anger reached its climax when he threatened to burn Fatima's home and then broke the door of her home, crushing her and causing physical injuries leading to her child being stillborn and her eventual demise.[6] This was Fatima, Muhammad's only beloved daughter. To hurt her was equivalent to hurting Muhammad and Allah[7]. She died within six months of her father's death from injuries inflicted during the siege of her home.

Allah's Apostle said, "Fatima is a part of me, and he who makes her angry, makes me angry."[8]

Soon before his death, Umar formed a committee of six to select the next Khalifa. This was a total abandonment of the first two selection processes, which were defined as *Shura*, although in reality, all were a grave misuse of the term for political maneuvering. These inconsistencies indicate that the basis of selection was consistent neither with the Quran nor

ahadith.[9] Ali was offered Khilafath on the condition that he would follow the Quran and Sunnah of the first two Khalifas: Abu Bakr and Umar. Ali said he would follow the Quran and Sunnah of Muhammad but not the first two Khalifas. Uthman, after Ali rejected the position of Khalifath, accepted all provisions put forth by the committee. Thus, the political system was once again used to put Uthman in the position of Khalifath and to push the *Bani Hashims* (family of Muhammad) aside.

This new regime was selected in the hope that it would, as promised, follow the past two Khalifas. Uthman's Khilafath brought significant changes to administrative practices. Nepotism took center stage, and all his relatives were given key positions. The important aspect to note is the fact that all those appointed had been determined enemies of Islam and Muhammad all their lives. Muawiah ibn Abu Sufyan, Marwan Ibn Hakam, and Walid ibn Uqba, among others, were specifically mentioned by Maududi for their anti-Islamic activities and had converted to Islam at the last second under fear of Muhammad's triumphant march into Mecca. According to Maududi, they were classified as *Tulaqa* (Freed prisoners of war who had a status lower than that of slaves—the lowest status in the Arab world).[10] The Bani Ummayyas (Muawiah, Marwan, and others) dominated the scene. Rules and Islamic laws were broken, changed, and modified. The abuse of human rights and the rights of Muslims under the Islamic laws became commonplace. Uthman had appointed Marwan as his secretary with significant powers. He was placed as the right hand of Uthman and was given almost total control during Uthman's Khilafath, making him only a puppet Khalifa. Marwan was known for atrocities, embezzlement of funds, and the mistreatment of some of the most notable companions of Muhammad.[11] According to Aisha, the prophet Muhammad had cursed Marwan's father while his wife was carrying Marwan.

She said that the following verse was revealed at the time when Muhammad had cursed Marwan's father:

> But (there is one) who says to his parents, "Fie
> on you! Do ye hold out the promise to me that I
> shall be raised up, even though generations have
> passed before me (without rising again)?" And
> they too seek Allah's aid, (and rebuke the son):
> "Woe to thee! Have faith! for the promise of
> Allah is true." But he says, "This is nothing but
> tales of the ancients!" (Quran 46:17; translator,
> Yousuf Ali)[12]

وَالَّذِي قَالَ لِوَالِدَيْهِ أُفٍّ لَكُمَا أَتَعِدَانِنِي أَنْ أُخْرَجَ وَقَدْ
خَلَتِ الْقُرُونُ مِن قَبْلِي وَهُمَا يَسْتَغِيثَانِ اللَّهَ وَيْلَكَ آمِنْ
إِنَّ وَعْدَ اللَّهِ حَقٌّ فَيَقُولُ مَا هَذَا إِلَّا أَسَاطِيرُ الْأَوَّلِينَ

Uthman further humiliated the family of Muhammad by gifting Fadak to Marwan. Fadak, which had been illegally seized from Fatima by Abu Bakr, was now in the hands of a criminal and a tyrant. Later, the deceitful, cunning, and manipulative Muawiah split Fadak between his son Yazid—a drunkard and a horrifically cruel ruler—and Marwan.[13]

Abu Darr, one of the most revered companions of Muhammad who was well respected by the Muslims, sadly ended up paying a heavy price for being vocal in his criticism of Uthman's policies. Uthman's punishment of Abu Dhar was a painfully horrific ordeal. Abu Dhar died from a long string of unjustified punishments in a desert.[14] Revolt and dissention were brewing in the background. Muawiah, the governor of

Syria, was gaining a foothold. He had managed somehow to distance himself from Uthman at a time when Uthman needed Muawiah's help. Muawiah had amassed a large contingent of forces which were at his disposal to protect Uthman, but instead, he positioned himself safely away from the predictable coup that led to Uthman's assassination.[15] It is ironic to note that later, when Ali became Khalifa, Muawiah blamed Ali for not coming to Uthman's aid and for not punishing those who had killed him.[16]

Aisha, in spite of Uthman's request for help, abandoned Uthman at a time when he needed her support. She left for Hajj anticipating Uthman's end and hoping that Zubayr, her brother-in-law, would become the next Khalif. She was instrumental in turning people against Uthman. In a display of anger, she once waved Muhammad's shirt in the Mosque while Uthman was delivering a sermon and said, "Oh Muslims behold the garment of the Messenger of God! It is still not worn out and yet Uthman has already ruined his Sunnah. Kill the old man! May God kill the old man."[17] All supporters and appointees of Uthman, especially Muawiah and some others (Aisha, Talha, and Zubayr), had abandoned him and were intentionally negligent, demonstrating that they wanted him out of office, even if it meant creating fertile grounds for murder.[18] They later conveniently turned against Ali for not taking revenge on Uthman's murderers.

Ali was elected by a majority as Khilafa, and those who revolted against him for not punishing the "murderers of Uthman" were actually either instigators or indirect participants in Uthman's assassination. Aisha, Talha, and Zubayr had openly declared that Uthman was incompetent and should be killed. Al Zubayr used to say, "Kill Uthman. He has altered your faith." People said, "Your son is standing at his door guarding him." He replied by saying,

"Even my son may be lost, but Uthman must be killed. Uthman will be lying like a carcass on Siret tomorrow."[19]

In fact, it was only Ali who had helped Uthman by mediating an accord between the angry mobs of people from Egypt, Kufa, and Basra who were unhappy with Uthman's unjust policies and practices. Marwan, after Ali had settled the dispute between Uthman and the revolting peoples, intervened and undermined the deal that Uthman had agreed to with the unhappy mobs by making the following statement:

> Why have you assembled here? Do you intend
> to attack, or to ransack? Remember you cannot
> easily snatch away power from our hands; Take
> out the idea from your hearts that you would
> subdue us. We would not be subdued by anyone.
> Take away your black faces from here. Allah may
> disgrace and dishonor you.[20]

On another occasion, Marwan, addressing the unhappy mobs, shouted the following:

> What is the matter with you that you assemble
> as if you came for plunder? May your faces be
> disfigured! . . . You have come coveting to wrest
> our property (Mulk-Khilafath) from our hands.
> Be off from us. By God, if that is what you want,
> something from us will fall upon you which
> will not please you, and you will not praise the
> outcome of your fancy. Go back to your houses,
> for, by God we will not be overwhelmed and
> deprived of what we have in our hands.[21]

Marwan's irresponsible and arrogant statements had already turned the nonviolent protest into an angry and ferocious assembly. Uthman's wife, Nailah, was weary and scared of Marwan's influence on her husband. She was certain that Marwan's deceitful tactics would eventually lead to her husband's death (see note 1).

The emergence of Ali as Khalifa after Uthman was an unexpected blow to Aisha, who was hoping to secure that position for Zubayr. Her disappointment took a dreadful turn. She started a campaign to overthrow Ali. She tried everything in her means to remove Ali, which led to a war that she orchestrated and lost, but she still managed to politically maneuver conditions that later facilitated Muawiah to grab power, which he would soon use to form a traditionally despotic regime. Bertrand Russell, in his book *A History of Western Philosophy,* made the following statement about the Bani Umayyahs: "The first dynasty, that of the Umayyads which lasted until 750, was founded by men whose acceptance of Mahomet [Muhammad] was purely Political."[22]

Muawiah belonged to a family who fought against Islam and Muhammad, and upon their grievous failure, they surrendered and were labeled as *Tulaqa.* They eventually infiltrated the fold of Islam with the help of Umar and Uthman and formed a political base to gain power. Maududi, in response to a question, said that *fitna* (sedition, dissension, creating discord, temptation) did not start in the period of Ali. Ali was a fair and just Khalifa with an unblemished record of piety, devotion, and dedication to Islam. He said that it began during the time of Uthman, who had appointed to key positions his relatives, whose records were as disgraceful as their characters. People like Marwan, Muawiah, and many others who were known for cunningness, coercion, fraud, intimidation, torture, and murders of innocent and pious

devoted companions of Muhammad, stood as only part of their dark *resumé*. Maududi pinned Uthman for seeding the *fitna* during his khilafath.[23]

Ali, who was deprived of fair selection practices, was a man of significant talent as a warrior, commander, negotiator, and possessor of in-depth knowledge and command of the Quran, Islam, and jurisprudence. He was also a just administrator and was beginning to emerge as the most deserving of them all. In fact, he was the first one who should have stood out as an obvious choice in a truly democratic sense. Ali was selected with an overwhelming majority that surpassed those of past Khalifas. In spite of the obvious animosity of Aisha against Ali, her cousin Talha, and her brother-in-law Zubayr, pledged their allegiance to him. Ali's goal was to restore the Islam of Muhammad according to the Quran and his Sunnah. His past successes had made him a target of animosity of Aisha and the Bani Ummayahs, as he had killed quite a few of the Bani Ummayah clan members in the Battle of Badar. Ali reluctantly accepted the Khilafath presented to him. Aisha was desperately seeking assistance to overthrow Ali, hoping to appoint Talha or Zubayr in Ali's place. The Battle of Jamal brought a direct clash between Aisha and Ali. She lost the battle and then asked Ali for exculpation.[24] Aisha had been his enemy from the beginning. Her action to participate in a war was prohibited according to Shariah. Not only did she act against the principles of Islam, but she also played the role of a leader in waging this war. She even tried to persuade Umm Salma, Muhammad's other wife, to join her in her bid to dislodge Ali from Khilafath in the Battle of Jamal (The Battle of the Camel). The following is an excerpt from *The Accounts of Aisha and Umm Salamah Dialogue* by Ibn A'tham al-Kufi about the conversation between Aisha and Umm Salma.

Umm Salma angrily responds to her invitation:
"Woe to you, O' Aisha, would you rebel against
Ali the cousin of the Messenger of God, after
both the Muhajirun and the Ansar willingly
offered him Bayah?" While Umm Salma
recounted Ali's excellence, Abd Allah son of Al-
Zubayr stood listening at the door. He cried out
"We know well your animosity toward al'Zubayr!"
Umm Salma retorted "Do you think that the
immigrants and supporters would accept your
father Zubayr and his fellow Talhah while Ali
Ibn Abi Talib, who is the master (wali) of every
man and women of faith, lives?" Abd Allah
denied having heard such a designation of Ali
by the prophet. Umm Salma insisted that his
aunt, Aisha, had heard the prophet say, "Ali is my
representative (Khalifa) over you, both during
my life and after my death. Anyone who disobeys
him disobeys me". She then asked Aisha, "Do you
testify or not, O'Aisha that you heard this?" "Yes, by
God I did," She replied.[25]

Aisha knew that the Khilafath belonged to Ali in the first place,
yet she did everything she could against the will of Muhammad
and the directive of Allah to stop him from becoming the
Khalifa.

She was responsible for creating an environment conducive
to breaking up the Umma and creating conditions favorable for
Muawiah to form a despotic dynasty in the name of Islam. He
refused to pay allegiance to Ali for the reasons stated above.
Muawiah thus categorically disobeyed every principle of Islam
and the Quran. Muawiah—through deception, fraud, and

coercion—declared himself Khalif and started his reign with the systematic elimination of all his opposition with indiscriminate violence and merciless murders. All the revered and respected companions of Muhammad were rounded up and vindictively punished. Ammar-e-Yasir, about whom Muhammad had said "Ammar will be killed by bandits," became Muawiah's victim in the Battle of Siffin. Similarly, Hujr Ibn Adi, another highly regarded companion of Muhammad, was brutally murdered along with his supporters by Ibn Ziyad. Hujr was a very open and fearless critic of Muawiah's Khilafath and a supporter of Ali who refused to pledge his allegiance to Muawiah. Muawiah's men killed Hujr and his companions. Muawiah expressed his guilt for killing a pious and devoted Muslim like Hujr at the time of his own death, when he said, "My day was three times as long because of Ibn Adbar [Hujr]." Even Aisha questioned Muawiah for Hujr's murder when she said, "O Muawiah, don't you fear God because of the killing of Hujr and his companions." A detailed narrative of all these merciless killings is recorded by Al Tabari.[26]

History is witness to all the deceptive methods Muawiah readily used to retain his rule, which he then transferred to his son Yazid.[27] Yazid was a drunkard, a womanizer, a tyrant, and a dictator who turned his empire into a monarchy that violated all the laws of Islam.[28] Karbala was the culmination point of Yazid's tyranny in hopes of keeping his Khilafath. Ali's son Husain and his his family members, followers, and supporters were violently massacred. Husain's sacrifice in defense of Islam thus became known as the "definitive sacrifice"—the sacrifice in which evil's victory turned into a chaotic political failure. The verse below mentions this sacrifice as *Zibhun azeem*. He thus restored the Islam of Muhammad to its original intent. Husain's movement against Yazid became a model of revolution for the future generations (see note 2).

We called out to him: "O Abraham, thou hast already fulfilled [the purpose of] that dream-vision!" Thus, verily, do We reward the doers of good: for, behold, all this was indeed a trial, clear in itself. And We ransomed him with a <u>tremendous sacrifice</u>, and left him thus to be remembered among later generations: "Peace be upon Abraham!" (Quran 37:104–109)

وَنَادَيْنَاهُ أَنْ يَا إِبْرَاهِيمُ قَدْ صَدَّقْتَ الرُّؤْيَا إِنَّا كَذَلِكَ نَجْزِي الْمُحْسِنِينَ إِنَّ هَذَا لَهُوَ الْبَلَاء الْمُبِينُ

وَفَدَيْنَاهُ بِذِبْحٍ عَظِيمٍ

وَتَرَكْنَا عَلَيْهِ فِي الْآخِرِينَ سَلَامٌ عَلَى إِبْرَاهِيمَ

Muawiah found a strong supportive Aisha on his side to combat Ali. Her malice against Ali and his children steered her energy to flow in sync with that of the crafty, deceitful Muawiah, indirectly helping him to gain power. He gained control and transformed the Khilafath into a successive chain of immoral, brutal rulers by making his incompetent son Yazid his successor. Aisha protested against Yazid's succession to no avail. She is believed to have been murdered by order of Muawiah as he was conferring the reign to Yazid. Aisha was also considered by many as an important contributor to the collectors of hadith and Sunnah of Islam. Her marriage to Muhammad at the age of nine years is completely debatable. Whether one considers her marriage as a political move is still disputable. The political moves made by her in coordination with Abu Bakr and Umar for Khilafath at and after the death of Muhammad are clear indicators of her political ambitions. Her role as a wife is full of controversies often downplayed by her admirers. Aisha was

not the most devoted wife. History shows that Muhammad was uncomfortable with her and Hafza's (Umar's daughter married to Muhammad) behavior and that he was often angry at them for causing distress. Even her father, Abu Bakr, expressed his dissatisfaction for her attitude toward Muhammad. [29]

> If ye two turn in repentance to Him, your hearts
> are indeed so inclined; But if ye back up each
> other against him, truly Allah is his Protector, and
> Gabriel, and (every) righteous one among those
> who believe,- and furthermore, the angels - will
> back (him) up. (66:4 Quran; translator, Yousuf
> Ali)

إِن تَتُوبَا إِلَى اللَّهِ فَقَدْ صَغَتْ قُلُوبُكُمَا وَإِن تَظَاهَرَا عَلَيْهِ فَإِنَّ اللَّهَ هُوَ مَوْلَاهُ وَجِبْرِيلُ وَصَالِحُ الْمُؤْمِنِينَ وَالْمَلَائِكَةُ بَعْدَ ذَلِكَ ظَهِيرٌ

The above verse of the Quran bluntly speaks against her and Hafsa (daughter of Umar), as they are the two mentioned in the beginning of the above verse. Aisha was also an open adversary of Ali, which was displayed in the Battle of Jamal, in which she led a revolt against him in violation of the laws of Islam. She later regretted having gone to war against Ali.[30] One has to read the history with an open mind to characterize her role from a religious viewpoint. Political and military victories in wars waged against the principles of Islam are considered a deterrent to the process of the propagation of Islam. Incidentally, her appeal to the *Mohatheseen* (hadith compilers) has been significant because of the nature of the ahadith against Ali, Fatima and their family

(Ahlul Bayth) she narrated for the sake of pleasing the ruling parties.

Some of the ahadith by and about her are painfully repulsive. Unfortunately, a lot of this fabricated material has found its way into *Bukhari* and other books. Misuse of the Quran in combination with ahadith became a convenient tool to mislead the community that was willing to accept it if there were any underlying benefits. Interpretations of the Quran out of context were brewing deviations from its textual intent. Fatima was aware of these deviations. She was also aware that there would be misuse and abuse of the original principles and laws of a supreme system that her father had put forth in service of Allah.

In this chapter it has been demonstrated that every rule established in Chapter 2 was violated by the parties who were responsible for adhering to the Quran and *Sunnah*. As we move into the next chapter, we will begin the examination of events under the scope of the Quran, using it as an analytical tool to classify deviations from the principles of Islam.

CHAPTER 6

Quranic Exegesis

"but none save God knows its final meaning. Hence, those who are deeply rooted in knowledge say: "We believe in it; the whole [of the divine writ] is from our Sustainer - albeit none takes this to heart save those who are endowed with insight" (Quran 3:7; translator, Muhammad Asad).

تَأْوِيلِهِ وَمَا يَعْلَمُ تَأْوِيلَهُ إِلاَّ اللّهُ وَالرَّاسِخُونَ فِي الْعِلْمِ يَقُولُونَ آمَنَّا بِهِ كُلٌّ مِّنْ عِندِ رَبِّنَا وَمَا يَذَّكَّرُ إِلاَّ أُوْلُواْ الأَلْبَابِ

For a Muslim, the Quran is absolute and final. This is a revealed text from Allah that produces guidelines, a code of conduct, and constitutionality. The Quran is egalitarian; it is codified to protect human rights, women's rights, and the principles of justice under all circumstances. Realistically, the complexities arising from its interpretations can be attributed to a lack of understanding and knowledge about the complex connectivity within the Quran and between the Quran (being the absolute), ahadith, Sunnah, and history. The exegesis and hermeneutics that have emerged over the past 1,400 years have not been simple. Decoding the Quran and deriving its intended denotations is further complicated if it is not properly interpreted. To further this challenge, one is faced

with the process of *Tawil* relating to the allegoric nature of verses with layers of depth. The *Zahir* (obvious things), just as the *Batin* (masked things), sometimes are not easily understood. The human mind is invited to reflect and contemplate upon the intended purpose of the text. The Quran refers to this challenge to the human mind to explore and seek knowledge through reasoning and through consultation with those who have knowledge as "Ahel az Zikr." The process of *Ijtehad* (hermeneutics) is an alternate channel available to advance one's basis of understanding the Quran. This approach is configured to promote, reinforce, and consolidate one's beliefs. Muhammad was sent not just to deliver the message, but also to practice and preach interactively such that his actions would reflect the practical aspect of the Quran to enable his followers to emulate his actions and draw conclusions about, as well as find solutions to, complex problems.

Many scholars recently engaged in the debates over human rights and women's rights in Islam have demonstrated the need to revisit these areas for better understanding. In particular, the Muslim scholars Amina Hudud,[2] Abdul Karim Saroush,[3] Khalid abou Fadl,[4] and Asma Barlas[5] have made genuine attempts to target the intended purpose of *ayas* (verses) that are usually quoted in negative connotations both by Muslims and non-Muslims, the non-Muslims including John Espasito,[6] Bernard Lewis,[7] and Karen Armstrong.[8] These objections and counterarguments have been unable to provide convincing solutions. A more persuasive approach to unfold the hidden meaning can be drawn from within the Quranic text and from what is known as the practical Quran—the life of Muhammad. The few ayas that are generally quoted out of the 6,236 ayas of the Quran deal with slavery and the inheritance and legal status of a women as a witness, and one is specifically about a noncompliant situation leading to physical punishment in a situation concerning a married woman who is in

a conflicting relationship with her spouse. These ayas have been attributed unfairly to the religion as a whole. The core problem lies in the inability to connect the Quran, history, and Sunnah to synthesize meaningful interpretations.

A viable approach to address these issues is to establish criteria using the Quran as a source for deconvoluting the complexities involved. There are three rules that can help to resolve this problem. The first rule is to accept the fact that Muhammad and the Quran are one and the same based on the ayas and ahadith quoted in Chapter 2. Secondly, one must accept that the Quran has provided guides who have the background and ability to solve the complexities in the Quran. These are referenced as Ahel az Zikr and "Rasequoona fil Ilm," and they are explained in the notes. The final rule is to apply the principles of justice repeatedly referenced in the Quran.

Slavery in Islam as normally put forth by critics is a misconception excogitated from the misinterpretation of the Quran and Sunnah. This relationship between a master and his subordinate as established by Muhammad appeared to be similar to that of an employer and an employee. After being trained by Muhammad, Zayd Ibn Haritha (freed slave of African origin) and his son, Usama ibn Zayd, were placed as commanders of his army on two different expeditions. Muhammad demonstrated through his praxes that his subordinates were given freedom, respect, and equality at the level that any other Muslim would receive. In fact, Muhammad cared and respected the rights of his subordinates as he would those of any other Muslims. This was a colossal achievement for human rights and dignity, because he not only preached, but also transformed his practices into an Islamic code of law applicable to both Muslims and non-Muslims living within the domain of Islam. Muhammad was the first prophet in

world history who codified the resolution of the issue of racial discrimination. He provided dignity and respect to every human being regardless of race and gender. Technically, this code of conduct became a law to be followed by all Muslim administrators and managers of the affairs of the Umma. Incidentally these were the times the world was beleaguered with brutality, barbarianism, and injustice. Muhammad was challenging and changing the past policies and rules to establish human and women's rights. Just to demonstrate the honor and respect that every human being deserves, he broke the barriers of racial discrimination by allowing his cousin sister to marry his freed slave, Zayd Ibn Haritha, who was of African origin. Just before his death, he made Usama, Zayd's son, commander of his expedition to Abil.[9] This was a huge step in the direction of removing racial bias.[10] Umar and others refused to obey Muhammad's orders to join Usama because of racial bias, which infuriated him.

Paradoxically, western scholars who criticize Islam about slavery are drawn into comparing it to an image they acquired from their own horrific experiences of slavery. For hundreds of years, the exploitation of African labor in the form of slavery was committed, and every nature of abuse, crime, torture, horrific mistreatment, psychological damage, immoral behavior, and trauma was inflicted on a race that has left indelible marks on the history of the western society. Even the world events of the twenty-first century lays witness to these mistreatments that jar the myth of human rights and human dignity about nations that claim and sermonize egalitarianism. Colonization was yet another form of subjugation indistinguishable from slavery. Residual effects from this still exist.

A second major attack on Islam and the Quran deals with the status of women. A whole chapter in the Quran, "An-Nisa,"

is dedicated to women. This chapter outlines freedom, dignity, and equality in the status of women when examined under its intended purpose. The Quran has uplifted women to heights never before achieved in human history. A small portion of the verse that has been the basis for criticism is about the mention of a voluntary response to a relationship between a disgruntled husband and wife as a last resort for reconciliation.[11] Muhammad, as mentioned before, was the practical representation of the Quran. As history and Sunnah indicates, Muhammad treated women in general with great respect. His behavior with his wives was exceptionally honorable and caring.[12] History, ahadith, and Sunnah supports the fact that Muhammad never hurt any women in his life. It is ludicrous to state that Islam permits a husband to beat his wife. This statement would be against both Sunnah and the intent of the Quran. Since justice is the ultimate goal of Islam and a determining factor in the treatment of any person, this act would violate the code of conduct as demonstrated by Muhammad. A true Muslim would look at Muhammad's life, learn from it, and adopt his praxes, because the Quran embodies Muhammad's life.

Another litmus test and another victory of the Quran and Islam relates to the question of heritage and the continuance of lineage through women. Fatima was the only surviving child of Muhammad and his only line of continuance of his progeny. This was a drastic change in a society where women were treated as subhumans and the continuance of lineage and heredity was allowed only through the male's surname. Allah changed that and made Fatima a point of focus from which Muhammad's progeny would continue. Allah had put to rest the taunting that Muhammad was facing for not having a son by demonstrating the importance of his daughter, Fatima. An entire chapter of the Quran is concerned with this special arrangement:

Lo! We have given thee Abundance; -

So pray unto they Lord, and sacrifice.

Lo! It is thy insulter (and not thou) who is
without posterity(Quran 108:1-3; translator,
Yousuf Ali).

إِنَّا أَعْطَيْنَاكَ الْكَوْثَرَ فَصَلِّ لِرَبِّكَ وَانْحَرْ إِنَّ شَانِئَكَ
هُوَ الْأَبْتَرُ

The Quran assures Muhammad abundance, symbolically
referring to a long line of Imams in the progeny of Fatima
through whom Islam will spread across the world. This lineage is
believed to continue till the Day of Judgment.

The Quran is egalitarian, non-misogynic, and a protector of
human rights and women's rights. It is simple yet complex. As
we have seen, some of its verses have deep-seated concepts that
require knowledge and education to unravel the mysteries hidden
in them. Allah has provided guides who know and understand
the deep meaning and have been put among us to interactively
share their knowledge and lead us in the right direction.

Before thee, also, the apostles We sent were but
men, to whom We granted inspiration: If ye
realize this not, ask of those who possess the
Message. (Quran 21:7; translator, Yousuf Ali)

وَمَا أَرْسَلْنَا قَبْلَكَ إِلاَّ رِجَالاً نُوحِي إِلَيْهِمْ فَاسْأَلُوا
أَهْلَ الذِّكْرِ إِن كُنتُمْ لاَ تَعْلَمُونَ

The critical source of information about these verses, as the Quran implies, is guides identified by the Quran as those who possess the inner knowledge. These experts have been endowed with special enlightenment from Allah that qualifies them as *Ahel az Zikr;* this can be seen in the above verse.

> All this have We expounded in this blessed
> divine writ which We have revealed unto thee, [O
> Muhammad,] so that men may ponder over its
> messages, and that those who are endowed with
> insight may take them to heart. (Quran 38:29;
> translator, Muhammad Asad)

كِتَابٌ أَنزَلْنَاهُ إِلَيْكَ مُبَارَكٌ لِيَدَّبَّرُوا آيَاتِهِ وَلِيَتَذَكَّرَ أُوْلُوا الْأَلْبَابِ

An in-depth look at the Quran is seen to provide answers to all problems. Society's complex issues begin to unfold as one explores the conditions responsible for generating problems if *Ahel az Zikr* are used as sources to decipher these complications. Exoteric verses usually deal with principles, practices, ethics, and social aspects. These provide clear regulations about daily practices in both the social and religious environment. These building blocks of personality and character are tools that bolster self-esteem, self-confidence, and the development of conscience and motivation that is seen to come from the Quran. Hidden in these principles and practices is a complete, automated program that rejuvenates, strengthens, and escalates self-esteem through spirituality. The blessings of spirituality lead to discoveries of hidden treasures of the power of the mind. As we explore the meanings and various philosophic dimensions of the lives of all the prophets that have been mentioned in the Quran, we begin to

see a trend emerging out of it. The trend, broadly speaking, shows that the Prophets were created to reform, train, teach, condition, and prepare people to receive the message of Allah, starting with the concept of *Tawheed* (unity). The crux of their creation lies in the reinforcement of the belief in the one and only Creator of the Universe, Allah. Their blending into societies and presenting an exemplary and idealistic way of living was designed to convince those around them to voluntarily embrace their lifestyle, and therefore Islam. However, the process was never simple.

Hardship, difficulties, and torture became part of their lives as they began the propagation process. From Adam, Noah, Abraham, Jacob, Zakariah, Moses, and Jesus to Muhammad, a common bond was established. This bond of patience, tolerance, and perseverance was formed for the propagation of Islam in different formats tailored to fit the needs of particular times and environments. Suffering and hardship came as part of the package connected with the ultimate sacrifice in Karbala. Their families and loved ones were put through a barrage of terror that never ceased to end. As we examine each prophet's life, we see similar patterns. Abraham suffered at the hands of Namrood; Moses at the hands of Pharoah; Jesus at the hands of the Jews and Romans; Muhammad initially at the hands of the Quresh; his daughter, Fatima, at the hands of the early Khalifas; and his progeny through Fatima later at the hands of Bani Ummayahs (the progeny of Abu Sufyan) and Bani Abbas (Abbasids).

These emerging trends had a definite pattern. There were two distinct diametrically opposite groups. In the first group were Prophets, and associated with them were the Islamic principles of compassion, love, peace, and the word of Allah. The price they had to pay to accomplish their goals was one of hardship, humiliation, torture, murder, and death. In contrast, the second

group had an exact opposite agenda, and associated with it was a categorical denial of Allah, the torturing of the innocent, murders of prophets, acts of demoralization, and the execution of their opponents. By examining Muhammad and his immediate family (Ahlul Bayth) under the lens of Quran, a trend can be seen similar to that of the Prophets of the Quran. The span of time from *Zul-e-sheera* (first call for Islam) to the events before and after Muhammad's death—the confiscation of Fadak; the burning of Fatima's home; the poisoning of her firstborn son, Hasan; and the violent massacre of her second son, Husain, along with his entire family, his friends, and his followers in the hot plains of Karbala—was a relentless congeries of atrocities. The massacre at Karbala was alluded to in the Quran below as a sacrifice that awakened mankind:

> And We ransomed him with a momentous sacrifice. (Quran 37:107; translator, Yousuf Ali)

> And We left (this blessing) for him among generations (to come) in later times. (Quran 37:108; translator, Yousuf Ali)

وَفَدَيْنَاهُ بِذِبْحٍ عَظِيمٍ

وَتَرَكْنَا عَلَيْهِ فِي الْآخِرِينَ

Husain Ibn Ali refused to pledge his allegiance to Yazid Ibn Muawiah, a drunkard, an infiltrator, and a traitor of Islam. Husain's sacrifice in Karbala was referenced in the Quran as "Zibhun Azeem". Yazid's side, in the view of the Quran, was directly connected to his line of predecessors; his heritage is traced all the way from Muawiah, Abu Sufyan, Marwan, Ferro, Namrood, and

Shaddad. Yazid was merciless and evil, and his ancestors mutated and adopted deceitful tactics to fall into the fold of Islam as a last resort to pave their way to Khilafath, monarchy, and dictatorship, in the process obliterating the Islam of Muhammad. Their mutilated religion legitimized treason, murder, drinking, and womanizing under the name and banner of Islam. The chapter "Munafeqoon" (hypocrites) in the Quran outlines this difference between the righteous and the hypocrites.

Allah had sent Muhammad, who was aware of all shades of converts and had safeguarded Islam by creating a line of individuals from his progeny who would rise to protect Islam with all their might when needed. Muhammad thus carried out the final task of making the Umma recognize who these individuals were by creating the following hadith:

> Zayd Ibn Arqam has recounted that the prophet
> said: "It seems that Allah has called me unto
> himself and I must obey His call. But I leave two
> great and precious things among you: the book
> of Allah and my household. Be careful as to how
> you behave with them. These two will never be
> separated from each other until they encounter
> me at *Kawther*.[13]

In the above hadith, *book* refers to the Quran and *household* refers to Ahlul Bayth, which was comprised exclusively of Fatima, Ali, and their progeny. This fact has been agreed upon by all Sunni and Shia scholars. A list of Sunni sources is presented under Appendix 2.

Quran and Islam were introduced and employed with such solid footing that the conditions were set to rule out any possibility of the change in its direction. Just like in the past, every twist

and bend induced by the forces of corruption was repulsed with an equal and opposite force. Whenever and wherever the Quran and Islam were in danger, the Ahel az Zikr stood up against the enemies of Islam with an equal and opposite force. Thus the world was able to recognize the difference between these two opposite forces. Any time the corrupted and the power-hungry people gained some ground, ammunitions of compassion, kindness, mercy, love, respect, and morality neutralized the advance. In the end, sadly, justice was not served, and the corrupting forces of evil—starting from the initial khilafath and continuing now with Osama bin Laden—have been able to effectively cast their dark shadow over the true Islam.

Materialists seek success through wealth, force, power, manipulation, coercion, and intimidation as long as the results are favorable. The trickery and bribery that was prohibited in Islam was one of the assets of the Bani Ummayahs line represented by Muawiah ibn Abu Sufyan. Abu Sufyan was a staunch enemy of Muhammad and Islam throughout his life, but when Muhammad entered Mecca as a victor, Abu Sufyan begged for mercy by accepting Islam as an alternative to protect his life.

> Verily, as for those who deny the truth of God's messages, and slay the prophets against all right, and slay people who enjoin equity - announce unto them a grievous chastisement. (Quran 3:21; translator, Muhammad Asad)

إِنَّ الَّذِينَ يَكْفُرُونَ بِآيَاتِ اللَّهِ وَيَقْتُلُونَ النَّبِيِّينَ بِغَيْرِ حَقٍّ وَيَقْتُلُونَ الَّذِينَ يَأْمُرُونَ بِالْقِسْطِ مِنَ النَّاسِ فَبَشِّرْهُم بِعَذَابٍ أَلِيمٍ

The Quran has thus given us the tools and techniques to analyze conditions and backgrounds that we may easily differentiate between the righteous and the unrighteous. It has also provided us with the Ahel az Zikr to seek answers from the hidden wealth of information encapsulated in the esoteric parts of the Quran to be learned through Ahlul Bayth, who are Ahel az Zikr, as suggested in the Quran (see note 1 for more detail).

Show us the straight path. The way of those on whom Thou hast bestowed Thy Grace, those whose (portion) is not wrath, and who go not astray? (Quran 1:6, 1:7; translator, Yousuf Ali)

اهدِنَـــــا الصِّرَاطَ المُستَقِيمَ

صِرَاطَ الَّذِينَ أَنعَمتَ عَلَيهِمْ غَيرِ المَغضُوبِ عَلَيهِمْ وَلاَ الضَّالِّينَ

The Quran is comprehensive. The depth and breadth of coverage relating to every element of life is provided for those who believe in it, some times clearly and sometimes with new dimensions to challenge the mind. The challenge is intended to invoke the desire to explore, research, and draw conclusions on the basis of reason. The impressions inscribed on one's memory from this process are indelible. The Quran generates an impetus capable of taking one into new aspects and directions with each verse. The Quran is therefore an ideal measuring, testing, and evaluating device capable of identifying and isolating false Ahadeeth, Sunnah, and events from the History of Islam.

CHAPTER 7

Ahadith, Sunnah and History

*"O ye who believe! If a wicked person comes to you
with any news, ascertain the truth, lest ye harm people
unwittingly, and afterwards become full of repentance for
what ye have done"* (Quran 49:6; translator, Yousuf
Ali).

يَا أَيُّهَا الَّذِينَ آمَنُوا إِن جَاءكُمْ فَاسِقٌ بِنَبَإٍ فَتَبَيَّنُوا أَن
تُصِيبُوا قَوْمًا بِجَهَالَةٍ فَتُصْبِحُوا عَلَى مَا فَعَلْتُمْ نَادِمِينَ

(A second translation from another source is below)

*"Verify the truth before giving credence to any such
report or rumour. The tale-bearer is characterized
as "iniquitous" because the very act of spreading
unsubstantiated rumours affecting the reputation of other
persons constitutes a spiritual offence"* (Quran 49:6).

The science of hadith and Sunnah are unique to Islam. The
process to build, construct, deconstruct, and rebuild from a vast
source of information relating to who said what, what was said,
whom it was said to, the context in which it was said, and the
conditions and circumstances that catered the development of
theses, conjectures, results, and conclusions reached is daunting.
The challenge of filtering and examining the end product and

then correlating and authenticating it against the test of the Quran could be simplified if the sources and narrators were identified as honest and reliable. The task of pulverizing 1,400 years of calcified strata of information cannot be undertaken without an open mind.

There are some basic building blocks to be identified that can significantly be effective. A hadith, in simple terms, is a saying of Muhammad that was transmitted through a chain of narrators for the compilation of a *Sahih* some two hundred years later. This gap of two hundred years or more is in itself a reason to be apprehensive. A qualitative breakdown of a hadith is dependent upon its *Silsila* (number of chains of narrators) and the reliability of sources with which each chain is referenced; these are referred to as *isnad*. A hadith could be Sahih, *Hasan* or *daif*. Sahih occupies the highest level of reliability and daif is the weakest in the group, with Hasan taking an intermediary position. A *Mutawatir* hadith is considered reliable and generally acceptable, and an *ahad* hadith is one acquired by a single source or, in some cases, by multiple chains (*isnad*).

Matn (text of the hadith), on the other hand, is a term assigned to a narrative dealing with the actions from Muhammad's life. It relates to actions taken by Muhammad in performing both personal and administrative tasks dealing with the community as well as personal matters. These helped in the building of Shariah, the codes of law derived from a combination of the Quran, ahadith, and Sunnah. Matn, or the textual content of a hadith, is generally used to place the hadith into categories, such as *ameliya* (Praxes), *qawliyah* (sayings), and *teqririyah* (spoken words relating to actions or deeds). Qawliyah and teqriryah are relatively less important.

Hadith, Sunnah, and history thus appear to be essential elements in the understanding of early monolithic Islam. The validity and accuracy of these components are to be focused upon if one has to extract information in consolidating one's comprehension of the religion in its entirety. These essential sources of information have to be subjected to an investigative process for the sake of accuracy. The main source of concern arises from the narrator's and the collector's honesty, degree of freedom of expression, personal bias, and idiosyncrasies. Above all, the impact of the conditions and the environment of the time become crucial. Unfortunately, bias and selectivity that have slipped into the process have to be identified and removed objectively. Fundamentally, the *Sahih Sitta,* or the six compilers of ahadith that are generally accepted, should be individually evaluated, which is beyond the scope of this book. The focus here is on some of the important aspects of Sahih Bukhari and Sahih Muslim and some of their narrators.

These evaluations provide the basis for the analysis of the case of Fadak. The arguments and the counterarguments about Fadak have been going on for centuries. Over the years, each side has provided justification for its view, often masked under prejudice and bias. A solution is furnished on the basis of information taken from history, ahadith, and the Quran in a logically convincing approach of presenting facts to make the analysis discernable. It is important to keep in mind that the ahadith in the backdrop of history can be convincing yet unacceptable in the view of the Quran. Fatima demonstrated that the hadith quoted to reject her claim did not stand up against the test of the Quran, and she often used this to deflect criticism.

As it turns out, the processes that Sahih Bukhari and Sahih Muslim applied were not robust, and therefore the criterion of

acceptance and rejection of a hadith was in itself questionable, which made their narrations and reporting troublesome. There are processes that were adopted and developed later, but they are vague and unsatisfactory, as well as open to criticism. Some of the reporters that were acceptable, according to Bukhari and Muslim, turned out to be unreliable, as was demonstrated by other ahadith. The list of Bukhari's main sources starts with frequent characters, such as Abu Huraira, Anas ibn Malik, Aisha ibn Abu Bakr, and Ibn Abbas. Besides examining these sources, one has to also look at the compilers (Bukhari and Muslim) themselves; one must examine their views, their employers, and their financial supporters, all of which might have impacted negatively on the process. Politics and dictatorial regimes obviously had a major influence on the compilation processes. The works of both Bukhari and Muslim were compiled during the times of the Bani Abbas, who were hostile to the Family of Muhammad, particularly to Fatima and Ali. An example that stands out is the case of Abu Huraira, who was appointed and financially supported by Muawiah ibn Abu Sufyan, a staunch enemy of Islam and the family of Muhammad, Ali, and Fatima who was well known for his manipulative methods of governance.[1] Abu Huraira is known for his expertise in the fabrication of ahadith on a basis of need. He was punished and prohibited from reporting false hadith by Umar.[2] Ibn Qutayba, in *Ta'wil-e-Mukhtalifu'l-Hadith*; Hakim in *Mustadrak,* Volume III; Dhahabi in *Talkhisu'l-Mustadrak;* and Muslim in *Sahih,* Volume II, reported about the characteristics of Abu Huraira, claiming that A'yesha repeatedly contradicted him and said, "Abu Huraira is a great liar who fabricates ahadith and attributes them to the Holy Prophet".

> And cover not Truth with falsehood, nor conceal
> the Truth when ye know (what it is). (Quran 2:42;
> translation, Yousuf Ali)

وَلاَ تَلْبِسُوا الْحَقَّ بِالْبَاطِلِ وَتَكْتُمُوا الْحَقَّ وَأَنْتُمْ
تَعْلَمُونَ

Accordingly, the Sheikhs of the Mu'tazilites and their Imams and the Hanafi ulema generally reject the hadith narrated by Abu Huraira. Moreover, in Volume IV of his commentary on Muslim's Sahih, Nadwi emphasizes this point:

> Abu Hanifa said, 'The companions of the
> Prophet were generally pious and just. I accept
> every hadith with evidence narrated by them, but
> I do not accept the hadith whose source is Abu
> Huraira, Anas ibn Malik, or Samra Ibn Jundab.[3]

Admittedly, Sahih Bukhari and Sahih Muslim are recognized by a majority of Muslims as being next to the Quran. There are several reasons this has turned out to be the case. The first reason is based on the early propaganda and support of the ahadith created during Bani Ummayah's period and those created later by Bani Abbas. The common goal of these regimes was to promote material that was in the interest of the policymakers whose intention was to mislead the public about the character of Muhammad by making him out to be one capable of making mistakes that even an ordinary Muslim would hesitate to do. The second reason was to simultaneously bring down the value and respect of the Ahlul Bayth—Ali, Fatima, and their family— and to glamorize Islamic underperformers, such as some of the early three Khalifas, Bani Ummayahs, and other popular figures of Islam. The knowledge and background of a common Muslim who is more involved in his or her day-to-day life and is dependent on the few hours of exposure he or she gets at the

Masjid and religious schools is a contributing factor in accepting ahadith as given. Basically, these guardians of religion control the information distribution process.

A reasonable approach, therefore, is to evaluate the collection and compilation of ahadith in an objectively subjective dimension. As Tejani[4] has rightly pointed out, neither Bukhari nor Muslim thought that his work would get this level of acceptance among the Muslims across the world. Realistically, these are only collections of statements by individuals relating to the actions, policies, and day-to-day incidences during the time of Muhammad that were published without any formal scrutiny. Sadly, the criteria for acceptance were either nonexistent or poorly defined in general, and they usually lacked scholarship. To make things worse, a lot of these narrators were classified as liars and fabricators of stories. Contradictions within a collection were an obvious pitfall. The honest, however, lacking political clout, were intentionally ignored or occasionally used when the benefits of doing so were in favor of the compiler's viewpoint.

Imagine Abu Huraira's maximum contributions going into Sahih Bukhari, knowing that he fabricated stories, was punished for lying by Umar, and was rebuked by Aisha for generating degrading remarks and ahadith about Muhammad in contradiction to the Quran. Muawiah, in a ridiculously debased turn of events, promised Abu Huraira heavy rewards for fabricating ahadith against Ali.[5] Similarly, there were others, like Anas ibn Malik, who fabricated ahadith for personal recognition and benefit. In other words, this period was a period during which anyone could present ahadith favoring the existing regime if he or she was in any remote way connected to Muhammad. These ahadith generators were established, dishonest people, yet they were given credibility as narrators. The interesting thing about Abu Huraira is that he

accepted Islam roughly about three years before the death of Muhammad but was able to pitch in 1,100 ahadith acceptable to Bukhari, including some involving events that he was neither directly involved with nor was a witness to. Abu Huraira's ahadith prior to accepting Islam should, technically speaking, be automatically characterized as invalid because it is based on hearsay and not verifiable. It is sad to see that some of the ahadith from Abu Huraira degrade the character of Muhammad. The situation is so disturbing that one wonders whether Bukhari or Muslim ever considered the evaluation of these ahadith against the Quran as suggested by Muhammad, who had predicted its misuse as follows:

A hadith, narrated by Imam Fakhru'd-Din Razi in his *Tafsir Kabir*, reports that the Prophet said, "When a hadith from me is reported to you, put it before the Book of Allah. If it agrees with the Holy Qur'an, accept it. Otherwise, reject it."[6]

And the Quran, on the other hand, presents the character of Muhammad as flawless and pure.

> And thou (standest) on an exalted standard of character. (Quran 68:4; translator, Yousuf Ali).

$$وَإِنَّكَ لَعَلَى خُلُقٍ عَظِيمٍ$$

The admission of such ahadith does not speak too highly of Bukhari and Muslim as believers who confided in the basic principles of Islam.

Ilm-e-rijal, strictly an intensive screening approach, was developed as a result to evaluate the ahadith not only on the basis

of the honesty and integrity of the narrator, but also, and more importantly, on the basis that it agrees with the Quran as the first test. If this process was applied to Sahih Bukhari and Sahih Muslim, these treaties would be reduced to only a few hundred pages. Tejani has cited some of the most interesting ahadith from Bukhari and Muslim that are representative of the type of hadith base that has negative connotations about Muhammad, whom Allah described as a perfect creation with the highest level of purity, a man free of any flaw, and an ideal role model for the purpose of preaching and propagating his chosen religion of Islam[7]. Muhammad was a role model for all generations; therefore, Allah would not have accepted any impurity creeping into the character and behavior of Muhammad. It is believed that care was taken by Allah to present his last and final version of the chain of messengers in the perfect form of Muhammad. By injecting the venom of impurity and degradation, the infiltrators were successful in making his character open to debate. The ahadith mentioned are so incredibly denigrating and debasing of the character of Muhammad that it is not appropriate to present them here. A concerned reader is recommended to read chapters seven and eight from the above book by Tejani.

Attention will now be on the character of Muhammad and his Ahlul Bayth in the context of the Quran as follows:

> And stay quietly in your houses, and make not a dazzling display, like that of the former Times of Ignorance; and establish regular Prayer, and give regular Charity; and obey Allah and His Messenger. And Allah only wishes to remove all abomination from you, ye members of the Family, and to make you pure and spotless. (Quran 33:33; translator, Yousuf Ali)

وَقَرْنَ فِي بُيُوتِكُنَّ وَلَا تَبَرَّجْنَ تَبَرُّجَ الْجَاهِلِيَّةِ الْأُولَى
وَأَقِمْنَ الصَّلَاةَ وَآتِينَ الزَّكَاةَ وَأَطِعْنَ اللَّهَ وَرَسُولَهُ إِنَّمَا
يُرِيدُ اللَّهُ لِيُذْهِبَ عَنكُمُ الرِّجْسَ أَهْلَ الْبَيْتِ وَيُطَهِّرَكُمْ
تَطْهِيرًا

The above verse from the Quran states that Allah kept Muhammad away from all acts of immorality and any forms of sin, creating him in the role of an ideal human being who superceded all the previous models he had sent down to earth as messengers. It is not possible that he would display any objectionable behavior at any time. In the previous verse of the Quran, the word Ahlul Bayth is used exclusively in reference to Fatima, Ali, Hasan, and Husain (In the Quran translated by Yousuf Ali, the notes explain that *Ahlul Bayth* in this verse refers to Fatima, Ali, Hasan, and Husain).[8] There are numerous Sunni scholars who have vividly and assertively demonstrated that the Ahlul Bayth mentioned here is exclusively in reference to Fatima, Ali, Hassan, and Husain. Appendix 3 has a list of at least thirty of those well-known Sunni scholars. As the verse indicates, Ahlul Bayth have been kept away from all impurities. In other words, their characters are free from all forms of fault and are therefore pure and clean. There have been debates and exchanges of ideas about the words *Ahlul Bayth,* but this issue is put to rest once one goes through the small list in Appendix 3 that comes from a vast collection of these well-respected scholars.

One has to keep in mind that the hadith collectors, producers, and creators had a two-fold goal; they were first to please their employers and providers by generating ahadith to cater their needs, and second to bring Muhammad down to their own level to enable the justification of their own acts of immorality condemned

by the Quran. In spite of all the negative effort put forth by these hadith collectors against Ahlul Bayth, if one comes away with nothing but praises in their sanctity, honesty, fairness, and sacrifices to uphold Islam, one is genuinely persuaded to accept them as role models. Thus Fatima, Ali, Hasan, and Husain stand above anyone known to history except Muhammad himself.

Muhammad's character covered all aspects of life. He offered respect to women both inside and outside his household. Women who were implanted into his home with the purpose of extracting information to be used against him became proponents of his infallible disposition. His enemies were confounded by the strength of his character as a leader, husband, father, brother, son, and friend. His sincerity, truthfulness, manners, and attitude provided a perfect model of scholarship and virtue. Every act of his was in synchrony with the Quran. His kindness toward widows (widows were treated as outcasts), orphans, the destitute, and the sick exemplified perfection. He married a widow to set an example for Muslims to help such women by uplifting them and returning them to society. Bilal, who was of African origin, was one of his most respected followers. History shows the respect and special treatment he received from Muhammad, his family members, and his relatives. By treating Bilal as his equal, Muhammad was demonstrating the teachings of equality in the Quran and Islam.

That the compilers and recorders of the biography of Muhammad and the early history of Islam assembled about eighty to three hundred years after Muhammad's death has to be dealt with in an analytical approach with the objective that all material reported has to first corroborate with the Quran, and second be proven to be derived from a reliable source. A sincere attempt has been made to take the information strictly from

non-Shia sources to prove a point irrefutable. Ibn Ishaaq, who is considered by many as one of the more reliable sources about the life of Muhammad, has also had issues that are in conflict with the Quran and Islamic legislation. J. Guillium, the translator of the *Sirah* (biography) of Muhammad by Ibn Ishaaq, cautions the reader in his introduction with the following statement by the author:

> The phrase 'God knows best' speaks for itself and needs no comment. It is sometimes used when the author (Ibn Ishaaq) records two conflicting traditions and is unable to say which is correct. Another indication of the author's scrupulousness is the phrase 'God preserve me from attributing to the apostle words which he did not use', His report of Muhammad's first public address at Medina and his order to each of his companions to adopt another as a brother are prefixed by these words and hedged by *fi ma balaghani* [A phrase used by Arabic biographers to denote doubt or uncertainty].

> If any, after this, invent a lie and attribute it to Allah, they are indeed unjust wrong-doers. (Quran 3:94; translator, Yousuf Ali)

فَمَنِ افْتَرَىٰ عَلَى اللَّهِ الْكَذِبَ مِن بَعْدِ ذَٰلِكَ فَأُوْلَـٰئِكَ هُمُ الظَّالِمُونَ

Nor does he say (aught) of (his own) Desire. (Quran 53:3; translator, Yousuf Ali).

وَمَا يَنطِقُ عَنِ الْهَوَى

This demonstrates an extremely important point; biographies and histories are to be evaluated for the reliability of such reports. From the above two verses, it is made apparent that fabricating any saying by Muhammad is equivalent to inventing a lie against Allah.

The danger of these ahadith and reports is incredibly alarming. It provides the opportunity for evil minds to adversely exploit this information. Salman Rushdie's *Satanic Verses,* the sources of which appear to be Bukhari and Muslim, should not be a surprise, given the quality of material that these compilations are known for. Whether it be Karen Armstrong or Bernard Lewis who ascertains information from these sources (which are considered by Sunni Muslims as next to the Quran), the information extracted from them is usually bound to be damaging to the fundamental beliefs and principles of Islam and the Quran. History and traditions (ahadith) quoted in Guillium's book *The Life of Muhammad* are often contradictory and distorted to selectively present antagonistic views.[9] Conclusions and analyses are based on traditions (ahadith) from questionable sources, and they do not, as such, authenticate the author's views by virtue of their fallacious nature.

Likewise, the concepts of Jihad and Caliphate presented by Bernard Lewis are irrational because of such bogus sources. An example is on page thirty-three of his book *The Crisis of Islam.* Here the author quotes the first tradition on jihad as follows: "Jihad is your duty under any ruler, be he godly or wicked."

This tradition (hadith) is baseless, counter to the Islamic concept of justice, and completely contradictory to the Quran. The author presents no supporting evidence, and since the Quran is the primary source of the religion, this view must be rejected. Similarly, most of the traditions cited in this book are from fabricated sources and present no substantiating evidence.

Karen Armstrong, in the chapter "Satanic Verses" in her book *Muhammad:A Biography of The Prophet,* makes an attempt to distance herself from the previous assertions by Tabari that led to the revelation of the alleged verses in the Quran that implied Muhammad's compromise for the temporary acceptance of other deities besides Allah. These traditions and reports are fabrications that were created to desecrate the image of Muhammad and Islam. The creation of Muhammad, according to the Quran, stands flawless with no room for any modification (Quran 68:4).

Fatima Mernissi, in her book *The Veil and the Male Elite*, systematically and selectively presents events that are unsubstantiated and erroneously quoted to enhance a point by masking facts and misleading readers in a way similar to that of the early Muhadeseen and historians, who did so as a result of their own prejudices. As an example, on page thirty-seven of Mernissi's book, Tabari is quoted as follows in a passage describing the events after the death of the prophet that led to the chaotic seizure of Khilafath: "The body of the Prophet , covered by a cloak, lay in his house. Everyone was caught up in the election (of a successor); no one thought about the washing of the body nor of the burial."[10]

Ibn Ishaq, from whom Tabari had acquired information, unequivocally establishes that the body and the preparations for burial of Muhammad were left in the hands of his family and that Ali took charge of burial preparations and burial.[11] The fact

is that Ali buried the Apostle. Abu Bakr and Umar abandoned the body of the messenger of Allah and rushed to Saqifa to grab leadership.[12] Mernissi's prejudice against the family of Muhammad—that is, Ali and Fatima—is obvious throughout her book. Her approach is similar to that of those who for more than 1,400 years have systematically covered up facts while still able to hoist a deceptive image of honesty and truthfulness.

As mentioned earlier, there were two groups with different philosophies and concepts of Islam. The divide between the two diametrically opposite groups has its roots in the very first call of Islam, known as Zul-e-sheera, and it continued throughout the history of the Muslim world. The treacherous road of dishonesty, dissension, violation of laws, and willful degradation of the principles of Islam and the Quran was one side of the story. The other side used Muhammad as its role model; displayed high levels of moral values, integrity, and honesty (even under threat of death); remained committed to the principles of the Quran under all circumstances; stood up against evil; spoke out against unfair practices; and helped the poor and the less fortunate. These were also the proponents of compassion and love. Peace played a central role in conducting the task of leadership in a similar way to that of Muhammad.

The hadith that Abu Bakr quoted to justify his decision in the case of Fadak has been a burning issue for several reasons. Here the narrator of this hadith is only Abu Bakr, and hence it is automatically classified as weak. It is also probable that this hadith could have been a strategic move to instantaneously gain political hegemony. The political fallout after the death of Muhammad and the violent display of force toward the family of Muhammad's daughter by Abu Bakr and Umar followed by the confiscation of Fadak has to be evaluated for its legitimacy. In order for the

hadith to hold its validity, it would have to pass the primary test of the Quran as we have set in the ground rules. Another test it has to pass is relating to the honesty and truthfulness of the narrator, who remains unaffected from any potential political gains. Fatima takes an interesting approach to challenge the status quo by moving above human susceptibility to fairness by placing her claim before Allah in a Masjid, where absolute justice was mandated. The case of Fadak, from Fatima's perspective, was a case before the court of The Almighty Allah and not before the community and its representative selected by them. Fatima thus built a Quranic defense that could not be shaken.

CHAPTER 8

Inheritance and Women's rights

"And you devour the inheritance [of others] with devouring greed" (Quran 89:19; translator, Yousuf Ali).

وَتَأْكُلُونَ التُّرَاثَ أَكْلًا لَّمًّا

Islam establishes firm rules on inheritance. Inheritance and justice are intentionally and seamlessly balanced such that one compliments the other. Extreme care has been placed on inheritance to address three important issues. The inheritance of an offspring in general, legal establishment of the rights of females to inheritance and the implementation of fairness in the distribution of wealth are designed to create a healthy, stable society. The responsibility of society is to provide values to intrafamily and interfamily relationships. Any deviation from proper distribution is looked down upon as an act of injustice, which is then subject to retribution.

The chapter "An-Nisa" in the Quran deals with important values and preferences about women. It plays a major role in eliminating gender preference. The pre-Islamic society evolved on the basis that man was superior, and Islam and the Quran broke down that ego that was created during the period of *jahiliah*. "An-Nisa" contains several verses relating to inheritance in general.

The case of Fadak is a significantly important issue challenging the justice system of a regime unfamiliar with constitutionality and the laws of Islam. The principle of justice is well defined in Islam, and there are no loopholes that one can think of to circumvent the demanding need for justice in the Shariah. In fact, on numerous occasions the Quran emphasizes the significance of justice to safeguard human rights under all circumstances. Muhammad, being the executor and the implementer of the will of Allah, would never have worked against the Quran.

Fadak was the property of Muhammad. Muhammad had gifted this to Fatima during his life, and she was in possession and control of it until it was confiscated by Abu Bakr through a premeditated plan for political leveraging. Fatima was upset at this action and was perhaps not surprised by it, having just gone through a traumatic ordeal at the hands of Abu Bakr and Umar. She went to Abu Bakr and claimed her rights to Fadak. Abu Bakr, in his defense, responded by saying that Fadak was public property because he had heard Muhammad say "Our property will not be inherited, whatever we (i.e., prophets) leave is Sadaqah (to be used for charity)." Fatima sensed that this was a tactical attempt by Abu Bakr to use this hadith to hold on to Fadak. Since he had used the word *inheritance,* Abu Bakr was hoping to quell her claim, not realizing that this hadith would fall apart on the basis of the Quran. Fatima's immediate response was to quote verses of the Quran to disqualify the quoted hadith as fallible in view of the Islamic system of justice. The two verses of the Quran quoted by Fatima will be held off for a later chapter (Chapter 9).

The following are those verses on the basis of which legislation relating to inheritance was developed. Most of these verses are clear. They defined the guidelines on the distribution of wealth, property, etc. of the deceased.

And let them stand in awe [of God], those [legal heirs] - who, if they [themselves] had to leave behind weak offspring, would feel fear on their account - and let them remain conscious of God, and let them speak [to the poor] in a just manner. (Quran 4:9; translator, Yousuf Ali)

وَلْيَخْشَ الَّذِينَ لَوْ تَرَكُوا مِنْ خَلْفِهِمْ ذُرِّيَّةً ضِعَافًا خَافُوا عَلَيْهِمْ فَلْيَتَّقُوا اللّٰهَ وَلْيَقُولُوا قَوْلاً سَدِيدًا

The above verse reinforces the significance of the welfare of the offspring. It is not only the stability of financial status, but also the strong commitment to the upbringing of a child robust in faith and compassion that enables him or her to become an asset to society.

CONCERNING [the inheritance of] your children, God enjoins [this] upon you: The male shall have the equal of two females' share; but if there are more than two females, they shall have two-thirds of what [their parents] leave behind; and if there is only one daughter, she shall have one-half thereof. And as for the parents [of the deceased], each of them shall have one-sixth of what he leaves behind, in the event of his having [left] a child; but if he has left no child and his parents are his [only] heirs, then his mother shall have one-third; and if he has brothers and sisters, then his mother shall have one-sixth after [the deduction of] any bequest he may have made, or any debt [he may have incurred]. As for your parents and your children - you know not which

of them is more deserving of benefit from you:
[therefore this] ordinance from God. Verily, God
is all-knowing, wise. (Quran 4:11; translator,
Yousuf Ali)

يُوصِيكُمُ اللَّهُ فِي أَوْلَادِكُمْ لِلذَّكَرِ مِثْلُ حَظِّ الأُنثَيَيْن
فَإِن كُنَّ نِسَاءً فَوْقَ اثْنَتَيْن فَلَهُنَّ ثُلُثَا مَا تَرَكَ وَإِن
كَانَتْ وَاحِدَةً فَلَهَا النِّصْفُ وَلأَبَوَيْهِ لِكُلِّ وَاحِدٍ مِّنْهُمَا
السُّدُسُ مِمَّا تَرَكَ إِن كَانَ لَهُ وَلَدٌ فَإِن لَّمْ يَكُن لَّهُ وَلَدٌ
وَوَرِثَهُ أَبَوَاهُ فَلأُمِّهِ الثُّلُثُ فَإِن كَانَ لَهُ إِخْوَةٌ فَلأُمِّهِ
السُّدُسُ مِن بَعْدِ وَصِيَّةٍ يُوصِي بِهَا أَوْ دَيْنٍ آبَاؤُكُمْ
وَأَبناؤُكُمْ لاَ تَدْرُونَ أَيُّهُمْ أَقْرَبُ لَكُمْ نَفْعاً فَرِيضَةً مِّنَ
اللَّهِ إِنَّ اللَّهَ كَانَ عَلِيما حَكِيمًا

The important point to note in this verse is that it provides
specific instructions on the handling of inheritance if the deceased
is left with one daughter. It appears that this verse is explicitly
created for the situation with Muhammad, who was left with
only one daughter, Fatima. Since Fatima was the only daughter
of Muhammad, on the basis of Shariah, she would technically
inherit all the properties of Muhammad. This is true according
to both Sunni and Shia jurists.

And you shall inherit one-half of what your
wives leave behind, provided they have left no
child; but if they have left a child, then you shall
have one-quarter of what they leave behind, after
[the deduction of] any bequest they may have
made, or any debt [they may have incurred]. And
your widows shall have one-quarter of what you
leave behind, provided you have left no child;
but if you have left a child, then they shall have

one-eighth of what you leave behind, after [the deduction of] any bequest you may have made, or any debt [you may have incurred]. And if a man or a woman has no heir in the direct line, but has a brother or a sister, then each of these two shall inherit one-sixth; but if there are more than two, then they shall share in one-third [of the inheritance], after [the deduction of] any bequest that may have been made, or any debt [that may have been incurred], neither of which having been intended to harm [the heirs]. [This is] an injunction from God: and God is all-knowing, forbearing." (Quran 4:12; translator, Yousuf Ali)

وَلَكُمْ نِصْفُ مَا تَرَكَ أَزْوَاجُكُمْ إِن لَّمْ يَكُن لَّهُنَّ وَلَدٌ
فَإِن كَانَ لَهُنَّ وَلَدٌ فَلَكُمُ الرُّبُعُ مِمَّا تَرَكْنَ مِن بَعْدِ
وَصِيَّةٍ يُوصِينَ بِهَا أَوْ دَيْنٍ وَلَهُنَّ الرُّبُعُ مِمَّا تَرَكْتُمْ إِن
لَّمْ يَكُن لَّكُمْ وَلَدٌ فَإِن كَانَ لَكُمْ وَلَدٌ فَلَهُنَّ الثُّمُنُ مِمَّا
تَرَكْتُم مِّن بَعْدِ وَصِيَّةٍ تُوصُونَ بِهَا أَوْ دَيْنٍ وَإِن كَانَ
رَجُلٌ يُورَثُ كَلَالَةً أَو امْرَأَةٌ وَلَهُ أَخٌ أَوْ أُخْتٌ فَلِكُلِّ
وَاحِدٍ مِّنْهُمَا السُّدُسُ فَإِن كَانُوا أَكْثَرَ مِن ذَلِكَ فَهُمْ
شُرَكَاء فِي الثُّلُثِ مِن بَعْدِ وَصِيَّةٍ يُوصَى بِهَا أَوْ دَيْنٍ
غَيْرَ مُضَارٍّ وَصِيَّةً مِّنَ اللَّهِ وَاللَّهُ عَلِيمٌ حَلِيمٌ

The above verse outlines all the necessary details about the conditions and methods of distribution of wealth and property to the heirs.

And unto everyone have We appointed heirs
to what he may leave behind: parents, and near

kinsfolk, and those to whom you have pledged
your troth give them, therefore, their share.
Behold, God is indeed a witness unto everything.
(Quran 4:33; translator, Yousuf Ali).

وَلِكُلٍّ جَعَلْنَا مَوَالِيَ مِمَّا تَرَكَ الْوَالِدَانِ وَالأَقْرَبُونَ
وَالَّذِينَ عَقَدَتْ أَيْمَانُكُمْ فَآتُوهُمْ نَصِيبَهُمْ إِنَّ اللّهَ كَانَ
عَلَى كُلِّ شَيْءٍ شَهِيدًا

This verse is a reiteration of other verses about the distribution
of wealth and property left for parents and kinsfolk if the
deceased had no heirs.

THEY WILL ASK thee to enlighten them.
Say: "God enlightens you [thus] about the laws
concerning [inheritance from] those who leave
no heir in the direct line: If a man dies childless
and has a sister, she shall inherit one-half of what
he has left, just as he shall inherit from her if she
dies childless. But if there are two sisters, both
[together] shall have two-thirds of what he has
left; and if there are brothers and sisters, then the
male shall have the equal of two females' share."
God makes [all this] clear unto you, lest you go
astray; and God knows everything" (Quran 4:176;
translator, Yousuf Ali).

يَسْتَفْتُونَكَ قُلِ اللَّهُ يُفْتِيكُمْ فِي الْكَلَالَةِ إِنِ امْرُؤٌ هَلَكَ
لَيْسَ لَهُ وَلَدٌ وَلَهُ أُخْتٌ فَلَهَا نِصْفُ مَا تَرَكَ وَهُوَ يَرِثُهَا
إِن لَّمْ يَكُن لَّهَا وَلَدٌ فَإِن كَانَتَا اثْنَتَيْنِ فَلَهُمَا الثُّلُثَانِ مِمَّا
تَرَكَ وَإِن كَانُوا إِخْوَةً رِّجَالًا وَنِسَاءً فَلِلذَّكَرِ مِثْلُ حَظِّ
الْأُنثَيَيْنِ يُبَيِّنُ اللَّهُ لَكُمْ أَن تَضِلُّوا وَاللَّهُ بِكُلِّ شَيْءٍ
عَلِيمٌ

The above verse makes it obvious that inheritance is an important factor in the welfare of any offspring and near relatives. Special reservations are placed on the responsibility of the distributor of the inheritance in the case that the deceased is not left with anyone directly in his line.

> and you devour the inheritance [of others] with
> devouring greed. (Quran 89:19; translator, Yousuf
> Ali)

وَتَأْكُلُونَ التُّرَاثَ أَكْلًا لَّمًّا

This verse has already been discussed. Suffice it to say that this sounds more like a warning for not giving the ascribed inheritance to the proper individuals.

> IT IS ordained for you, when death approaches
> any of you and he is leaving behind much wealth,
> to make bequests in favor of his parents and
> [other] near of kin in accordance with what is
> fair: this is binding on all who are conscious of
> God. (Quran 2:180; translator, M. Asad)

كُتِبَ عَلَيْكُمْ إِذَا حَضَرَ أَحَدَكُمُ الْمَوْتُ إِن تَرَكَ خَيْرًا
الْوَصِيَّةُ لِلْوَالِدَيْنِ وَالأَقْرَبِينَ بِالْمَعْرُوفِ حَقًّا عَلَى
الْمُتَّقِينَ

And when [other] near of kin and orphans and
needy persons are present at the distribution [of
inheritance], give them something thereof for
their sustenance, and speak unto them in a kindly
way. (Quran 4:8; translator, Yousuf Ali)

وَإِذَا حَضَرَ الْقِسْمَةَ أُوْلُواْ الْقُرْبَى وَالْيَتَامَى وَالْمَسَاكِينُ
فَارْزُقُوهُم مِّنْهُ وَقُولُواْ لَهُمْ قَوْلاً مَّعْرُوفًا

Compassion, kindness, and fairness are the recommended
approaches when dealing with orphans. Severe consequences for
the mistreatment of orphans are guaranteed in general, and they
are particularly guaranteed if their property is improperly seized.

MEN SHALL have a share in what parents and
kinsfolk leave behind, and women shall have a
share in what parents and kinsfolk leave behind,
whether it be little or much - a share ordained [by
God]. (Quran 4:7; translator, Yousuf Ali)

لِّلرِّجَالِ نَصِيبٌ مِّمَّا تَرَكَ الْوَالِدَانِ وَالأَقْرَبُونَ
وَلِلنِّسَاء نَصِيبٌ مِّمَّا تَرَكَ الْوَالِدَانِ وَالأَقْرَبُونَ مِمَّا قَلَّ
مِنْهُ أَوْ كَثُرَ نَصِيبًا مَّفْرُوضًا

The instructions are very clear and tenacious regarding
inheritance; there is no indication anywhere of any exceptions.

Muhammad, being a role model for society, was sent to demonstrate obedience to Allah under all circumstances and was assigned the task of adhering to all the rules within the Quran; therefore, it was incumbent upon him to place significant importance on this issue. In fact, as was mentioned earlier, Muhammad's actions and spoken words were direct orders from Allah to be carried out by Muhammad. The verse above is very clear about this. One who believes in the Quran has to accept the fact that under the conditions presented above and in view of the verses of the Quran referenced above, it is not possible that Muhammad would disinherit his only daughter, whom he loved so dearly that he considered her to be a part of him. It is not possible that Muhammad would go against the Quran. Therefore, the statement of Abu Bakr that Muhammad said to him "We the group of prophets do not inherit, nor are we inherited " does not agree with the personality of Muhammad and contradicts the Quran. It appears that this was a pure fabrication to deprive Fatima and her family for political gain.

The above nine verses of the Quran are straightforwardly quoted. The interpretations, likewise, have no internal conflicts. There are a few important observations to be noted. All these verses corroborate with each other and, in fact, lend support to one another. Inheritance and fairness in distribution is repeated emphatically. So are the consequences for not carrying out the prescribed instructions.

Verse 4:11 is worth paying special attention to. The share of the only surviving daughter is unmistakably mentioned for a special reason, as this part of the verse applies directly to Muhammad's only surviving daughter, Fatima. Fadak, which was Muhammad's property, was already established in the previous chapter on the basis of history and *Tafasirs*. This property was in Muhammad's possession and belonged to him;[1] thus his only

surviving daughter, according to the Quran, was the sole inheritor of the properties of Fadak and some properties from Khaibar.

Bukhari and Muslim have dedicated chapters to inheritance that are presented to substantiate the above statements. The selected few ahadith listed below are taken from Bukhari:

Volume 8, Book 80, Number 716

Narrated Jabir bin 'Abdullah:

I became sick so Allah's Apostle and Abu Bakr came on foot to pay me a visit. When they came, I was unconscious. Allah's Apostle performed ablution and he poured over me the water (of his ablution) and I came to my senses and said, "O Allah's Apostle! What shall I do regarding my property? How shall I distribute it?" The Prophet did not reply till the Divine Verses of inheritance were revealed.

Volume 8, Book 80, Number 738

Narrated Ibn 'Abbas

The Prophet said, "Give the Fara'id (the shares of the inheritance that are prescribed in the Qur'an) to those who are entitled to receive it; and whatever is left should be given to the closest male relative of the deceased."

Volume 8, Book 80, Number 728:

Narrated Huzail bin Shirahbil

Abu Musa was asked regarding (the inheritance of) a daughter, a son's daughter, and a sister. He said, "The daughter will take one-half and the sister will take one-half. If you go to Ibn Mas'ud, he will tell you the same." Ibn Mas'ud was asked and was told of Abu Musa's verdict. Ibn Mas'ud then said, "If I give the same verdict, I would stray and would not be of the rightly-guided. The verdict I will give in this case, will be the same as the Prophet did, i.e. one-half is for daughter, and one-sixth for the son's daughter, i.e. both shares make two-thirds of the total property; and the rest is for the sister.

"Afterwards we came to Abu Musa and informed him of Ibn Mas'ud's verdict, whereupon he said, "So, do not ask me for verdicts, as long as this learned man is among you."

Volume 8, Book 80, Number 734

Narrated Huzail:

Abdullah said, "The judgment I will give in this matter will be like the judgment of the Prophet, i.e. one-half is for the daughter and one-sixth for the son's daughter and the rest of the inheritance for the sister."

Out of the above four, one narrated by Ibn Abbas and one narrated by Jabir Ibn Abdullah direct attention to the specific verses of the Quran addressing the issue. The remaining two by Huzail appear to be reiterations of the same hadith, which specifically cites the Quran about the case of a single surviving

daughter. An interesting observation of the hadith by Ibn Abbas suggests that whatever property is left after distribution should be given to the nearest male relative. In this situation, the only closest male relative was Ali, who was Muhammad's first cousin and son-in-law. There was no other male as close to Muhammad as Ali.

The four ahadith below that are in conflict with the Quran are also in conflict with each other. In one case—the hadith immediately below—according to Saad ibn Abi Waqaas, a third of the property is to be inherited by an only surviving daughter. Technically, this is also in conflict with the Quran and hence is automatically disqualified.

Volume 8, Book 80, Number 725:

Narrated Sa'd bin Abi Waqqas:

I was stricken by an ailment that led me to the verge of death. The Prophet came to pay me a visit. I said, "O Allah's Apostle! I have much property and no heir except my single daughter. Shall I give two-thirds of my property in charity?" He said, "No." I said, "Half of it?" He said, "No." I said, "One-third of it?" He said, "You may do so though one-third is also to(o) much, for it is better for you to leave your off-spring wealthy than to leave them poor, asking others for help. And whatever you spend (for Allah's sake) you will be rewarded for it, even for a morsel of food which you may put in the mouth of your wife." I said, "O Allah's Apostle! Will I remain behind and fail to complete my emigration?" The Prophet said, "If you are left behind after me,

whatever good deeds you will do for Allah's sake, that will upgrade you and raise you high. May(be) you will have (a) long life so that some people may benefit by you and others (the enemies) be harmed by you." But Allah's Apostle felt sorry for Sa'd bin Khaula as he died in Mecca. (Sufyan, a sub-narrator said that Sa'd bin Khaula was a man from the tribe of Bani 'Amir bin Lu'ai).

Volume 8, Book 80, Number 755

Narrated Abu Huraira:

The Prophet said, " If somebody dies (among the Muslims) leaving some property, the property will go to his heirs; and if he leaves a debt or dependants, we will take care of them."

Volume 8, Book 80, Number 718

Narrated 'Aisha

Fatima and Al 'Abbas came to Abu Bakr, seeking their share from the property of Allah's Apostle and at that time, they were asking for their land at Fadak and their share from Khaibar. Abu Bakr said to them, " I have heard from Allah's Apostle saying, 'Our property cannot be inherited, and whatever we leave is to be spent in charity, but the family of Muhammad may take their provisions from this property." Abu Bakr added, "By Allah, I will not leave the procedure I saw Allah's Apostle following during his lifetime concerning this

property." Therefore Fatima left Abu Bakr and did not speak to him till she died.

Volume 8, Book 80, Number 719

Narrated 'Aisha

The Prophet said, "Our (Apostles') property should not be inherited, and whatever we leave, is to be spent in charity".

Two of the above narrations are from Aisha. hadith number 719 is intended to establish the validity of the other hadith (number 718), which she narrates about what she heard from her father. The hadith from Aisha (number 719) reads as follows: "The Prophet said, 'Our (Apostles') property should not be inherited, and whatever we leave, is to be spent in charity." This is presented such that it appears that she heard it directly from Muhammad. This is false, because Abu Baker was the first to claim he heard this from Muhammad. In fact he was the only one who heard it, and therefore doesn't fall under the category of reliable ahadith. As we shall see in the later chapters, both these ahadith are in conflict with Quran and with the above ahadith.

Abu Bakr claimed that he would adhere to the procedure that he saw Muhammad practice. If, in fact, he saw Muhammad practice this, why then was he not able to provide the citation and references of a similar case in his defense? This hadith appears to be on shaky ground, and it is surrounded by a plethora of unanswered questions.

In addition, the above hadith is unacceptable because it contradicts the Quran, as stated above. A second flaw about this hadith is that the only person who heard it from Muhammad

was Abu Baker and no one else, so it is unsubstantiated and nonverifiable.

Volume 8, Book 80, Number 721

Narrated Abu Huraira

Allah's Apostle said, "Not even a single Dinar of my property should be distributed (after my deaths to my inheritors, but whatever I leave excluding the provision for my wives and my servants, should be spent in charity.

The above hadith, narrated by Abu Huraira, reveals that Muhammad specifically excluded Fatima from inheritance but allowed the inheritance of the property owned by him to his wives. This hadith does not hold up against the Quran and is also against the principles of justice in Islam. Muhammad, being the perfect role model to the society and the Muslim community, would not speak anything in conflict with the Quran. Therefore, this hadith is a fabrication of Abu Huraira to please the ruling parties, and hence it should be rejected as false.

The eight ahadith that are cited above are to be examined closely. The science of hadith was outlined in the previous chapter and should be kept in mind to enable proper interpretation and application to the case of Fadak. As previously shown in a hadith from Muhammad, "the hadith in conflict with Quran is to be rejected" is a guideline that must be followed for the hadith to be valid. It is to be noted that out of the eight ahadith presented above, only four are in agreement with the Quran. The following conclusions are of importance for the final analysis:

The Quran is clear about the inheritance unequivocally being in favor of Fatima. Statistically speaking, 75 percent of the ahadith taken from Bukhari establish Fatima's inheritance of Fadak. The only two ahadith that are in favor of Abu Bakr, whose soul narrator is Abu Bakr, happen to be ridiculously in conflict with the Quran. Of course, it's easy for a person in a position of power to make statements in his own support with extreme narcissism. This clearly does not validate such a ludicrous hadith, but instead highlights only the surface of the deception embedded within the regimes of Abu Bakr, Umar, and Uthman. The above ahadith are mainly in favor of Fatima, and those of them that stand against Fatima are also against the verdict of the Quran, invalidating them and making them moot points. Fatima was an essential component of Muhammad's life. Muhammad treasured her and would never allow her to suffer under any circumstances. He would never have disinherited her against the will of Allah, and above all, according to the Quran, Muhammad would not say or do anything against the Quran. The evidence and arguments presented in previous chapters and in this chapter confirm that this hadith from Abu Baker is invalid from any conceivable approach. Fatima, in her speech (which will be discussed later), presents very specific verses of the Quran that she uses to overthrow Abu Bakr's hadith. The important point to note is that Fadak was exclusively Muhammad's property; hence, it only belonged to Fatima.

CHAPTER 9

The Statement That Shook the World

After Muhammad's death, the precipitous thrust hurled Fatima to martyrdom within six months. This was a heart-wrenching event in the early history of Islam. Muhammad's last few days witnessed aggressive changes in the behavior of his companions. Abu Bakr and Umar's refusal to obey his orders to follow Usama bin Zayd's command was initiated to debilitate Muhammad's plan. Islam and the Quran were totally ignored. Muhammad's end was imminent. Fatima and Ali were helping Muhammad to get through the illness while their adversaries surrounded Muhammad. Aiyasha and Hafza, Muhammad's wives, were working from inside to help their parents, Abu Bakr and Umar, to pave their way for a takeover bid. They appeared to be least concerned about Muhammad's chances of recovery. Political upheaval was guaranteed to take the center stage, and Muhammad was aware of it. The refusal to provide paper and pen for him to write his will was a clear indication of a takeover bid.

Abu Bakr and Umar rushed to Saquifa for the selection of a Khalifa, deliberately leaving the body of the apostle of Allah in the hands of Fatima and Ali, which appears to be in accordance to a well thought-out plan. Ali, Fatima, and Fatima's family and close relatives and friends were left out of the process in Saquifa, eliminating any threat to Abu Bakr and Umar's long-term ambitions. After the burial given by Ali, Fatima became a target of atrocities. Her home was attacked. The door to her home

was broken and set on fire. Fatima was crushed by the attacker, and this killed her unborn child. Her husband was harassed. The family that needed support and condolence was instead subjected to torture, causing both physical and mental anguish. Fatima was systematically attacked and emotionally and physically drained.

Islamic values were ignored; laws and principles of Islam were broken. Islamic morals were disobeyed, and the sanctity of human rights and women's rights were dishonored. The most pious, devoted follower of Islam, Fatima, was in distress. The only daughter of Muhammad, whom Muhammad adored, was helpless and in pain. Quranic teachings were violated, trampled, and destroyed. The community that was responsible for protecting the sacredness of Islam and the Quran was on the brink of dissolution.

Fatima was facing a challenge that even Muhammad did not encounter. Fatima, physically hurt and emotionally shattered, had to rise up to protect Islam, the Quran, and women's rights. The honor and respect given to women for the first time in the history of mankind was at stake. Fatima was the only one who could revive it. Her property, Fadak, was seized specifically to avert all possibilities of challenge to Abu Bakr and Umar's illegitimate assumption of Khilafath from Muhammad's family.

Fatima realized the gravity of the situation and stepped up to protest and set the record straight by claiming her rights to Fadak, a property owned by her father Muhammad that was given to her as a gift, according to some reports. Nonetheless, the property belonged to her whether as a gift or legally through the Islamic code of inheritance. This was a moment at which Ali had to exercise control over his rights to vicegerency. His actions were dictated by the political conditions at that time, and he had decided to soften his position. Many scholars have

given explanations suggesting that Ali's interests were beyond establishing his own power; it was Islam that he had decided to protect under all circumstances. Fatima, however, was ready for a face-off. The place was Masjid-e-Nabavi—the mosque built, managed, and administered by Muhammad. Fatima selected the Masjid for a specific purpose. She was symbolically entrusting the judgment to the divine court of justice. Therefore, the party claiming to assume the authority to rule would in fact be morally and Islamically bound by the tenets of the Quran and would have to be prepared to face the consequences should the party fail to deliver a lucid and absolute judgment mandated by the Quran and Islam.

Fatima and Ali represented virtue, honesty, and piety. Their ultimate surrender to Allah, the Quran, and Islam was an already established fact. This level of unwavering commitment to Allah was only found in Muhammad, Ali, and Fatima. Fatima's deep-rooted knowledge of Islam and the Quran was displayed in her speech for the claim of Fadak. The execution, clarity, and effectiveness of the delivery of her speech bolstered her claim. The invincibility and courage she displayed in an unfriendly environment was amazing. She was aware that her appeal was going to fall on deaf ears. Perhaps she took into account that their minds were already made up.

Fatima was embarking on a movement that was sure to turn the heads of those who were against the policies that were Quranically and morally unjust. Her speech, as we shall see, covered all of the core components of Islam. The deep insights to the philosophy of Islam, the meticulously concocted elements of justice, the significance of human rights, the revolutionary regulative laws enforcing honor and respect for women, full and equal right's for women, and the maintenance of law and order

were some of the highlights of her famous speech for the claim of Fadak (see the full speech in note 1).

Fatima:

> Praise be to Allah for that which He bestowed (upon us); And thanks be to Him for all that which He inspired; and commended in His Name for that which He Provided: Form prevalent favors which He created, And abundant benefactions which He offered and perfect grants which He presented; (such benefactions) that their number is much too plentiful to compute; Bounties too vast to measure; Their limit was too distant to realize; He recommended to them (His creatures) to gain more (of His benefaction) by being grateful for their continuity; He ordained Himself praiseworthy by giving generously to His creatures; I bear witness that there is no God but Allah Who is One without partner, a statement which sincere devotion is made to be its interpretation; hearts guarantee its continuation, and illuminated in the minds is its sensibility. He Who cannot be perceived with vision; neither be described with tongues; nor can imagination surround His state.

Fatima began by declaring her faith and conviction in Allah as the absolute authority over mankind and the universe. She then dove into the deep chasms of the world of metaphysics, inventing superbly precise terminology to express the concept of Tawheed (the belief that Allah, singular, without any equal, is the absolute, infinite, and perfect divine creator of the universe),

thereby establishing her command over language by selectively linking words carefully balanced to convey the first fundamental principle of Islam. As she advanced in her presentation, she assertively reminded her audience about Allah's attributes, paving her way as she attempted to cleanse their minds from past paganistic malevolence while simultaneously preparing them to recognize and honor Islamic justice—the second most important principle of Islam. Fatima was consequently scouting and preparing her audience to ensure that in the end, her message would be effectively delivered and justice would be recognized and served.

Fatima:

> Allah has sent him (Muhammad) (peace be
> upon him) as perfection for His commands,
> a resolution to accomplish His rode, and an
> implementation of the decrees of His Mercy.

As she continued her pursuit to reestablish the forgotten past, she introduced Muhammad, her father, as a perfect creation and a perfect operator of the will of Allah who had personally introduced and identified the role models[1] created by the Almighty to lead the future generations. She methodically outlined a detailed set of beliefs and practices as an indicative requirement of an ideal Muslim.

Fatima:

> Obeying us (Ahlul-Bayt)-Management of the
> nation. Our leadership (Ahlul-Bayt): Safeguard
> from disunity.

O People ! Be informed that I am Fatimah, and
my father is Muhammad

(p.b.u.h.) I say that repeatedly and initiate it
continually; I say not what I say mistakenly, nor
do I do what I do aimlessly. Now hath come unto
you an Apostle from among yourselves It grieves
him that you should perish; Ardently anxious
is he over you; To the believers he is most kind
and merciful. Thus, if you identify and recognize
him, you shall realize that he is my father and not
the father of any of your women; the brother
of my cousin (Ali (AS)) rather than any of your
men. What an excellent identity he was, may the
peace and blessings of Allah be upon him and his
descendants.

Thus, he propagated the Message, by coming
out openly with the warning and while inclined
away from the path of the polytheists, (whom
he) struck their strength and seized their throats,
while he invited (all) to the way of his Lord with
wisdom and beautiful preaching, He destroyed
idols, and defeated heroes, until their group fled
and turned their backs. So night revealed its
dawn; righteousness uncovered its genuineness;
the voice of the religious authority spoke out
loud; the evil discords were silenced; The crown
of hypocrisy was diminished; the tightening of
infidelity and desertion were untied,

So you spoke the statement of devotion among a
band of starved ones; and you were on the edge
of a hole of fire; (you were) the drink of the

thirsty one; the opportunity of the desiring one;
the fire brand of him who passes in haste; the
step for feet; you used to drink from the water
gathered on roads; eat jerked meat.

Fatima then turned her focus to introducing herself as the
direct link to Muhammad and explaining that she had witnessed
and supported the propagation, growth, and expansion of Islam
with a concerted effort on behalf of herself and her husband,
Ali. She thus introduced Ali as the destroyer of idols and the hero
of all major battles whose righteousness and genius silenced the
enemy on all fronts. She reminded them of her status and the
status of her family members, the Ahlul Bayth, whom, according
to her explanation in the Quran, had special privileges over
Muslims. She also strategically established her status as the only
daughter of the prophet of Islam in the process.

Fatima:

> You were despised outcasts always in fear of
> abduction from those around you. Yet, Allah
> rescued you through my father, Muhammad
> (p.b.u.h.) after much ado, and after he was
> confronted by mighty men, the Arab beasts, and
> the demons of the people of the Book Who,
> whenever they ignited the fire of war, Allah
> extinguished it; and whenever the thorn of the
> devil appeared, or a mouth of the polytheists
> opened wide in defiance, he (p.b.u.h.) would strike
> its discords with his brother (Ali (AS)), who
> comes not back until he treads its wing with the
> sole of his feet, and extinguishes its flames with
> his sword.

But how, for a people whose faith is assured,
can give better judgment than Allah? Don't you
know? Yes, indeed it is obvious to you that I am
his daughter. O Muslims! Will my inheritance
be usurped? O son of Abu Quhafa! (Abu Bakr
identified through his paternal linage) Where
is it in the Book of Allah that you inherit your
father and I do not inherit mine? Surely you have
come up with an unprecedented thing. Do you
intentionally abandon the Book of Allah and cast
it behind your back? Do you not read where it
says: And Sulaiman inherited Dawood ? (Quran
27:16)And when it narrates the story of Zakariya
and says: 'So give me an heir as from thyself (One
that) will inherit ones and inherit the posterity of
Yaqoob'.(Quran 19:4-6)

You claim that I have no share! And that I do not
inherit my father!

What! Did Allah reveal a (Quranic) verse
regarding you from which He excluded my
father? Or do you say:

At this point she challenges Abu Bakr to identify a verse
in the Quran that singles out Muhammad from the rest of the
Islamic community. Abu Bakr's failure to produce any verse of
the Quran in his defense indicates that the hadith he presented
was baseless.

Almost halfway through her speech, as she reminisced about
her status and position in Quran and history, her attention turned
toward the attributes of an ideal just leader who could fill in
as a Khalifa to lead the Umma. She then delved into how the

firepower of the enemy was extinguished by Muhammad and Ali's coordinated and synchronized actions to crush and counterattack the enemy within to establish the doctrines of Islam.

Fatima changed her stratagem and began to focus on Muhammad's contributions to the human race and myriad techniques he employed to bring people into the fold of Islam. Her speech was also a reminder of their dark, appalling past of *jahilliah* (the times of ignorance before Islam) that her father Muhammad had lightened up with humanity and respect.

> 14:1 A Book which We have revealed unto thee, in order that thou mightest lead mankind out of the depths of darkness into light - by the leave of their Lord - to the Way of (Him) the Exalted in power, worthy of all praise!-

الر كِتَابٌ أَنزَلْنَاهُ إِلَيْكَ لِتُخْرِجَ النَّاسَ مِنَ الظُّلُمَاتِ
إِلَى النُّورِ بِإِذْنِ رَبِّهِمْ إِلَى صِرَاطِ الْعَزِيزِ الْحَمِيدِ

Indeed, God bestowed a favor upon the believers when he raised up in their midst an apostle from among themselves, to convey His messages unto them, and to cause them to grow in purity, and to impart unto them the divine writ as well as wisdom - whereas before that they were indeed, most obviously, lost in error. (Quran 3:164; translator, Yousuf Ali).

لَقَدْ مَنَّ اللَّهُ عَلَى الْمُؤْمِنِينَ إِذْ بَعَثَ فِيهِمْ رَسُولًا مِّنْ
أَنفُسِهِمْ يَتْلُو عَلَيْهِمْ آيَاتِهِ وَيُزَكِّيهِمْ وَيُعَلِّمُهُمُ الْكِتَابَ
وَالْحِكْمَةَ وَإِن كَانُوا مِن قَبْلُ لَفِي ضَلَالٍ مُّبِين

Fatima's graceful formulation of words was transforming into Quranic verses. Her expertise on different branches of Islam and her eloquence was emulating Muhammad's Quranic teachings. She carefully directed the attention of the public toward the characteristics of a supporter of and an ideal successor to Muhammad. She brought Ali into the equation as the first male convert and supporter who was responsible for the victories of all the wars during the time of Muhammad. Ali's unique position and his attributes as a vicegerent for the Muslims after Muhammad's death were skillfully cited to an attentive congregation as she discussed the outcome of Saquifa as a violation of the Quran and the will of Muhammad and therefore of Allah.

Her claim for Fadak and their denial of her rights took center stage as she started to build up justification for her claim under the auspices of the Quran and on the basis of the disqualification of the hadith that Abu Bakr had presented as his rationale to take Fadak from her. The verses of the Quran that she presented in her speech invalidated the hadith below, which is quoted from Abu Bakr.

Abu Bakr's hadith that "We the group of prophets do not inherit, nor are we inherited" was the basis for his taking Fadak from Fatima. Another version of the same hadith with a slight change in the use of words was as follows; 'Our property will not be inherited, whatever we (i.e., prophets) leave is Sadaqah." The following discussion from the book *Peshawar Nights*[2] actually

goes into some detail to show that his hadith does not hold up against the Quran:

> First, whoever contrived this hadith uttered it
> without thinking about the words he used. If he
> had been careful about it, he would never have
> said: "We prophets do not leave any inheritance,"
> because he would have known that his lying
> would be exposed by the very wording of this
> concocted hadith. If he had used the words "I
> have not left behind any legacy," his attempted
> hadith would have been more plausible. But
> when he used the plural "We prophets . . ."we are
> obliged to investigate the truth of the hadith and
> refer to the Holy Qur'an for guidance. We find
> that there are a number of verses which tell us
> that the prophets in fact did leave inheritances.
> This proves that this hadith is to be rejected
> outright.

Fatima began to quote the Quran in her defense to counter any arguments laid down by the defense to prevent her from claiming her rights of inheritance.

Fatimah then turned toward the Ansars and said:

> O you people of intellect! The strong supporters
> of the nation! And those who embraced Islam;
> What is this short-coming in defending my right?
> And what is this slumber (while you see) injustice
> (being done toward me)? Did not the Messenger
> of Allah (p.b.u.h.) my father, used to say: "A man
> is upheld (remembered) by his children ?!" O

how quick have you violated (his orders)! How
soon have you plotted against us? But you still
are capable (of helping me in) my attempt, and
powerful (to help me) in that which I request and
(in) my pursuit (of it).

Fatima's spoken words in the Masjid-e-Nabavi as an
opening statement from a plaintiff possessed the hallmark of
a revolutionary speech that reinvigorated women's rights. The
depth and breadth of the coverage of the past, present, and
future were skillfully presented with a flawless delivery that
left the opponent confused, vulnerable, weak, and speechless.
Her arguments and reasoning were exceptionally well balanced
and expertly choreographed. The structure of her speech was
brilliantly cast into sections that first started with Tawheed—
the belief in one God, Allah—and as she delved deeper in, she
brought out the attributes of Allah that addressed every angle
that needed to be covered from the metaphysical corollaries that
were expertly utilized in confirmation of Tawheed. She then
identified Muhammad, her father, as the divine representative
whose role in the introduction, preaching, and propagation of
Islam was given to the uninformed, unprepared society whose
culture was vehemently resistant to accept a comprehensive
system designed to create an environment promoting peaceful
coexistence, respect, and love. She backed this with the Quran
as a call to peace, order, and absolute justice. She expounded
on its glory as an ultimate testimony to a code of conduct with
comprehensive, multi-dimensional coverage able to address every
conceivable issue. To make sure that all aspects were covered,
she delivered a list of core beliefs and practices that a Muslim is
required to follow.

According to recorded historical events, it appears that Fatimah (AS) was successful at the beginning in persuading Abu Bakr to hand back Fadak to her.

Abu Bakr:

O daughter of the Messenger of Allah . . . Surely the Prophet is your father, not anyone else's, the brother of your husband, not any other man's; he surely preferred him over all his friends and (Ali) supported him in every important matter, no one loves you save the lucky and no one hates you save [the] wretched. You are the blessed progeny of Allah's Messenger, the chosen ones, our guides to goodness, our path to Paradise, and you-the best of women-and the daughter of the best of prophets, truthful is your sayings, excelling in reason.

You shall not be driven back from your right . . . But I surely heard your father saying: "'We the group of prophets do not inherit, nor are we inherited.'" Yet, this is my situation and property, it is yours (if you wish); it shall not be concealed from you, nor will it be stored away from you. You are the Mistress of your father's nation, and the blessed tree of your descendants. Your property shall not be usurped against your will, nor can your name be defamed Your judgment shall be executed in all that which I possess. This, do you think that I violate your father's (will)?

Fatimah then refuted Abu Bakr's claim that the Prophet (p.b.u.h.) had stated that prophets do not leave any property for inheritance:

> Glory be to Allah ! Surely Allah's Messenger
> (p.b.u.h.) did not abandon Allah's Book nor did
> he violate His commands. Rather, he followed its
> decrees and adhered to its chapters. So do you
> unite with treachery justifying your fabrications?
> Indeed this-after his departure-is similar to the
> disasters which were plotted against him during
> his lifetime. But behold ! This is Allah's Book, a
> just judge and a decisive speaker, saying One that
> will (truly) inherit Me, and inherit the posterity of
> Yaqub, and Sulaiman inherited Dawood. Thus,
> He (Glory be to Him) made clear that which
> He made share of all heirs, decreed from the
> amounts of inheritance, allowed for males and
> females, and eradicated all doubts and ambiguities
> (pertaining to this issue which existed with the) by
> gones.
>
> Nay! But your minds have made up a tale (that
> may pass) with you, but (for me) patience is most
> fitting against that which ye assert; it is Allah
> (alone) whose help can be sought.

Abu Bakr responded by stating the following:

> Surely Allah and His Apostle are truthful, and
> so has as (the Prophet's) daughter told the
> truth. Surely you are the source of wisdom, the
> element of faith, and the sole authority. May
> Allah not refute your righteous argument, nor

invalidate your decisive speech But these are
the Muslims between us-who have entrusted
me with leadership and it was according to their
satisfaction that I received what I have. I am not
being arrogant, autocratic, or selfish, and they are
my witnesses.

Upon hearing Abu Bakr speak of the people's support for
him, Lady Fatima Zahra (AS) turned toward them and said, "O
people, who rush toward uttering falsehood and are indifferent
to disgraceful and losing actions !"

It appears as though Abu Bakr was finally persuaded to return
Fadak to her. He was prepared to hand the claim of Fadak to
Fatima.

Nevertheless, when Fatimah (AS) was leaving
Abu Bakr's house, Umar suddenly appeared and
exclaimed :

What is that you hold in your hand ?

Abu Bakr replied :

'A decree I have written for Fatimah (AS)
in which I assigned Fadak and her father's
inheritance to her.

Umar then said :

With what will you spend on the Muslims if the
Arabs decide to fight you.

Umar then seized the decree and tore it up!!![3]

And when they who were bent on evildoing
behold the suffering [that awaits them, they will
realize that] it will not be lightened for them [by
virtue of their pleading] ; and neither will they be
granted respite. (Quran 16:85; translator, Asad)

وَإِذَا رَأَى الَّذِينَ ظَلَمُوا الْعَذَابَ فَلاَ يُخَفَّفُ عَنْهُمْ وَلاَ
هُمْ يُنظَرُونَ

It is not surprising that Fatima's speech in the Masjid brought
more suffering to her and her family. Fatima was hurled into an
inexorable onslaught. It was only yesterday that Fatima had been
the princess of the heart of Muhammad. Muhammad always
rose up to greet Fatima. According to Aisha, her staunch enemy,
who said:

> I have seen no one more resembling in manner,
> guidance and conduct of the noble Prophet than
> Fatima? Whenever she came to him, he used to
> stand up for her and then take her by the hand
> and kiss her and make her sit in his seat. And
> whenever he went to her, she used to stand up
> for him, take him by the hand, kiss him and make
> him sit in her seat.[4]

It is recorded in history that Muhammad's day would not start
without his first paying a visit to Fatima. It was not Muhammad
who was giving her this special treatment that he never gave
to anyone else; it was Allah, according to the Quran, who was
making him honor Fatima.

"Nor does he say (aught) of (his own) Desire."
(Quran 53:3; translator, Yousuf Ali)

وَمَا يَنطِقُ عَنِ الْهَوَى

The icon of purity honored by the Quran was engulfed in the clouds of despair only but a few days after the passing of Muhammad. Fatima's actions epitomized the Quran's teachings, and the Quran condemned every evil act intended to harm Fatima in any way. The Quran had made it clear that the Ahlul Bayth of Muhammad, as we have already stated in the previous chapters, were special.

> That is (the Bounty) whereof Allah gives Glad Tidings to His Servants who believe and do righteous deeds. Say: "No reward do I ask of you for this except the love of those near of kin." And if anyone earns any good, We shall give him an increase of good in respect thereof: for Allah is Oft-Forgiving, Most Ready to appreciate (service). (Quran 42:23; translator, Yousuf Ali)

ذَلِكَ الَّذِي يُبَشِّرُ اللَّهُ عِبَادَهُ الَّذِينَ آمَنُوا وَعَمِلُوا
الصَّالِحَاتِ قُل لَّا أَسْأَلُكُمْ عَلَيْهِ أَجْرًا إِلَّا الْمَوَدَّةَ فِي
الْقُرْبَى وَمَن يَقْتَرِفْ حَسَنَةً نَّزِدْ لَهُ فِيهَا حُسْنًا إِنَّ اللَّهَ
غَفُورٌ شَكُورٌ

"Love of those near to kin" in the above verse is a reference to Fatima, Ali, Hasan, and Husain.

for God only wants to remove from you all
that might be loathsome, O you members of
the [Prophet's] household, and to purify you to
utmost purity. (Quran 33:33; translator, Asad)

إِنَّمَا يُرِيدُ اللَّهُ لِيُذْهِبَ عَنكُمُ الرِّجْسَ أَهْلَ الْبَيْتِ
وَيُطَهِّرَكُمْ تَطْهِيرًا

The verses from the Quran quoted above in support of the
statement are verifiable by both Sunni and Shia sources.

The above episode was only a prelude to an everlasting,
torturous path laid for the members of the family of the prophet
by their foes. Unfortunately, history under the tyrannical rulers
of the Bani Ummayah (Ummayads) and Bani Abbas (Abbasids)
was extraordinarily sympathetic to these oppressors and despots
who changed the course of Muslim history in a diametrically
opposite direction to the will of Allah and Muhammad. These
and later autocrats under the banner of Islam did the exact
opposite of Quran, hadith and Sunnah. The ungrateful grandson
of Abu Sufyan, Yazid ibn Muawiah, who terrorized the family
of Muhammad in Karbala, had forgotten that Muhammad, the
last grand prophet, was merciful and beneficent to his staunch
enemies Abu Sufyan, Muawiah, Khalid Ibn Walid, and others at
his triumphant entry into Mecca by releasing these hopeless and
beaten misfits as Talaq.[5]

Ali remained silent during the early chaotic times only for
the safety and protection of Islam. Ali, an unrivaled commander
and graceful warrior who had destroyed legends, such as Amr
ibn Abduad, Marhab, and many other giants, was holding back

to prevent Islam from losing its ground. Ali was a determined combatant who would not run and hide as did Umar and Abu Bakr in the Battle of Uhad and other battles. History, in an insinuating tone, illustrates that Umar was boisterously ruthless only in a safe and protected environment and not in the combat zone. During the battle of Saffin, Ali had challenged Muawiah to a duel to resolve the conflict, but Muawiah swiftly backed out, afraid of dying at the hands of an established legendary warrior like Ali[6].

Numerous scholars have written books to explain why Ali did not take action against the architects of Saquifa. He turned down Abu Sufyan's offer of support to gain Khilafath against Abu Bakr. It is worth noting that history and evidence indicates that with or without Abu Sufyan's support, Ali could have taken Khilafath if he had so desired.

CHAPTER 10

Reformists, Modernists and Current Crisis

*"But the Unbelievers,- their deeds are like a mirage in
sandy deserts, which the man parched with thirst mistakes
for water; until when he comes up to it, he finds it to be
nothing: But he finds Allah (ever) with him, and Allah
will pay him his account: and Allah is swift in taking
account"* (Quran 24:39; translator, Yousuf Ali).

وَالَّذِينَ كَفَرُوا أَعْمَالُهُمْ كَسَرَابٍ بِقِيعَةٍ يَحْسَبُهُ الظَّمْآنُ
مَاء حَتَّى إِذَا جَاءهُ لَمْ يَجِدْهُ شَيْئًا وَوَجَدَ اللَّهَ عِندَهُ
فَوَقَّاهُ حِسَابَهُ وَاللَّهُ سَرِيعُ الْحِسَابِ

The very vision of Islam and the Quran are not what they
once were. The original Islam stood as a means of peaceful
interpretation and cooperation, with the message of Muhammad
being the guidance by which to understand and implement what
the Quran taught. The deviance from the originally established
Islam of Muhammad began in a systemic fervor through Muslim
history; it has lasted from the death of Muhammad to this very day.
Many disguised their misinterpretations and misrepresentations
of what was the original Islam as claims of Islamic reform.
Though the reforms themselves usually proved not to be violent
(with the exception of Wahhabism) but merely new ways of
looking at the Islamic belief system, history has demonstrated
that these reforms have instead led to new brands of extremism,

the followers of which are willing to push such reforms by taking up the sword.

The beliefs that often drove these reforms in and of themselves stood to be narrow minded in their nature; they were sometimes flagrant misunderstandings of the original Islam that had once driven the Cultural Revolution. Originally, Islam had stood as a religion that was a representation of peace, its teaching proving time and time again that the only war to be fought that was ruled Islamically justified was strictly a defensive war. Muhammad himself demonstrated this in grand nature, as historically scrutinized, one will see that Muhammad only fought wars that were defensive in their nature, and he only fought such wars after he had already attempted to reach peaceful solutions through treaties and negotiations. An example of such negotiations was the Hudaibiah Treaty, which was designed to resolve the outbreak of war by allowing for peaceful coexistence with the aggressors. To demonstrate the immediate level of misinterpretations that were taking place even in Muhammad's lifetime, Umar, one of Muhammad's companions, had himself blatantly disagreed with Muhammad's treaty, even though Muhammad justified it with revelation and scripture.

> Verily We have granted thee a manifest Victory:
> That Allah may forgive thee thy faults of the past
> and those to follow; fulfil His favour to thee; and
> guide thee on the Straight Way; And that Allah
> may help thee with powerful help: And that He
> may punish the Hypocrites, men and women, and
> the Polytheists men and women, who imagine
> an evil opinion of Allah. On them is a round
> of Evil: the Wrath of Allah is on them: He has
> cursed them and got Hell ready for them: and

evil is it for a destination. (Quran 48:1–48:6;
translator, Yousuf Ali)

إِنَّا فَتَحْنَا لَكَ فَتْحًا مُّبِينًا

لِيَغْفِرَ لَكَ اللَّهُ مَا تَقَدَّمَ مِن ذَنبِكَ وَمَا تَأَخَّرَ وَيُتِمَّ نِعْمَتَهُ
عَلَيْكَ وَيَهْدِيَكَ صِرَاطًا مُّسْتَقِيمًا

وَيَنصُرَكَ اللَّهُ نَصْرًا عَزِيزًا

وَيُعَذِّبَ الْمُنَافِقِينَ وَالْمُنَافِقَاتِ وَالْمُشْرِكِينَ
وَالْمُشْرِكَاتِ الظَّانِّينَ بِاللَّهِ ظَنَّ السَّوْءِ عَلَيْهِمْ دَائِرَةُ
السَّوْءِ وَغَضِبَ اللَّهُ عَلَيْهِمْ وَلَعَنَهُمْ وَأَعَدَّ لَهُمْ جَهَنَّمَ
وَسَاءتْ مَصِيرًا

The disagreement by Umar was proved to be based on a
far more materialistic point of view, while Muhammad's treaty
was one of a moral nature. Umar even went as far as to say that
the treaty raised large doubts on Muhammad's decision-making
ability, questioning the very prophet of Islam himself, and through
Islamic belief, questioning Allah as well.[1]

Verily those who plight their fealty to thee do no
less than plight their fealty to Allah. the Hand
of Allah is over their hands: then any one who
violates his oath, does so to the harm of his
own soul, and any one who fulfils what he has
covenanted with Allah,- Allah will soon grant him
a great Reward. (Quran 48:10; translator, Yousuf
Ali)

إِنَّ الَّذِينَ يُبَايِعُونَكَ إِنَّمَا يُبَايِعُونَ اللَّهَ يَدُ اللَّهِ فَوْقَ
أَيْدِيهِمْ فَمَن نَّكَثَ فَإِنَّمَا يَنكُثُ عَلَى نَفْسِهِ وَمَنْ أَوْفَى
بِمَا عَاهَدَ عَلَيْهُ اللَّهَ فَسَيُؤْتِيهِ أَجْرًا عَظِيمًا

Ali, on the other hand, had supported this treaty along with Muhammad on moral lines, considering the necessity of moral peace and fiber more important than the gains of power and wealth. The treaty became a social and idealistic landmark in Muhammad's time for its successful aversion of war and the social order it led to between Islam and other religions.

Developments and Difficulties

From this point and beyond, the dissention from the beliefs Muhammad had once put in place as the standards of Islam were clearly becoming far more brazen and frequent. What had once stood as a white flag for peace and justice was sullied with the dark crimes of humanity under a falsified banner that hung with the name of Islam but lay hollow with the lack of the religions core beliefs, a banner that was waved in blind, twisted faith for movements that amassed thousands of innocent blood-bathed bodies and resulted in flagrant violations of the original faith. The Kharajites lay claim to one such instance that drew its misanthropic beliefs from misguided interpretations of the Quran and hadith. This group believed that Ali, who was the Khalifa of the time, should never have agreed to arbitration with Muawiah, the governor of Shaam (Syria), who had refused to pledge his allegiance to Ali. This turned them against Ali and led to the heinous assassination of the brother of the prophet in the Mosque as he was finishing the prayer that his brother had led not too long before.

In the eighth and ninth centuries (767–855 AD), four new Sunni theological schools of thought emerged. These four schools of thought were led by four men who were responsible for the development of the Sunni shari'ah:[2] Abu Hanifa, Malik Ibn Anas, Al Shafai, and Ahmed Ibn Hambal. Abu Hanifa and

Malik Ibn Anas were both students of Imam Jafar al-Sadiq, who will be discussed in the next paragraph; they combined the methodologies and processes of the Quran, Sunnah, and the ahadith of Muhammad to create a final jurisprudential order that would become their shariah. The developments resulting from these jurists after their extensive research was complete were considered absolute and final by the Sunnis. Any further innovations and interpretations or Ijtihad (hermeneutics) of such material was completely banned. Hence, no change has occurred in these four schools of thought in the last 1,100 years or more. Some of the current scholars have pushed for reincarnating Ijtihad upon believing that a great many difficulties have taken place because of such a lack of change.

The Shia school of Shari'ah was developed under the guidance of Muhammad's descendent Imam Jafar al-Sadiq, known as Fiqh-e-Jafariah. Ijtihad for the Shia faith was never forbidden or restricted as long as it existed within the perimeters that were established by the Quran, reliable ahadith, and Sunnah.

The listed differences, in terms of direct splits in the faith's core tenets, began here. The Sunni jurists had stated that there were five main pillars of Islam that all had to accept to be Muslim. The order of these five pillars was not crucial, though the ideas behind them were. These five pillars were the profession of faith (known as the shahada), ritual prayers, purification through charity, fasting, and Hajj (the required pilgrimage to Mecca). For Shias, there are five core pillars of Islamic belief as established through Jafar al-Sadiq, and there are ten core practices as well. The Shia belief set has an order of importance. These beliefs are, in order: Tawheed (belief in Allah as singular and absolute), Adal (justice), Nabuwath (belief in prophethood), Imamath (belief in the Imams/Legatees after Muhammad), and Khayamath (belief

in the Day of Judgment). It is important to note that justice comes directly after the stated absoluteness of Allah, tying justice to a level in god's judgment and also making injustice a core demerit within the Shia faith, which has in some cases given the Shias a reputation for rebelliousness. All of the Shia principles of belief are intermingled, as each connects to the next intricately. For example, there is the belief of the absoluteness of Allah, which ties directly to his absolute justice, from which was established the prophethood that allowed the spread of Islamic law and belief, which paved way for the Imamath to continue where Muhammad left off, ending it with a final day of justice—the Day of Judgment. The Sunni beliefs are not bound in such a way and are more open in their manner and levels of importance.

The Dawn Of A New Dark Age

350 years after the time of Ibn Hambal, Ibn Taiymmiah began to grow in reputation, lending change to the teachings of Ibn Hambal and driving them toward a far more restrictive and controversial direction, creating immense tension, vastly expanding the chasm that was the sectarian divide, and also laying the groundwork for the most extremist version of Islam—Wahhabism. It is also possible that the Deobandi movement of India involving the advocates of the early Khilafath, who were referred to as Salafi, led to the foreboding birth of Wahhabism[3]. Thus, the Wahhabi belief system appears to be a hybrid of both the Deobandi movement of India and the polarizing teachings of Ibn Taiymmiah.

The teachings of Ibn Taiymmiah, though, were popularized, and upon further research, it was found that they seemed to clearly stand incongruous to the original Islamic beliefs that stood under the Quran and the ahadith. Though the Deobandi movement played a role, the movement of Ibn Taiymmiah laid a

powerful foundation for the narrowed down and far more violent translated beliefs of Abdul Wahhab.[4] Abdul Wahhab's traditions were considered so dangerous that his own father and brother opposed any chance of him spreading his word. Wahhab's brother Sulayman wrote in detail about his father's clear opposition to Wahhab's radical beliefs and prevented Wahhab from promoting or uttering them as long as he was alive.[5] Sulayman continued to detail how Wahhab rarely ever read the complete works of other schools of thought within his sect of Islam and only picked and chose certain aspects from the works of Ibn Taiymmiah to support his radical views. Ibn Humaydi, a very noteworthy Sunni who was also a firm supporter of Ibn Taiymmiah's views, made similar accusations against Abdul Wahhab as well.[5] When Abdul Wahhab fought against the belief in *Taqlid* (the following of Muslim jurists or scholars), he in effect promoted his own Taqlid of Wahhabism to a completely different level. Wahhab stated that his brand of Islam was the only path that was allowed and that all other paths in Islam were considered wrong, even heretical and therefore punishable by death.[5]

Wahhabism began to take off, especially under the Saudi government, which was continuing to grow and become more violent and which had begun standardizing, if not glorifying, the practices of Al-Qaeda and other extremist terrorist organizations. The message drew on old resentments and battle lines, creating the basis for wanton murder, massacre, rape, and genocide against the Shi'ites and other non-Wahhabis.[3] One need only look at the despicable attacks on 9/11 against the World Trade Center, the Pentagon, and Flight 93 to see how twisted the Wahhabi tradition has become. These same groups have proven responsible for the deaths of thousands in Iraq and Afghanistan, as well as Spain, England and many other countries of the world.

Of course, there are few to no parallels that can be drawn between the original state of Islam under Muhammad and that of the Wahhabi branch. Islam had never allowed flagrant massacres and senseless force in establishing Muslim right, neither according to the Quran nor the beliefs of the Prophet himself. Yet the misinterpretations are clear, with the likes of Osama bin Laden and others claiming misrepresented Quranic quotes and sadistic ramblings coined from the traditions of Abdul Wahhab. In the history of Islam (not so much the religion, but those that used it for political strength and power over the people), this was the way of the world. Conquests and forceful conversion through violence were the only means of conversion; this often led to slaughter, which of course was usually committed under the guise of the name Islam, though often beneath this thin superficial layer lay the gargantuan fact that it was all steeped in political and economic gain.

> It is He Who hath sent His Messenger with guidance and the Religion of Truth, to proclaim it over all religion, even though the Pagans may detest (it). (Quran 9:33; translator, Yousuf Ali).

هُوَ الَّذِي أَرْسَلَ رَسُولَهُ بِالْهُدَى وَدِينِ الْحَقِّ لِيُظْهِرَهُ عَلَى الدِّينِ كُلِّهِ وَلَوْ كَرِهَ الْمُشْرِكُونَ

When Jesus delivered the early Islam that later developed separately into Christianity through peace, we saw this peace met with the vehement aggression and misguided religiosity leading to extreme levels of torture, violence, and murder in the name of religion. It was clear, though, that politics and power were deeply embedded in the death of one of the great prophets. Later in Islamic history, the same was seen with Hussain Ibne Ali ibn Abu

Talib, the grandson of Muhammad who attempted to peacefully preach the original and just version of Islam and was violently murdered with his companions and whose women-folk were tortured by Yazid ibn Muawiah.

Such reform movements as Abdul Wahhab's are grossly exaggerated in their presentations as being for the advancement of Islam. The political undertones of the Saudi family's backing of such beliefs should lay proof enough of the true purpose behind following such beliefs. As all Muslims believe, the Quran is the ultimate word of Allah. If this word is complete, flawless, and perfect by Allah, then where is the need for the reformation of the original, unadulterated ways of Islam? The reforms that have taken place and the reformers behind them have proven time and time again that there is a strong political undercurrent to it that manifests itself in Muslim rulers, non-Muslim appeasement, and/or the proliferation of foreign cultures that made these reforms of a cultural nature rather than a religious nature. It has never been Islam that has needed reformation; it has been the Muslim community that has needed it. As was clearly shown above, it is the so-called Islamic reformation movements that have themselves caused the blatant violence and destruction we have seen. It has been such misrepresentations and misinterpretations of Islam, as well as fabricated hadith, that have been passed off as Islamic reforms when they clearly represented political agendas, much as a wolf in sheep's clothing.

The original catalyst for the growth of Islam was on a far more pure level—that of peace, love, and justice. The Islam that had been spread by the so-called sword was relatively short lived, while the original message continued to flourish in areas few expected it to. The Muslim representatives that went to India

converted masses of people through the word of Islamic peace rather than the sword.

The spread of Islam, though, caused several problems in and of itself. The expansion of Islam through the world outlet led to a blending of culture and religion, as many wanted to embrace their religion but at the same time wanted to hold on to what they could of their cultures. The original blending of culture and Islam itself was not a problem. The problem came about with the melding into the cultures of their peoples while still staying completely true to their Islamic philosophies and regulations. Of course, in most situations, there was a clash between such cultures and the religion itself, and this led many to feel threatened because their stakes in their religion were being forced to go before the battalion of culture and society. In Islam, this was not an important issue, as Islam does not force its religious principles, rules, and beliefs on others from different faiths, but some Muslims saw this culture clash as a serious threat to their integrity and solace as Muslims, and thus they began a conflict that ran down a bloody road.

The Modern Reformations

The beginning of the twentieth century lay witness to the severity of the cultural impact on Islam. The so-called revivalist movements began to grow in nature on both political and religious fronts, often in unison, as the world began to decolonize and new borders and boundaries created new freedoms and conflicts. What many had envisioned as a new frontier into a civilized world away from the tyranny of colonization instead grew into bitter, bloody wars within nations that had been misguidedly divided not by religion or culture, but by rivers, lakes, and arbitrary lines drawn without thought to the possible brutality that could arise.

It was only a matter of time before the Muslim populace began to draw religion into the situation.

The starters of the revivalist process were from all around the world: Qutub in Egypt, Maududi in India, and Taha in Sudan. Taha and Qutub both saw the bloody hand of political executions.[6] Maududi, who claimed to be the descendent of Fatima, the daughter of Muhammad, went through several different stages with his religious ideologies. These stages of changes, no doubt, were at least partially led by changes in the political weather depending on their prevalence in India at that time. Vali Nasr, in his book *The Vanguard of Islamic Revolution*, describes the many changes Maududi went through at the time as he moved from India to Pakistan to Saudi Arabia and eventually settled in the United States at the time of his death. Before his arrival in the United States, Maududi clearly was supported by the monarchy of Saudi Arabia, which he saw as mutually beneficial.[7] In the last phase of his life, though, the realization came to Maududi that there was a strong conflict between the philosophies of the House of Saud and his own deeper respect to Islam's core beliefs.

Maududi's book *Khilafath and Mulukiath* (Khilaphat and Monarchy) became a controversial epitaph.[8] It became an intensely controversial book because in it, Maududi sets a guideline according to the standards of the Quran of what attributes and character a Khalif should have, and further, through his analysis, he comes to realize that Uthman (the third Khalif) had actually deviated on a grand scale from the Quran and mishandled the Khilapath. Maududi concluded that Uthman had in fact gone against his duties as Khalif by creating a system which would allow his clan members and relatives to command his administration and in turn help Muawiah to rule

and create a dictatorial dynasty that would then disrespect the teachings of the Quran and Islam. Maududi quotes the Quranic verse below to support Abu Haneefa's view quoting the exegesis of a Hanafi expert, Abu Bakr Al-Jasas, which states that a *Zalim* (unjust evildoer) cannot be in any leadership position, including that of Khilafath. He claims that in view of the verse, a Khalifa who has been unjust and known for evil acts does not qualify for allegiance. The trend set by Abu Bakr, Umar, and Uthman, as well as the Khalifas of Bani Ummayah and the Bani Abbas, all fall into this category.[9]

And remember that Abraham was tried by his Lord with certain commands, which he fulfilled: He said: "I will make thee an Imam to the Nations." He pleaded: "And also (Imams) from my offspring!" He answered: <u>"But My Promise is not within the reach of evil-doers.</u> (Quran 2:124; translator, Yousuf Ali)

وَإِذِ ابْتَلَى إِبْرَاهِيمَ رَبُّهُ بِكَلِمَاتٍ فَأَتَمَّهُنَّ قَالَ إِنِّي جَاعِلُكَ
لِلنَّاس إِمَامًا قَالَ وَمِن ذُرِّيَّتِي قَالَ لاَ يَنَالُ عَهْدِي الظَّالِمِينَ

According to this verse, Khilafath and Imamath cannot be in the hands of someone considered wicked or bad. Injustice as well is also considered an attribute that is unacceptable in terms of both the Quran and core Islamic principles. Thus, Maududi demonstrates that all Kulafa (plural of Khalifa) proven to be unjust are no longer acceptable Khalifas. This book, as can be expected, led to a strong backlash against Maududi's words and ended up costing him dearly.

Taha instead drew upon the Quran itself and its interpretations. Taha argued that the Quran's revelation was split between the verses that were revealed in Mecca and those verses that were

revealed in Medina. The conclusion that this argument leads to, according to Taha, is that some of the verses given during the revelations in Mecca should not be abrogated by verses given during the revelations in Medina. Taha's ideas stated that the Quran itself was timeless, and that to separate its ideas within the confines of time would be a contradiction to the essence of the Quran. One student of Taha, An Naim, had written the book *Toward an Islamic Reformation,* which continues, in essence, the works of Taha by detailing the developmental aspects of this theory to attack the regimes that had justified the execution of Taha.

Though the understanding of Islam was in conflict among the revisionists, the understanding of Islam, human rights, and women's rights was debated on a separate, two-front line. On one side, there were the non-Muslim commentaries on Islamic human rights and women's rights. These commentaries, more often than not, came from a heavily Westernized sphere of ideas and beliefs. It was, and is still not, uncommon for many of the Western commentators to look at Islam through the actions of dictators, monarchs, and other Muslim leaders of state rather than to look at Islam from its own perspective and see the severe difference between the two. Many entered the discussion hoping to achieve some sort of fact-finding goal, though in the end most were left with a subconscious bias toward Islamic law and the Quran itself and ended up debating issues through misinterpretation and misrepresentation.

Because of a high level of interest after many of the horrific terrorist events that have recently taken place under the banner of Islam, several "experts" on Islam have emerged. Through a discussion about the intricacies of state and Islam, the religion, and its development is necessary to understand Islam, many of

these "experts" have instead used selected verses of the Quran out of context and have used a loose understanding of the faith to venture into the intense job of understanding ahadith, the Quran, Jihad, and the Khilafath, a responsibility many others have spent their entire lives studying. The result of such lackadaisical research and fact finding is a great deal of confusion, contradiction, and blatant misrepresentation of the ahadith and the Quran. In the modern era, Islam has become a cultural and universal phenomenon, both through its powerful teachings and also, sadly, through the misguided people who use it for political violence and malevolence. Because of this large upsurge in interest for the religion, a vast amount of information on Islam, Quran, and ahadith has come to exist. The problem with such a vast mass of knowledge is that few are able to decipher it and take away the impartial meanings from this level of information; they instead twist and jumble what they find into a foundationless house of an argument that's sure to collapse at the slightest refutation.

The Battle of Women's Rights

When the issue of women's rights comes up, the misrepresentations of Islam are found far more than the realities of the religion and its beliefs about women. Many notable female Muslim authors though have taken it upon themselves to fight back against those who claim Islam has no standing when it comes to women's rights. One such author is Amina Wudud, who goes into detail with the Quran to demonstrate that the allegations against Islam's stand on Women's rights are baseless and that Islam in fact holds a high place for women's rights. Similarly, Asma Barlas, though prejudiced at times,[9] goes into a detailed analysis of Quranic exegesis and the intricacies that relate to the early development of ahadith and Sunnah and their impact on the current status of women in the Muslim world, and it also

ventures into the various stereotypes and negative connotations that have been argued against women's rights in Islam and continues by disproving them. The influence of various exegetes of the Quran, as well as experts on ahadith and Sunnah, was also discussed to explain the evolution and creation of the negative nuances that cause misrepresentation of the Quran and Islam.

Such analyses, like that of Hudud and Abdul Fadl, provide a forward-moving understanding into the original intents of the religion of Islam as well as the Quran by vindicating them of the several negative allegations that have been tacked on to them because of the centuries of patriarchal influences that biased themselves against the proper understanding of Islam and instead used the religion for political cronyism and support.

The problem becomes, though, that many of these same authors fall victim to the same political and tribal biases that would have caused the very collapse of women's rights itself. As many of these authors began developing arguments for women's rights, they still fell prey to arguing in areas that they knew little about, and they argued without any formal facts or basis. For example, in the same book in which Barlas comes out as fair and understanding regarding women's rights, Barlas interjects an unnecessarily prejudiced statement in its midst: "with the Shi'ites claiming that the Prophet backed Ali's claim to the caliphate and the Sunnis that Ali's father was condemned to hell."[11]

As was shown earlier, after the death of the Prophet Muhammad, Abu Bakr and Umar followed through on a plan to enact a coup for the power of Khilafath by leaving Ali out of the process of selection. A clearly unbiased and valid argument would have taken into account exactly why Ali should not have been in the place of Khilafath or should have been in the place of Khilafath rather than leading to his own father. There was

clearly no need for the invective remarks that claim Ali's father, Abu Talib, would go to hell. In the context of Abu Talib, it is more plausible to rise beyond the biases of Sunni or Shiah and go directly to the Quran and ahadith for understanding of what exactly the place of Abu Talib in Islam was. Abu Talib, Ali's father, was also Muhammad's paternal uncle. Abu Talib historically was the one who proved instrumental to the early propagation of Islam by Muhammad. Going specifically to the Quran though, one finds the Quran states that Allah had provided Muhammad guidance, living quarters, and support during his development.

> Thy Guardian-Lord hath not forsaken thee, nor is He displeased. And soon will thy Guardian-Lord give thee (that wherewith) thou shalt be well-pleased. Did He not find thee an orphan and give thee shelter (and care)? And He found thee wandering, and He gave thee guidance. (Quran 93:3–93:5, Translator, Yousuf Ali).

مَا وَدَّعَكَ رَبُّكَ وَمَا قَلَى

وَلَسَوْفَ يُعْطِيكَ رَبُّكَ فَتَرْضَى

أَلَمْ يَجِدْكَ يَتِيمًا فَآوَى

وَوَجَدَكَ ضَالًّا فَهَدَى

These ayas are given as a huge credit to what Abu Talib had undertaken with Muhammad. At the time, it was none other than Abu Talib himself that was giving all of these amenities to Muhammad in his development. Thus, his status was no different than say, that of Muhammad's own father, Abdullah.

According to the Quran, Allah claims the responsibility of the raising of Muhammad and, most importantly, the development of Muhammad. Clearly, Muhammad developed and grew in the household of Abu Talib, so to say that Abu Talib himself was a nonbeliever or that he was deserving of hellfire would be absurd, as it would contradict the Quran, because the growth of the prophet has to be in a house that was provided by Allah for Muhammad's development. Thus, rather than being, as some claim, a *kafir* (nonbeliever), Abu Talib was in fact carrying out the will of Allah according to the Quran, similarly to Asiya's performing her task of raising Moses. Therefore, Abu Talib was no less a Muslim than Ishmael or Abdullah.

Truth Past Swords

Such blatant misrepresentations and lies in the face of the Quran, ahadith, Sunnah, and history continue to be strong reasons that the Muslim community stays so bitterly divided. For those that aren't Muslim, this becomes an easy opportunity for finger-pointing and deriving shariah that are made from false and misconstrued hadith and Quranic exegesis. The issue still remains that most Muslims have yet to find a constructive manner in which they can reorganize and reform what it is they represent, their core values and beliefs, and the power of those beliefs. It is the responsibility of the Muslim world to enter the fray of resolving these large issues rather than spilling senseless blood over them, to debate peaceably rather than with guns and suicide bombs, and to push the truth of Allah and the Prophet forward, past the swords of stubbornness and thoughtless violence.

CHAPTER 11

Freedom, Democracy, Education and Islam

"Let there be no compulsion in religion (see below for details): Truth stands out clear from Error: whoever rejects evil and believes in Allah hath grasped the most trustworthy hand-hold, that never breaks. And Allah heareth and knoweth all things" (Quran 2:256; translator, Yousuf Ali)

لاَ إِكْرَاهَ فِي الدِّينِ قَد تَّبَيَّنَ الرُّشْدُ مِنَ الغَيِّ فَمَنْ يَكْفُرْ بِالطَّاغُوتِ وَيُؤْمِن بِاللّهِ فَقَدِ اسْتَمْسَكَ بِالْعُرْوَةِ الْوُثْقَىَ لاَ انفِصَامَ لَهَا وَاللّهُ سَمِيعٌ عَلِيمٌ

Race and religion admittedly are two major factors in most of the conflicts in the world. In the light of the above verse, it can be seen that nondefensive armed conflicts with non-Muslims and violent clashes between sects within Islam are baseless and unacceptable. Muslim jurists, without any exceptions, agree that forcible conversions are un-Islamic. The modern wave of terror led initially by Saddam in Iraq and now conducted on a daily basis by Al-Qaeda is condemnable according to the laws of Islam. On June 13, 2007, Al Qaeda operatives bombed the Al-Askari Shrine in Samarah to once again provoke the Shia and destabilize Iraq. According to David McKeeby, USINFO White House Correspondent, Bush said: "This barbarous act was clearly aimed at inflaming sectarian tensions among the peoples

of Iraq and defeating their aspirations for a secure, democratic, and prosperous country."[1]

For four years after the fall of Iraq, Al Qaeda and Bin Laden operatives from Saudi Arabia, Egypt and Jordan that were responsible for the attacks of 9/11 have terrorized and killed thousands.[2] The gruesome, chilling beheading of journalist Daniel Perle and many others ought to be condemned by all versions of Islam. These acts of cruelty by Al-Qaeda and the Taliban trace their origins to the Wahabi trademark of misguided interpretations of the Quran, Sunnah, and ahadith. Karbala, a dark, frightening chapter in the history of Islam which resulted in the murder of the paragon of Islam and the grandson of Muhammad, Husain Ibn Ali, by a dictator, Yazid—the grandson of Abu Sufyan, cousin of Uthman (third Khalifa)—is a reminder of the deep-seated roots of such terror. The shrine of Husain Ibn Ali was bulldozed with thousands of Shias inside it during eighteenth century.[3] Similar acts of terror directed toward certain targeted sects characterized falsely as apostates have caused misery and suffering in the past and continue to terrorize the present. Muhammad Talbi, in *Liberal Islam,* presents an in-depth analysis on this subject to prove that killing an apostate is unjustifiable and in conflict with the Quran.[4] All Muslim jurists concur that forcible conversion is a grievous sin and that killing another Muslim or non-Muslim is therefore even more outrageous. These acts are usually the result of groundless, forged ahadith. Regardless of how conflicts between different sects, races, religions, or civilizations are characterized, the history of the world is gorged with killings of every nature and form for power and control of land, riches, and resources.

The apartheid in the late twentieth century in South Africa is a painful reality, and so is the situation in Darfur. This is now the twenty-first century, and sadly speaking, we are still discussing

the apartheid of the Palestinian people. Chapters 16 and 17 of President Carter's book titled *Palestine Peace or Apartheid* make one realize the gravity of the suffering the Palestinians have endured for more than sixty years. President Carter's brave expression of this gratuitous human tragedy, that, sadly, continues to be an ongoing event, has pushed forward a powerful argument to the issue.[5]

A 1,400-year history of the genocide of the Shia people since the death of the prophet of Islam cannot be buried under layers of centuries of anti-Shia propaganda to justify continued genocide on the basis of disagreements in the exegeses of the Quran and ahadith.

The massacre of Jews by Hitler; the massacre at Jallianwalla Bagh by the British in India; the killings of about a million in the wake of independence and partitioning of India and Pakistan; the million or more deaths in the Iran-Iraq War waged by Saddam; the recent genocides in Rwanda, Somalia, Bosnia, and Kosovo; the internal and external disputes in Lebanon; and the Saudi abuse of human rights and women's rights are only a few of the raw, barbaric displays of force and power ignited by religious and racial conflicts.

Islamic freedom and democracy are the foundations of the religion. Islam's strength lies in the statement "La ikraha fiddin" (no compulsion in religion). This is the first fundamental requirement to be met when one enters the fold of Islam. Self-determination sets the tone and mode for a truly liberal and free society erected on the foundation of submission to a just system of laws governing equality and the protection of human rights, specifically women's rights. This is the first religion that recognized one's right to select a religion without force, as its fundamental requirement is to honor free will.

The principle of complete freedom in the acceptance of Islam as one's religion that is enshrined in justice, dignity, and respect provides a stimulus not only for self-propagation, but also in the creation of a robust community. The propagation of Islam and the conversion to Islam of hundreds of millions with unwavering commitment were brought about through peaceful propagation and intellectual debates,[6] not through conquests. The expansion of the Muslim empire by force in different parts of the world was short-lived. Monarchy and dictatorship are unacceptable modes of operation in Islam, yet today's Muslim world is infested with them. Ironically, governments that pretend to promote democracy and freedom support these dictatorial regimes. Islam was sent to Arabia for a reason—to detoxify this part of the world of the use of raw brutal force, anarchy, and ruthlessness. Sadly, it has been more than 1,400 years and the Middle East is largely still at the same level of savagery in the same exact area.

Sabr (tolerance) is one of the virtues of Islam that made it an effective tool to curb violence. The first Khalifa who demonstrated sabr was Ali Ibn Abi Talib.

> "And do thou be patient, for thy patience is but
> from Allah. nor grieve over them: and distress
> not thyself because of their plots. (Quran 16:127;
> Yousuf Ali)

وَاصْبِرْ وَمَا صَبْرُكَ إِلاَّ بِاللّٰهِ وَلاَ تَحْزَنْ عَلَيْهِمْ وَلاَ
تَكُ فِي ضَيْقٍ مِّمَّا يَمْكُرُونَ

It was not easy for Ali to allow usurpation of his rights to Khilafath given the fact that he was the icon of Islam whose authority on the Quran and the principles of Islam was at its

apex, along with his degree of wisdom. His valor, courage, and unchallenged chivalry were established by his victories in all major battles of Islam. He was intellectually exceptional and certainly superior in knowledge among all of Muhammad's companions, even according to a hadith by Umar Ibn Khattab, the second Khalifa, who, according to Ahmad Humbal in his *Musnad,* said: "Ali is the best in judgment among us." Muhammad's hadith stating, "I(Muhammad) am the city of knowledge and Ali is its gate," provides validity to such a point.[7] Abu Sufyan, who spent his life waging war against Islam, approached Ali after the selection of Abu Bakr and offered his support in a bid to take the Khilafath back from Abu Bakr. Ali turned his offer down because he was skeptical about Abu Sufyan's intentions. He was convinced that it would be counter-effective in the interest of Islam, especially at its infancy. It is clear that even Abu Sufyan, father of Muawiah, believed that the Khilafath rightfully belonged to Ali. Ali exercised patience and remained altruistic, complying with the instruction of Quran.

There are more than seventy-two sects in Islam, and only one can be right. The evolution of all these sects is based on two factors; the first is harsh, firebrand politics, and the second is coercive schemes achieved through misinterpretations of the Quran, ahadith, and Sunnah. Opportunists, infiltrators, and leaders with hidden agendas have played a tremendous role in the split. Misguided leaders supported by their theocratic advisors were effective in creating dictatorial regimes with no connections to Islam.

> Therefore do thou hold Patience,- a Patience of beautiful (contentment)." (Quran 70:5; translator, Yousuf Ali).

فَاصْبِرْ صَبْرًا جَمِيلًا

"Except such as have Faith, and do righteous
deeds, and (join together) in the mutual teaching
of Truth, and of Patience and Constancy. (Quran
103:3; translator, Yousuf Ali).

إِلَّا الَّذِينَ آمَنُوا وَعَمِلُوا الصَّالِحَاتِ وَتَوَاصَوْا بِالْحَقِّ
وَتَوَاصَوْا بِالصَّبْرِ

Muslims need to assess the status quo. The choices are clear
and obvious. They can either compromise among themselves or
be consumed by the incubators of terror and indignation. They
need to realize that these differences are their own creations and
that they result from the lack of understanding of the Islam of
Muhammad, his preachings, his practices, and his plans for its
future. The violence ignited by these divisions has cost hundreds
of millions of lives of Muslims at the hands of Muslims.

Ilm (knowledge)

[Know,] then, [that] God is sublimely exalted.
the Ultimate Sovereign, the Ultimate Truth and
[knowing this,] do not approach the Qur'an in
haste, ere it has been revealed unto thee in full,
but [always] say: "O my Sustainer, cause me to
grow in knowledge! (Quran 20:114; translator
Yousuf Ali)

فَتَعَالَى اللَّهُ الْمَلِكُ الْحَقُّ وَلَا تَعْجَلْ بِالْقُرْآن مِن قَبْلِ أَن يُقْضَى إِلَيْكَ وَحْيُهُ وَقُل رَّبِّ زِدْنِي عِلْمًا

The following ahadith[8] of the prophet Muhammad alludes to the significance of education and knowledge in Islam:

a) The believer is unceasingly in search of wisdom. Wherever he finds it, he grasps it.

b) He looks for science everywhere, "even as far as china."

Seeking Ilm under all circumstances as a need for advancement has been directly and indirectly reiterated in Quran. Muslims have neglected this aspect for centuries and are hence dependent upon foreign technology. The desire to advance in different branches of science and technology is nonexistent in Muslim states. In the area of social sciences, most of the scholars of modern social sciences are trained in the western countries and are therefore influenced by the western views about Islam. This has some positive and some negative connotations. It is not surprising that oil-rich Muslim nations of the Middle East have not progressed for almost a century while the rest of the world has been moving forward with lightning speed. The attitude of being able to acquire anything in the open market has kept them dependent on the suppliers who indirectly control their assets. They have yet to realize that unless they make changes in their old behavior they are not going to catch up with the rest of the world. They need to realize that there is an urgent need for a radical productive change in order to compete for real growth.

Healthy criticism and ideas advanced from a constructive approach are needed and should be encouraged to compete for the best outcome. Muslims should espouse Western views that are productive and beneficial. Unfortunately, some of the trained Western scholars have fallen victim to views that are sometimes unrealistic and contradictory to the cultural and religious upbringing within Muslim nations, which must be thoroughly evaluated and progressively adjusted. Muslim nations and Muslims in general should focus on becoming leaders and world experts in all branches of social sciences, core sciences, engineering, and new technologies emerging in the field of medicine, genetic engineering, nanotechnology, electronics, and computer-based technology. Religion can be effectively used as a tool to induce the desire to learn, research existing views, confirm or discover new paths to explain religious texts, and modify Islam's applications to fit the modern needs of the Islamic community.

Education provides discipline of the mind, a necessary component of gaining knowledge. Moral values and respect for fellow humans is the essence of a healthy society, and respect for the rights of others is an essential condition of the promotion of peace. Muhammad was sent to address this issue in the pagan world of Arabia. Iraq is an example of a complete breakdown of all the fundamentals of Islam. Unfortunately, Iraq, under the influence of the outside elements, took a wrong turn at its onset and kept drifting away from those principles of Islam that were designed to bring the community together.

The claim that the escalation of Sunni and Shia violence in Iraq is being instigated by outside elements is a fact. These internal conflicts that are strategically carried out by outsiders are fueled by the fire of schism and derived from gross misinterpretation of the Quran, Sunnah, and ahadith by narrow-minded theocrats

and politicians looking to make personal and national gains. Iraqis will have to realize that their future is dependent on how the political dynamics unfolds amid the chaos created by these outside forces. Unless they put aside their differences and patch the road to healthy recovery from an era of brutality, their future will remain bleak and dismal.

In general, Muslims need to evaluate their past, change the present, and design a robust future. They need to reevaluate their views through the lens of the Quran to promote conditions that do not undermine the real Islam and its ideologies. Theologians, scholars, and leaders should coordinate discussions and resolve issues to promote the real Islam of Muhammad. Religious authorities can assume the responsibility of being positive influences if they break out of their ranks and promote the importance of education to adults and children. To do this, they will need to systematize their educational programs and set high goals.

Education should become their focus, because education is the ultimate solution to most of the problems that Muslims have experienced. They must realize that the crux of the purpose of their creation relies upon the quest for knowledge and the yearning for excellence in education. Education and knowledge is the future of Islam.

> "Travel through the earth and see how Allah did
> originate creation; so will Allah produce a later
> creation: for Allah has power over all things."
> (Quran 29:20)

From the above verse, the directive is clear; one must ponder upon the creation of things in Allah's multifarious plan and order and attain knowledge about their creation and beyond. Thus, the

human desire to explore and appreciate the intricate grid that makes up our world and the universe is encouraged.

The Quran challenges the human mind to develop the skills to seek answers not only to the mysteries of the universe, but also about the sophisticated composition of the human body, mind, and soul. William Chittick, in *The heart of Islamic Philosophy*, quotes Ali ibn Abi Talib in reference to the philosophy of the recognition of one's self (and soul) as a means to acknowledge the creator, Allah, as follows: "He who knows his soul knows his lord."[9]

Allah has meticulously embedded exemplary personalities among us to be admired, valued, and followed. Muhammad was created as the greatest among the apostles of Allah, and Ali was sent as an icon of knowledge and wisdom to be emulated. Historically, Ali has always been a powerful motivational force behind education and the acquisition of knowledge in the world of Islam. He served Islam from its inception in different roles. His strength as an educator, a teacher, and a visionary with command over a wide range of intricate, perplexing topics and intellectually challenging subjects has truly been a gift to the human race. His sermons are a collection of solutions to human curiosity. His loftiness in knowledge and wisdom can be appreciated in some of his sermons that delve into the complexities of the creation of the universe and the concept of time and space. Thus Ali belonged to the class of Ahel az Zikr and *Rasequoona fil Ilm*, which the Quran mentions on various occasions (see notes). After Muhammad, Ali, and Fatima established a standard for the qualification of Rasequoona fil ilm, or those gifted by Allah with knowledge of the inner dimension of the secrets of the creation of mankind and the universe. Below are few examples from his sermons that are mind blowing:

1. Ali, talking about the astronomy and the cosmos, states:

"He (Allah/The creator) put them in motion on their appointed routine and made them into fixed stars, moving stars, descending stars, ascending stars, ominous stars, and lucky stars."[10] .

As we step back and examine the history of astronomy, we appreciate what Ali said about astronomy in the seventh century AD. It is interesting to note that astronomy did not experience any major discoveries until the arrival of the sixteenth century, starting with Copernicus; Kepler; Galileo; and finally Newton, whose breakthrough in gravity in the seventeenth century pushed forward a new perspective regarding the understanding of the universe. Einstein drove forward astronomical science by epic proportions with his discoveries through the development of the theory of relativity in the early twentieth century—a theory that completely changed our perception of the universe. Erwin Hubble's revolutionary discovery in 1929 based on his red-shift studies demonstrated that the universe was expanding and hence dynamic in nature. His red-shift studies helped to put aside the previous concept of a static universe based on Einstein's theories.[11]

To human amazement, Ali, about 1,400 years back, presented a dynamic universe that scientists are now able to confirm. From what is stated above, it appears as though Ali had classified the celestial and extraterrestrial bodies into groups of stars in constant motion in different directions, suggesting the expansion of the universe. He introduced terms, such as "ominous stars," perhaps referring to black holes, and "fixed stars" and "lucky stars." He directs our attention toward our solar system and characterizes the sun as a fixed star with respect to the earth's orbit and also as a lucky star because Earth is the only living planet known to us. To

recapitulate, it was Ali who, in the seventh century, characterized the universe as being in a dynamic state of expansion, which was later to be experimentally verified by Hubble.

2. About the concept of time and space, Ali states:

"Allah is timeless and spaceless."

Therefore, Allah cannot be confined in the domain of time or space.[12]

Thus the beginning of our understanding of time and space is limited only to the theory of the Big Bang and the concept of singularity (singularity theorems, suggested by Stephen Hawking and Roger Penrose).[13] Accordingly, the origin of time and space is restricted to the point of initiation of the event of the Big Bang. These concepts are complex and require the systematic development of one's background in astrophysics, quantum physics, quantum gravity, the theory of unification, and mathematical interpretations relating to these areas. To elucidate these theories and experimental data is beyond the scope of this book. It is appropriate at this point to mention that Allah had already made arrangements for the future generations to realize that his representatives, the Ahel az Zikr, who were endowed with divine knowledge, will have already addressed the future issues as new discoveries become available.

Nahjul Balagha, which is a collection of Ali's sermons, is only a fragment of the whole that was able to reach us. Ali's knowledge, wisdom, and intellectual prowess was unmatched. It is obvious why Muhammad said "I am the city of knowledge and Ali is its door of entry." Islamic history is unable to produce an equal of Ali among the Khulafa (plural of Khalifa) and among the companions and relatives of Muhammad.

Islam's focus has always been on education and the development of knowledge. Heavy emphasis has been laid upon the community to motivate children and adults toward education and advancement of knowledge that is ordained to lead humanity out of darkness by energizing human minds with powers that can take one into uncharted territories of wisdom, which can then allow one to unravel the hidden treasures of the mind to appreciate the intricacies of the universe.

As the cultural upheaval with the closing of the intercontinental divide grips the world communities, and as the undercurrents churn, mix, and reshape various components of multicultural origin, a new culture is bound to emerge. This new culture specifically affecting the Muslim community can have all the elements of Islam only if we succeed in responding effectively to bring about a positive change through a carefully orchestrated agenda for our children, youths, and adults through counseling centers for careers in all branches of science, industry, and technology. We must understand that this is only the beginning and that it is perhaps our only chance to prepare a solid foundation and a safe future for our children. The introduction to the operating principles of Islam in a logical and systematic method can prepare us to endure the rigorous tests and challenges which we will ultimately face in our lives as we grow.

The dynamic nature of our society makes it difficult for our children to retain Islamic culture as they begin to evolve. The burden rests upon parents to attenuate these difficulties to ensure that their children retain the proper focus and direction toward the *Sirat-al-Mustaqeem* (right path). They need to utilize all their resources and use full throttle to move forward with even more vigor. *Inshaallah* (Allah willing), someday they may be able to build

internationally recognized, prestigious institutions of learning.
These institutions should be designed to provide adults and
children the stimulus necessary to challenge and reinforce each
other and build the intellectual fortitude desirable for propagating
a scientifically advanced, democratic, and free Islam across the
world.

Muslim nations and Muslims need to be receptive to the
people of other faiths and establish interfaith dialogue in a
constructive and productive way for the peaceful advancement
of society as a whole. Muhammad set examples of this
throughout his life. He was open to discussions and exchanges
of ideas. Muhammad established a nation and a constitution
based on the Quran to regulate and legislate a just administration
to accommodate non-Muslims with respect and dignity, invite
them to embrace his views and beliefs, set up just conditions
to address the issues of the needy and the less fortunate, and
send emissaries and letters to dignitaries and heads of states,
inviting them to Islam. His letters were sent to Hercules of
Rome; Kisra (Khusrau), the king of Persia; Negus; Al Mundhir
of Syria; Al-Muqawqis, king of Alexzandria; and many others
in the area.[14] Internally, he made sure that the people under
his care were looked after at every socioeconomic level.
Business ethics; social attitude; financial stability; interfamily
and intrafamily discipline, respect, and treatment of children
and parents; and cordiality in the treatment of one's spouse,
relatives, friends, and neighbors all stood as guidelines for his
people. He even left areas for possible modifications as needed
for the future generations.

Thanks to the American invasion of Iraq, the fallout
amazingly provided hope for a free Iraq. Iraq has now been
given an environment free from the tyranny of a butcher who

was finally served with justice. A systematic approach has to be formulated with a coherent body of ideas and principles evaluating the status quo and making all necessary adjustments to set aside all differences to salvage Iraq—a strategically important country.

CHAPTER 12

Reflections

"Lo! Allah enjoineth justice and kindness, and giving to kinsfolk, and forbiddeth lewdness and abomination and wickedness. He exhorteth you in order that ye may take heed" (Quran 16:90; translator, Picktall).

إِنَّ اللّٰهَ يَأْمُرُ بِالْعَدْلِ وَالْإِحْسَانِ وَإِيتَاء ذِي الْقُرْبَى وَيَنْهَى عَنِ الْفَحْشَاء وَالْمُنكَرِ وَالْبَغْيِ يَعِظُكُمْ لَعَلَّكُمْ تَذَكَّرُونَ

The four most distinguished and acclaimed women in the world of Islam according to well-known traditions and most of the Muslim scholars are Asiya (wife of pharaoh), Mary (Mother of Jesus), Khadija (Wife of Muhammad), and Fatima (Daughter of Muhammad). These four are honored as "the leaders of the women in heaven."[1] According to some traditions, Muhammad has placed Fatima above all others. Fatima is referred to as "The Greater Mary."[1].

Sir Muhammad Iqbal—a brilliant scholar, renowned philosopher, and distinguished poet—provides an exquisitely delicate spin to the above hadith as he sums up Fatima in the following poem, "Asrar-e-ramoose," translated by Arthur J. Arberry:

Mary is hallowed in one line alone,

That she bore Jesus; Fatima in three.

For that she was the sweet delight of him
(Muhammad)

Who came a mercy to all living things,

Leader of former as of latter saints,

Who breathed new spirit into this dead world

And brought to birth the age of a New Law.

His lady she, whose regal diadem

God's words adorn Hath there come any time

The chosen one, resolver of all knots (Ali)

And hard perplexities, the Lion of God,

An emperor whose palace was a hut,

Accoutred with one sword, one coat of mail.

And she his mother, upon whom revolves

Love's compasses, the leader of Love's train,

That single candle in the corridor (Hasan)

Of sanctity resplendent, guardian

Of the integrity of that best race

Of all God's peoples; who that the fierce flame

Of war and hatred might extinguished be,

Trod underfoot the crown and royal ring.

His mother too, the lord of all earth's saints

And strong right arm of every freeborn man,

Husain. the passion in the song of life,

Teacher of freedom to God's chosen few.

Reviewing the Past

The stage was set. The place was the Masjid, the court was the house of worship, the case was before Allah, and the claimant was Fatima. An incredibly grief-stricken Fatima only a few days back was harassed; her home was burned and her children were put through mental anguish by Abu Bakr and Umar. A determined Fatima, the daughter of Muhammad, rose out of the smoldering fire, brushed off pain, and defiantly stood up to protect Islam from a formidable internal threat. As Fatima entered a packed Masjid-e-nabavi, the Mosque built by Muhammad, people froze in awe, staring at the unexpected visitor who quickly took the center stage. Silence suddenly filled the air. Her words began to resonate in the Quranic language, and once again it appeared that Muhammad was back. Her flair, tone, and expression matched those of Muhammad. Those who once dared to contemptuously address the elite wife of Muhammad, Ume Salma, cringed in vain as silence took control. Fatima shook up the pagan world 1,400 years ago in a sermon in which she claimed her right to Fadak.

That voice of Fatima still produces giant ripples as it gains momentum and amplitude with time. Her voice still triggers chills among the oppressors and despots. Echoes of her voice still induce crisp doses of energy to human rights, adding nuances to a classic revolutionary movement that she started centuries

back. The revolutionary message transmitted by her speech for the claim of Fadak has become the voice of every woman, regardless of her nationality, creed, class, and culture. History has tried to turn its face away from its despicable indignations of past injustices inflicted upon women, but the explosive growth of this movement begun by Fatima has kept its resilience strong. Fatima's plight changed the world permanently when she made her groundbreaking speech for women's rights.

Islam was the first religion that legislated equality, fair treatment, and respect to women. The Quran is a living legislature that regulates and guarantees women's rights. The special respect that the Quran has given to women was a revolutionary mandate in favor of equal rights in Islam. Islam stands as the only religion in which a person's journey to heaven lies metaphorically under the feet of his mother in *Sahih* Al Tirmidhi. Fatima was up against reincarnated chauvinism. This was a society and culture that was unwilling to be stood up to by a woman. Fatima was challenging the status quo as well as the ego and pride of the pagan culture.

All the factual information presented demonstrates that Muhammad and his family members—Fatima, Ali, Hasan, and Husain—according to the Quran, had distinction and honor that no one else did. Scholars and exegetes of ahadith and Sunnah have recognized them as role models and perfect Muslims.

Jesus was a man of distinction, and the Quran has characterized him as a messiah and messenger of Allah whose life reflected love, compassion, and respect. According to the Christian belief, Jesus was put through the pain and torture of crucifixion by a regime hoping to put an end to his message. However, his message continued and was reawakened with charismatic flair by Muhammad, according to Islamic belief, which took Arabia by storm. Muhammad, the grand messiah, along with Ali, proffered

Jesus's task to astounding heights by adding the attribute of just leadership. Similar to Jesus's plight, the family of the apostle of Allah was ruthlessly subjected to terror and harassment immediately after Muhammad's death. Fatima became a target because the enemy was aware that she and her family would not compromise under any circumstances for anything that had the potential to inflict damage to the real Islam. For centuries, the progeny of Muhammad was put through different forms of terror, agony, and brutality.

The followers of Muhammad, Fatima, and Ali acquired the name of *Shia* (followers of Ahlul Bayth in accordance to the Quran and Sunnah). The ease with which ahadith, Sunnah, and history can be manipulated has been the main discussion of previous chapters. Regrettably, the misinterpretations of the Quran have, in most instances, impelled discord in the community, dividing the group into several sects and subsects. The gap between the actual events and their recording and composition almost a century thereafter sadly ended up working advantageously for the enemies of Islam, as they were thus able to easily twist and fabricate events with a carefully planned stratagem. Abu Bakr's hadith benefited him in two ways: By allowing him to take Fadak unlawfully and by allowing him to mislead people in the name of honesty by a hadith that helped him in his political ambitions. As many as 600,000 ahadith were known to have been presented by honest and dishonest men and women who were looking to gain favors from the ruling parties. Islam was only used by the ruling parties as a means to serve their political interests through implementation of power-sharing schemes with clan members and potential challengers.

In summary, it has been established that the split between the Muslim communities began even before Muhammad's death. The

basis of separation can be traced to the events before Muhammad's death. The Saquifa power struggle was exclusively a political move with no elements of Islam. This was the beginning of the end of the real Islam and the establishment of an autocratic form of governance bearing the name of Islam. The structure of this new form of government bore the markings of any other aristocratic dictatorships of the past and present history with a caveat: in this case Islam was used as a device to energize public support.

Ali, during his short Khilafath, tried to bring it back to its original status but was faced with an enemy steeped in coercion, fraud, and trickery that cost him his life. The political fallout after Muhammad's death undermined the true spirit of Islam. In all reality, the Islamic form of government in accordance to the Quran and Muhammad was gone.

Legal And Moral Considerations
About Khilafath And Fadak

The case of Fadak brings out the true qualities of the so-called companions of Muhammad. Fadak was Fatima's property on the basis of the Quran, ahadith, and history, and it was illegally confiscated by a regime incapable of implementing justice as required of a true Khalif (Quran 38:26). Fatima had demonstrated that the confiscation of her property by the state was illegal on the basis of the Quran and shariah, and the ensuing judicial disposition of this case was unfair and unacceptable according to Islam, and for that matter, according to any fair past and present system of justice. Juristically, Abu Bakar would not have been a defendant and a judge simultaneously.

Fatima established that the judicial body of one man (Abu Bakr) who also happened to be the defendant in this case could not have passed judgment in his own favor on the basis that

he alone heard Muhammad saying "Our property will not be inherited, whatever we [i.e., prophets] leave is Sadaqah [to be used for charity]," which was proven inconsistent with the Quran and hence unacceptable. This hadith also loses its credibility on the basis that it was unverifiable.

It was demonstrated on technical and religious grounds that the selection of the first Khalifa was un-Islamic. Abu Bakr's legitimacy to Khilafath was, by his own admission, flawed. His emergence as Khalifa at Saquifa was confirmed as erroneous by Umar, Abbas Ibn Abdul Muttalib, Ali, and many later scholars (See Chapter 3). Extensive analysis of the Saquifa events suggest that political dynamics were dominated by unfair, non-regulated processes bearing imprints of coercion, intimidation, and drama, ultimately setting the stage for a takeover.

It is interesting to note Abu Bakr's acknowledgement of regret for his mistakes on his deathbed[3]:

> I did three things that I now regret, they are:
>
> That I failed to show respect toward the house of Fatima . . .
>
> That I did not burn Fajaf Salmah . . .
>
> That At Saqifa I transferred Khilafath to Abu Ubaydah or Umar . . .

The following is a part of Abu Bakr's inaugural address:

> If therefore, I act uprightly, follow me; but if I deviate from the right course, then you must set me straight. As for the Messenger of Allah, he passed away without anyone accusing him of any

wrong doing, not even the light strike of a whip or any thing lesser than that. <u>But for me, I have a Satan who possesses me; avoid me when he comes to me.</u>[3]

It is left to the reader to determine the situations in which Abu Bakr may have been possessed by the satanic spells. Was it at the burning of Fatima's home, or while rushing to Saquifa for a coup?

Fatima's speech brought awareness to the Muslim Umma that the usurpation of Khilafath was a result of years of preparations by the opposing forces via Shura, a politically driven, highly misinterpreted concept for the selection of a Khalif. She successfully established that women's rights and human rights are central to the beliefs of Islam and that the respect granted to women by the Quran and Islam cannot be ignored. On the judicial front, Fatima demonstrated her fundamental right to ownership of inherited property, in this case Fadak, which belonged to Muhammad and therefore to Fatima—his only daughter, according to her Islamic right.

Fadak remains an ugly scar on the history of Khilafath. Abu Bakr's usurpation of Fadak against the Quran and Sunnah were a blow to women's rights. Later it landed as a gift in the hands of sinners, murderers, criminals, and tyrants. Uthman, during his Khilafath, humiliated the family of Muhammad by gifting Fadak to Marwan, a veteran criminal of the time. Muawiah, a self-declared Khalif, gifted it to his son Yazid, a drunkard; followed by Marwan and Umar ibn Uthman.[4] The injustice initiated by Abu Bakr exacerbated the hostilities against the family of Muhammad's daughter, Fatima. The tragic outcome of the case of Fadak and the events relating to it in the early Khilafath emboldened the later rulers to terrorize and repress the progeny of Muhammad.

The selection of Khilafath was a deviation from the path of Muhammad and the guidelines set by him during his life. Muhammad, on numerous occasions, had declared Ali as his successor or *Wasi* (legatee.) The denial of a pen and paper to Muhammad to execute the will of Allah to keep the Umma from going astray was a direct disobedience to Allah and the Quran as discussed before (see Chapter 4).

The information provided below is intended to facilitate the reader in establishing the severity of the emotional trauma that Fatima and her family had to endure. After reading all the evidence and proof, it is left to the reader's good conscience to make the final judgment. However, it is important to reemphasize the conditions that caused these sufferings.

The following is Fatima's expression of grief at Muhammad's grave:

> There were after you conflicting news and misfortunes.
>
> If you were, no misfortune would happen.
>
> Some men showed us what there was hidden in their hearts.
>
> When you left and the grave kept you away from us.

As it turns out, the hostilities against Muhammad before his death intensified several fold after his death and were directed against Fatima and Ali to coerce them to accept the illegally acquired Khilafath. Fatima was terrorized during the attack on her home by Abu Bakr and Umar. Her home was set on fire and then her door was broken in, causing her severe injuries that

resulted in the death of her unborn baby and her own death a few months after. A streak of suffering engulfed her, starting with her father's traumatic death, the burning of her home, the death of her unborn son, the excruciating pain she experienced from her injuries, and the confiscation of Fadak. These deplorable crimes at the hands of the new regime deserved harsh punishment under the Islamic code of justice.

The confiscation of Fadak was also a scheme designed to weaken Fatima by taking away her assets. Abu Bakr had cornered himself in violation of numerous Islamic laws by putting forward his infamous hadith on the claim of Fadak discussed in several previous chapters. The information provided below is intended to facilitate the reader in establishing the severity of the emotional trauma that Fatima and her family had to endure.

This hadith quoted by Abu Bakr in his defense was so poorly formulated that it readily failed the test of the Quran. In addition, it fell apart on every conceivable front, as discussed in chapters 8 and 9. In the end, the following episode will further clarify the gravity of the emotional trauma Fatima must have gone through:[5]

> Abu Baker and Umar tried to reconcile with Fatima for the damaged relationship, perhaps out of guilt. They visited Fatima. The following is the conversation between them:
>
> She (Fatima) said to them: "If I narrate to you a tradition from the prophet, will you acknowledge it?"
>
> They said: "Yes."

She said: "I adjure you by Allah. Did you hear
the prophet saying: 'Fatima's contentment is
my contentment. Whosoever Loved Fatima,
Loved me, who ever pleased her, pleased me and
whoever displeased her, displeased me.'"

They said: "Yes, we did."

She said: "I call Allah and his angels to witness
that you have displeased me and have never
pleased me . If I meet the prophet, I will
complain of both of you to him."

Reflections

It was three years ago that I stood in Janath-ul-Baqui, about
one hundred feet away from the barricaded grave of Fatima,
passionately reminiscing about the history of Islam with limited
knowledge to reconstruct the past in anticipation of understanding
the present. I was not able to envision how such hatred toward
the daughter of Muhammad was possible. This was the grave of
the daughter of Muhammad—the daughter whom he had called
part of him, whom he had risen up to greet, and for whom he
showed anger at those who displeased her. This was Fatima—an
icon of womanhood whose shortened life was dedicated to the
spread of Islam. Her father, the grand messenger of Allah, was
Muhammad, without whose services there would not be more
than a billion Muslims today. As I stood in Janath-ul-Baqui, I
kept asking myself, "How is it possible for anyone to go to such
lengths to have mistreated the family of Muhammad, whom he
loved so intensely and whom Allah presented in the Quran as
models of human perfection?" The question that kept pulsating
in my mind related to the conundrum behind the rationale of
such hate, which was attributable either to enviousness regarding

Muhammad's family's superior character, intellectual prowess, knowledge, and physical strength, or ignorance regarding the Quranic verses and ahadith in praise and acknowledgement of their services to Islam. If the Quran and ahadith have eulogized Muhammad and his family, then how is it possible that almost a billion Muslims missed the highlighted scriptures of the Quran and ahadith? The answer is simple: mankind has always focused its attention on conquerors, emperors, kings, monarchs, and rulers who, in most instances, were tyrants and dictators with no instincts of Islam. Admiration for power, authority, and supremacy through domination and subjugation has always been human nature, and Muslims have proven to be no different from the rest of the world. The guards in Baqui were also, in a similar way, victims of the same thought process. They walked around inside Baqui answering questions and defending the need for barricades; they recited two or three verses of the Quran that were grossly misinterpreted and a few misconstrued and dangerously misleading ahadith that they had been forced to memorize. My brief confrontation with one of the guards convinced me that he was more of a robot programmed to perform limited tasks rather than one who had actually looked into the subject matter that he was reciting. Looking around, I was persuaded by the fact that the power of petrodollars (money from petroleum) has played a major role in keeping a fair majority of the Muslims in line with the beliefs of Wahabbism. Wahhabism was only about two hundred or so years old, whereas Islam had a history of 1,400 years, yet the Wahabi doctrine had still significantly influenced Muslims and non-Muslims alike.

The early split in the community that has been present from Muhammad's death to the current crisis in Iraq and elsewhere in the world between Shias and Sunnis has widened recently because of the acquisition of power and control over petroleum-

based wealth and territories. Muslims have demonstrated that logic, common sense, the Quran, and Sunnah are secondary to dominance and riches. Islam was meant to lead mankind toward a perfect lifestyle based on equality, coexistence, peace, love, honor, respect for human rights and women's rights, and a mandate for a socioeconomic structure addressing issues at every level of the community. At the very first call to Islam, Zul-e-sheerah, the majority that declined the message began a counter-campaign. As the message started to spread, there were those who genuinely accepted it while there were others who saw the power of the message and fell into its fold for fear of being left out. Then there was a third group that infiltrated the fold with the intention to destabilize it from within in anticipation of a possible takeover. The Quran contains an entire chapter, "Munafeqoon," dedicated to hypocrites. It specifically cautions Muhammad about these individuals and their malice and hidden agendas against Islam. These were anti-Islamic forces working from within. Abu Sufyan, Muawiah, and their supporters were open enemies for their entire lives who accepted Islam after large-scale losses; they internally remained anti-Islamic. The real threat to Islam came from those opportunists who acted and behaved like Muslims waiting in abeyance to strike at the right time for a coup d'état.

Muhammad recognized this threat and had planned to send them away before his death. Abu Bakr and Umar and their supporters sensed this and set their own plans to counter Muhammad's plan with inside help from their daughters, Aisha and Hafasa, who kept them informed about changes in Muhammad's health conditions. Those who refused to go under the leadership of Usama ibn Zayd angered Muhammad. As we examine the sequence of events prior to Muhammad's death, we notice that Muhammad initially asked for Ali, and Ayisha said that she wished he asked for Abu Bakr, and Hafza (Umar's daughter) said

she wished that he had asked for Umar. Immediately after this, Tabari states that Muhammad asked Abu Bakr to lead the prayer, and when Abu Bakr was about to lead the prayer, Muhammad, in his serious illness, proceeded to the Masjid with Ali and Abbas. Noticing that Muhammad was entering the Masjid, Abu Bakr stepped aside, and Muhammad then led the prayer. The question arises that if Muhammad had asked Abu Bakr to lead the prayer, why would he then in his condition go to the Masjid and lead the prayer, effectively preventing Abu Bakr from doing so? These events create doubts about whether Muhammad ever gave permission to Abu Bakr to lead the prayer in the first place. The following is the explanation provided under reference 1248 in Tabari:[6]

> All the reports that Abu Bakr was asked by the
> prophet during his last illness to lead the prayer
> are tendentious and inconsistent. They are used
> by Sunnis to argue the succession in favour of
> Abu Bakr.

After Muhammad's death, Abu Bakr and Umar rushed to Saquifa for a takeover bid. After Saquifa, they became hostile to Fatima and her family. Khilafath was acquired by unfair methods, and the process continued until Ali's Khilafath. After Ali, Muawiah forcefully declared himself Khalifa and converted it into a dynasty of rulers who were drunkards and tyrants with no connection to Islam. As pointed out by Bobby Ghosh in his article in the March 5, 2007, issue of *Time*, the followers of Muawiah (Uthman's clansmen) who transferred Khilafath to his successors (his sons Yazid and Marwan) began to identify themselves as Sunnis.[7] Once this trend was set, the criterion of the concept of Khilafath changed from its Quranic intent into the hands of dictators, tyrants, murderers, and oppressors. Bernard Lewis, in

his book *The Crisis of Islam,* quotes a hadith that reads as follows: "Jihad is your duty under any ruler, be he godly or wicked." This fabricated hadith, anti-Quranic in nature, appears to be the work of a Khalif who was safeguarding his position. This has been the trend for the last 1,400 years. Anyone who posed a threat to this dogma was disposed of.

Abdul Wahhab took it in a different direction by strategically aligning himself with the Saud family to advance his distorted views. The Quran declares that a *zalim* (unjust tyrant) like Saddam cannot be a Muslim. Ibn Taiymmiah and the Deobandi movement influenced Abdul Wahhab and his followers, such as Osama bin Laden and thousands of Al-Qaeda guerrillas who have connections to abhorrently devious concepts to end the lives of hundreds of thousands of Muslims.

After Muhammad's death, Fatima became a threat by challenging the new Khalifa and his illegal and unjust practices. Fatima was a threat then and is a threat today to any regime in the footsteps of Abu Bakr. Similarly, any publicity of Fatima is viewed as a danger and therefore has to be dampened. Shia who support and follow her and Muhammad's lineage have become targets for eradication and genocide by Muslim tyrants and dictators.

The insurgents in Iraq who are killing Shia also have ties to the same repugnant doctrine that have plagued Islam for centuries. A civil war that can maim the country and rob it off its wealth, culture, integrity, and religion does not appear to be in line with the Quran, ahadith, or Sunnah. The insurgents' attempts to destabilize the country for a possible takeover by someone like Saddam might be too far fetched now that the people of Iraq have realized the unlimited benefits of a free Islamic state. The crisis in Iraq is undeniably fueled by Sunni regimes surrounding the state whose goal it is to regain the power base from the

Shia. The Shia populace not only has to prove its capabilities as effective leaders, but also as a political power determined to stabilize the country by working cohesively with the Iraqi Sunnis to destabilize insurgents. American and coalition policymakers have to realize that a democratic Iraq cannot be accomplished without the support of the Shia. Historically, the Shia have demonstrated that they will compromise on all arrangements that do not in any way effect their core beliefs of absolute justice. To go one step deeper, one should bear in mind that the Shia will never negotiate on terms that are inconsistent with the ideal Islam of Muhammad and therefore of the Ahlul Bayth. The Shia have a lot to gain through open dialogue with the Sunnis and the Kurds, through mutual respect, and by showing the commitment to disintegrate the insurgent base and ideology. Sunnis, on the other hand, must recognize that it is in their interest to cooperate to build a nation similar to the one Muhammad had created.

GLOSSARY

A

Adl: Absolute justice.

Ahad: A Hadith that has been transmitted by a single source.

Ahel-az-Zikr: (see the section under Ahel-az-Zikr in the notes.)

Ahlul Bayth: Directly translated as *people of the house*. The bloodline progeny of Muhammad; his direct family.

Ameliya: Praxes

Ansar: The Muslims of Medina who accompanied the prophet. Directly translated as *helpers*.

Arafath: The plain near Mecca. A ritual relating to the required pilgrimage of Hajj is performed here.

Arabic: The language spoken by the Arab and Mesopotamian peoples. It is predominantly spoken within the Middle East, including parts of Africa.

Ayath or aya : A verse from the Quran.

Ayas (pl. Ayath) : Verses of the Quran. Directly translated as *sign*.

Azeem: vast, exquisite, immaculate, flawless, and unmatchable.

B

Badr: On March 17, 624 AD, the forces of the Quraish faced off against the forces of Muhammad in the Hejaz of

Western Arabia, now Saudi Arabia. The war became a decisive victory for the Muslims under the leadership of Muhammad and the bravery of Ali ibne Abu Talib.

Baqui: Cemetery in Madina, Saudi Arabia. It is a cemetery where martyrs, companions, and those related to the prophet Muhammad are buried. Fatima, Muhammad's daughter, is also buried within this cemetery.

Batin: Hidden.

Bani Ummayah: Descendants of Abu Sufyan and Muawiah's lineage. Abu Sufyan was a staunch enemy of Islam.

C

Caliph: (See Khilafath.)

Caliphate: (See Khilafath.)

D

Daif: A hadith that is weak.

E

Eeman: Strength of belief in Allah and Islam which is achieved through piety and devotion.

F

Fadak: Huge property owned by Muhammad who gifted it to Fatima. Abu Bakr confiscated this property from Fatima, denying her right to it. It remained in the hands of the enemies of the family of Muhammad. This issue is a matter of debate in this book.

Fajar: Morning prayers obligatory to all Muslims. Directly translated as *dawn*.

Falta: Unconstitutional; rushed into improperly.

Fitna: Dissension, sedition, subversion, destabilization, and sabotage. It is often used to refer to civil war, disagreement, and division within Islam, and it specifically alludes to a time involving trials of faith. The word also implies meanings including schism, secession, upheaval, and anarchy.

Figh: Jurisprudence

Fruh-e-Din: The Shiah practices of faith; also known as the "branches" of the religion. (See Usul-e-Din for the key beliefs in Shiah Islam.)

G

Ghadir-e-Khumm: A pool of water near Mecca. The prophet of Islam declared Ali as his legatee and successor before a crowd of more than 100,000 on his return from his last Hajj.

H

Hadith (pl. Ahadith): Generally prophetic traditions, narratives, or actions that are recorded from the recitations of the prophet's life.

Hajj: Required pilgrimage to Mecca that every Muslim must perform at least once in their lifetime.

Hasan: hadith categorized as fair. A Hasan hadith does not have the same level of authenticity as A Sahih hadith.

I

Ihram: Two pieces of cloth required to be worn by all males during the holy pilgrimage in Mecca. For women, the regular clothing worn at the beginning of the Hajj is considered Ihram.

Ijtehad: Interpretation of scripture and tradition in terms of judgment in a theological or judicial question. Directly translated as *innovation*. On a broader level, it also relates to hermeneutics as well as critical reasoning.

Ilm: Knowledge.

Imamath: Derived from the word Imam, which means *leader*. Imam is a designation assigned by Allah to a person who has excelled in knowledge and commitment to Islam. Ibrahim (Abraham), having passed all tests, was awarded the title of an Imam. Also, the imamath is the Shi'a belief in the leadership of the selected members from the prophet's family. Along the same lines, the imamath also refers to the transfer of vicegerency after Muhammad's death.

Isnad: Verification of the transmission record of a tradition.

J

Jahilia: Pre-Islamic period. Jahilia is the period before Islam in the Arab world where paganism and spiritual ignorance existed. This was also a state of anarchy.

Jamal: This battle took place in modern day Basra, Iraq in 656 AD between the rebel forces lead by Aisha bint Abu Bakr and the Islamic Khilafath of Ali ibne Abu Talib. Many forces within the city rose against Aisha, claiming her actions as a

slight against the memory of Muhammad. In the end she was defeated by Ali, and because she was Muhammad's wife, she was sent back to her home in respect, despite the great disrepute she received from even engaging in the battle.

K

Kaabah: A cubical building toward which all Muslims across the world pray five times each day. It is a symbolic building in Mecca that unifies the Muslims at the time of Hajj. It was originally built by Ibrahim and Ismaeel. It is a significantly important structure for the Muslims.

Kawther: The oft-represented fountain in heaven.

Khalifa/Khilafath: Vicegerency or successorship.

Khandaq: In 627 AD, a confederacy of non-Muslim forces joined under Abu Sufyan to battle against the Muslim city of Medina. The battle became known as Khandaq (trench) because of the large trench that was built around the city to protect it. Because of the strategic positioning of the trenches, as well as the resolve of the Muslim forces, the confederacy of non-Muslim forces was defeated, in large part due to the leadership of Muhammad and the battle prowess of Ali ibne Abu Talib.

M

Masjid (Also Mosque): The place of worship for Muslim peoples.

Masjid-e-Nabawi: Mosque originally built and run by Muhammad in Medina, which is in current Saudi Arabia.

Mat'n: Text; hadith and sunnah.

Maula: Directly translated as *master*, often used in reference to Muhammad regarding Ali in Ghadir-e-Khumm as: "whomsoever I (Muhammad) am maula, Ali is also his maula."

Minnah: A place near Medina at which part of the ritual for the Islamic pilgrimage of Hajj is performed.

Muhadiseen: Collectors of ahadith (traditions, usually of the prophet).

Muhajirun: Companions and followers of the Prophet Muhammad who accompanied him in his process of migration.

Munafiqoon (also Munafiq): Hypocrites in the eyes of Islam who practice Islam outwardly but inwardly hide their strong disbelief, sometimes even for the purpose of infiltration.

Musdalifa: A place between Minnah and Arafat where part of the required Islamic pilgrimage of Hajj takes place.

Mutawatir: A generally accepted hadith.

N

Nabuwath: The belief in prophethood. Allah's vicegerent; representative; deliverer of his message; one whose teachings, preachings, and praxes convey the complete way of life in accordance to the Quran. Muhammad being the last and the final prophet of Allah.

Naskh: to Abrogate.

P

Persian: People from the region of Iran, of Persian origin. Also, this is the spoken language in this region, also known as Farsi.

Q

Qawliyah: The traditions which are statements and sayings of the Prophet.

Qiyamath: The day of judgment, where each person will be judged upon. It is believed that punishment or rewards according to one's performance in this world will be established. Absolute justice will be served.

Khumm: (see Ghadir-e-Khumm.)

R

Rasequoona fil Ilm: (see notes.)

S

Sadaqah: Charity.

Sahih: Authentic and uncontested; having no possibility of error.

Sahih Sitta: The six collections of Hadith recognized by the Sunni Muslim sect as the most reliable for Ahadith. The six collections of Ahadith are Sahih Bukhari, Sahih Muslim, Sunan of Tirmidhi, Nasa'i, Ibn Majah, and Abu Da'ud.

Saquifa: A place where a small group of people gathered after the death of Muhammad to select a leader. The gathering and selection process is regarded as highly controversial.

The Shiah believe that key figures who should have been present at this meeting were left out intentionally, such as Ali ibne Abu Talib, while Sunnis claim that the desperation for leadership at the time justified the actions that took place. These issues have been partially discussed in chapters 4 and 5.

Shariah: The development of laws and regulations based on the Quran, ahadith, and Sunnah (see note 1, Chapter 2).

Silsila: The chain of narrators of any given hadith.

Sunnah: The actions and practices of the Prophet.

T

Tahajud: Non-obligatory midnight prayer for Muslims.

Tawheed: The belief in Allah. Allah the Supreme Being is the creator of the universe. Allah has absolute authority and power over everything in the entire universe.

Tawil: Interpretation of Quranic text as well as, to some degree, the commentaries on Quranic text.

Teqririyah: The spoken words—usually in reference to the Prophet's revelations and the Quranic revelations.

Taqwa: Piety, devotion, dedication, and durability of faith.

U

Uhad: On March 23, 625 AD, a battle took place between the combined forces of Quresh, Nasara (Christians), and Yahood (Jews) and the Muslims on the Mount of Uhad. The Muslim forces, led by Muhammad, lost the battle

after certain members of the Muslim forces broke ranks and retreated or hid.

Umma: The greater Muslim community at large.

Ummayah: The Progeny of Abu Sufyan.

Urdu: A widely spoken language of India as well as Pakistan.

Usul-e-Din: The five core Shi'a beliefs, known as the "roots" of the religion. (See fru-e-din for the practices of Shia Islam.) The Sunni sect also has a set of five core beliefs and practices that they declare as the Usul-e-Din, combining both practices and beliefs in one. This is discussed in greater detail in Chapter 10.

Z

Zahir: A blatantly obvious, undisputable interpretation of Quranic text.

Zalim: An unjust evildoer; one who transgresses other's rights.

Zul-a-Sheera: The first call of Islam as declared by Muhammad c. 613, in which he presented the religion before the public and prior to which Khadija had already become the first convert to Islam, followed by Ali ibne Abu Talib and later Zaid ibn Haarith.

NOTES

Preface, Note 1

Muhammad's Only Daughter, Fatima

Muhammad, according to the Quran (68:4), was a model of high-profile character. In view of the Quran, Muhammad was fair, just, merciful, compassionate, and egalitarian. Fatima was also special in Quranic terms. The following verses of the Quran were exclusively revealed to accentuate her unique position regarding the Quran and Islam. The following verses are discussed throughout the book, and are mentioned here only as a reference: Quran 33:33; 42:23; 16:43; 21:7. Fatima was very special to Muhammad. History, ahadith, and Sunnah show that Fatima was exclusive in receiving honor, respect, and love from her father. Muhammad rose up in respect to greet only Fatima. He declared that Fatima was part of him and hence inseparable. On numerous occasions he said "Whosoever hurts Fatima has hurt me and Allah." There were many more similar statements made by Muhammad that were exclusively for Fatima.

Sahih al Bukhari states in Volume 7, Book 62, Number 157 of *Bab ul Nikah:* "Fatima is a part of my body, and I hate what she hates to see, and what hurts her, hurts me." The same author states in Volume 5, Book 57, Number 61 of *Bab Fadail Fatima:* "Allah's Apostle said, 'Fatima is a part of me, and he who makes her angry, makes me angry.'"

Sahih Muslim states in Book 031, Number 6000 of *Bab Fatima Binte Rasul:* "Miswar b. Makhramah reported Allah's Messenger (may peace be upon him) as saying: Fatima is a part of me. He in fact tortures me who tortures her."

The claim that Muhammad had three more daughters besides Fatima appears to be baseless. If these three daughters were from Muhammad and Khadija, they would not have been married to Kafirs (un-believers). To make things even more suspicious, two of them were married to Abu Laheb's Kafir sons, and the third one was also married to a Kafir who fought against Muhammad in the Battle of Badar, which does not agree with the mandate that Muhammad was sent to fulfill. Abu Lahab was cursed by the Quran for his anti-Islamic activities. It is therefore not possible that Muhammad would give his own daughters to all Kafirs, especially Abu Lahab's sons.

More importantly, if these were Muhammad's daughters, he would have treated them the same way he had treated Fatima. As a model of excellence and justice, he would have had to be fair in his treatment of all his "daughters" equally. Neither history nor ahadith show that Muhammad addressed them the way he addressed Fatima. Fatima, in her claim to Fadak (see Chapter 9), states that Muhammad was her father and no one else's. When she made that statement in the Masjid-e-Nabavi, there was complete silence, and no one challenged her claim that "Muhammad was her father and no one else's." In addition, the claimant of Fadak was only Fatima, as established by Umar, Abu Bakr, Uthman, and all others present to accept her statement without contest. If there were other daughters, Fatima would have been challenged. The only person who claimed Fadak was Fatima. However, history suggests that these girls could have been Khadija's nieces (her sisters' daughters).

Chapter 2, Note 1

Shariah

Shariah is the development of laws and legislation derived from Quran, ahadith, and Sunnah. The jurists who developed these laws and regulation processes differed in their conclusions. Hence, among the Sunnis there were initially four schools of thought (we have discussed this in much greater detail in Chapter 10), and among the Shia, the Jafari (Imam Jafer-e-Sadiq) school of jurisprudence emerged as the leader. Sunnis suffered from restrictions of innovation (Ijtehad) for the last 1,000 years, whereas for the Shia, the doors of Ijtehad had always remained open.

Chapter 3, Note 1

Umar's Treatment of the Prophet

1. "The prophet was not happy with Umar because he did not cooperate with him when asked for pen and paper." See note 1,207 of The History of al Tabari, Vol IX.

Chapter 4, Note 1

Defining *Shura*

"Those who hearken to their Lord, and establish regular Prayer; who (conduct) their affairs by mutual Consultation; who spend out of what We bestow on them for Sustenance . . " (Quran 42:38; Translator, Yousuf Ali)

وَالَّذِينَ اسْتَجَابُوا لِرَبِّهِمْ وَأَقَامُوا الصَّلَاةَ وَأَمْرُهُمْ
شُورَى بَيْنَهُمْ وَمِمَّا رَزَقْنَاهُمْ يُنْفِقُونَ

An entire chapter in the Quran is named "Shura," which means *consultation*. Only one verse in this entire chapter contains the word *Shura*. Here the word *shura* is intended to promote brotherhood, friendship among followers, unity through congregations for prayers, discussions about the welfare of the community as a means of mutual support, and the coordination of ideas and views to better serve the community as a whole.

> It is part of the Mercy of Allah that thou dost
> deal gently with them. Wert thou severe or harsh-
> hearted, they would have broken away from
> about thee: so pass over (their faults), and ask for
> (Allah's) forgiveness for them; and consult them
> in affairs (of moment). Then, when thou hast
> taken a decision put thy trust in Allah. For Allah
> loves those who put their trust (in Him)." (Quran:
> 3:159; translator, Yousuf Ali)

فَبِمَا رَحْمَةٍ مِّنَ اللَّهِ لِنتَ لَهُمْ وَلَوْ كُنتَ فَظًّا غَلِيظَ
الْقَلْبِ لَانفَضُّوا مِنْ حَوْلِكَ فَاعْفُ عَنْهُمْ وَاسْتَغْفِرْ لَهُمْ
وَشَاوِرْهُمْ فِي الْأَمْرِ فَإِذَا عَزَمْتَ فَتَوَكَّلْ عَلَى اللَّهِ إِنَّ
اللَّهَ يُحِبُّ الْمُتَوَكِّلِينَ

Above is a second verse of the Quran in which the word *Shura* is used in reference to consultation about community affairs. Conveyed by the tone of this verse is advice to Muhammad to be considerate and generous in forgiveness and to consult them in affairs relating to any issues. However, as for the decision about

any action, Allah had granted only Muhammad the final authority for any action. There is no indication of any delegation of authority to anyone other than Muhammad, because the subject in the above verse is Muhammad.

Encouragement of consultation to resolve issues under the guardianship of Muhammad is limited only in regard to the community problem and not necessarily in the selection of a leader.

After Muhammad's death, Shura became a political tool, and it became beneficial to a certain group of people. Although Shura was not intended to be used regarding the selection of a Khalifa, it nonetheless became a means to an end. Abu Bakar was not selected fairly, and Umar played a crucial role in manipulating conditions to make Abu Bakr Khalifa, though he, by his own admission, did not deserve it. Umar was hand picked by Abu Bakar, perhaps by mutual agreement. Technically there was no Shura involved in this process. When Umar was departing, he again formed a council of six selectively picked people to guarantee the selection of Uthman. Therefore, in all three cases there were inconsistencies and unfair practices admitted by the planners of these processes.

Realistically, it was only during the time of Ali that anything close to Shura was instituted.

Chapter 5, Note 1

Uthman's Murder and Ali's Response

Uthman had unjustly given all key administrative positions to his relatives, i.e., The Bani Umayyas. Marwan was one of his closest advisors, and according to some historians, he was his mentor. These individuals (Muawiah; Marwan; Abd Allah Ibn Sa'd, his foster brother as governor of Egypt; Umayyad al Walid, his uterine brother who was governor of Kufa; and many other Bani Umayyas) were abusing the Islamic laws and misusing public wealth. Uthman had mistreated the most revered companions of Muhammad, sometimes causing public insults and degradation, physical torture, and many times, death. Abu Dharr, Amar-e-Yassir, and others were among those who became his victims. He had also planned to kill Muhammad ibne Abu Bakr. As a result, people were angry at the misuse of power and public funds under Uthman's government. People from Egypt, Basra, and other provinces gathered and marched toward the residence of Uthman to demand his resignation. Uthman was confused and scared, as all his supporters had abandoned him and maintained low profiles after instigating these attacks. Uthman felt that the only person who could help him was Ali ibne Abu Talib. He asked Ali for help, and Ali mediated a compromise by telling Uthman to admit to his mistakes and to apologize and pledge to discontinue past practices. Uthman agreed, went into the public, declared his mistakes, and apologized, as he was advised to do by Ali. The people were satisfied and had begun to disperse. Marwan, Uthman's right-hand man and mentor, learned of this and rushed to see Uthman immediately. He told him he had committed a grave mistake. Nailah Bint Farafisah, Uthman's wife, who was present at the time, specifically told Uthman not to listen to Marwan. She said, "He (Marwan) will get you killed!" There was a brief

argument between Nailah and Marwan, but Uthman, as usual, asked Marwan to handle the situation as he saw fit. Marwan made a speech that was already cited in Chapter 5. When people heard this speech, they felt deceived and were infuriated. While this was going on, Marwan and Uthman sent a letter to Abdullah ibn S'ad Abi Sahr, the foster brother of Uthman, who was infamous for torture and oppression, advising him to kill Muhammad Ibn Abu Bakr and others upon their arrival back in Egypt. The messenger, along with the letter, was caught. The people on their way home turned around and marched back toward Uthman's residence in anger. During an angry exchange of words, one of Uthman's men killed Niyar ibn Iyad, a companion of the prophet who had come to negotiate the stepping down of Uthman. Uthman was thus left alone and faced death at the hands of the angry mobs, and his body was left unburied for several days. It was only Ali who helped Uthman in his time of his need, and those who demanded the revenge against the murderers of Uthman in fact instigated the process of Uthman's death.[1]

Chapter 5, Note 2

The Reference of *Zibhun Azeem*

Ibrahim (Abraham) saw a dream in which he was instructed by Allah to sacrifice his son Ismaeel (Ishmael). Ibrahim told Ismaeel about his dream, and then Ismaeel told his father to act upon it. Ibrahim blindfolded himself and his son and performed the task he was assigned. When he opened his eyes, he found that a goat had been sacrificed and that Ismaeel had been saved. This was not an easy test, but Ibrahim succeeded in carrying out his task without hesitation. Both Abraham and his son Ismaeel demonstrated their devotion and commitment to the will of Allah. Allah was pleased by this and prevented harm to Ishmael.

As the Quran says, this sacrifice was replaced by a *Zibhun Azeem* (ultimate sacrifice) that he had postponed for later generations in the lineage of Abraham. The sacrifice of Husain Ibn Ali, grandson of Muhammad, fulfilled the destiny of Zibhun Azeem in 680 AD. This monolithic sacrifice on the plains of Karbala became the very definition of Zibhun Azeem. Husain Ibn Ali, along with his friends, family, and companions, sacrificed their lives in a battle to save Islam. The women accompanying him were taken captive and were punished and tortured by the brutal tyrant Yazid Ibn Muawiah. This only widened the ever-deepening split between the Shiah and the Sunnis.

Chapter 6, note 1

Ahel-az-Zikr – Rasequoona fil Ilm
(people with knowledge):

The Quran makes several references to the people whom the Quran has characterized as those who have the inner knowledge of the meaning, intent, and understanding of the principles and hidden wisdom of those verses that have agendas impervious to the common people. The people endowed with these gifts are referred to as Ahel az Zikr; they have attributes that put them in the category of Rasequoona fil Ilm, or people with knowledge of the inner dimension of certain verses.

The Quran has shifted the task of unfolding the complexities of Quranic text to the people with knowledge and has directed Muslims to seek their help. Muhammad repeatedly introduced and identified these individuals throughout his life. Ahadith, Sunnah, and history have explicitly revealed the identity and characteristics of Ahel az Zikr. Muhammad was obviously the central figure of this group, thus setting the standard of qualifications to be recognized as Ahel az Zikr and Rasequoona fil Ilm.

And before thee also the apostles We sent were but men, to whom We granted inspiration: if ye realise this not, ask of those who possess the Message. (Quran 16:43; translator, Yousuf Ali)

وَمَا أَرْسَلْنَا مِن قَبْلِكَ إِلاَّ رِجَالاً نُّوحِي إِلَيْهِمْ فَاسْأَلُواْ أَهْلَ الذِّكْرِ إِن كُنتُمْ لاَ تَعْلَمُونَ

Before thee, also, the apostles We sent were but men, to whom We granted inspiration: If ye realise this not, ask of those who possess the Message. (Quran 21:7; translator, Yousuf Ali)

وَمَا أَرْسَلْنَا قَبْلَكَ إِلاَّ رِجَالاً نُّوحِي إِلَيْهِمْ فَاسْأَلُوا أَهْلَ الذِّكْرِ إِن كُنتُمْ لاَ تَعْلَمُونَ

He it is Who has sent down to thee the Book: In it are verses basic or fundamental (of established meaning); they are the foundation of the Book: others are allegorical. But those in whose hearts is perversity follow the part thereof that is allegorical, seeking discord, and searching for its hidden meanings, but no one knows its hidden meanings except Allah. And those who are firmly grounded in knowledge say: 'We believe in the Book; the whole of it is from our Lord:' and none will grasp the Message except men of understanding. (Quran 3:7; translator, Yousuf Ali)

هُوَ الَّذِيَ أَنزَلَ عَلَيْكَ الْكِتَابَ مِنْهُ آيَاتٌ مُّحْكَمَاتٌ هُنَّ
أُمُّ الْكِتَابِ وَأُخَرُ مُتَشَابِهَاتٌ فَأَمَّا الَّذِينَ فِي قُلُوبِهِمْ زَيْغٌ
فَيَتَّبِعُونَ مَا تَشَابَهَ مِنْهُ ابْتِغَاءَ الْفِتْنَةِ وَابْتِغَاءَ تَأْوِيلِهِ
وَمَا يَعْلَمُ تَأْوِيلَهُ إِلاَّ اللّهُ وَالرَّاسِخُونَ فِي الْعِلْمِ يَقُولُونَ
آمَنَّا بِهِ كُلٌّ مِّنْ عِندِ رَبِّنَا وَمَا يَذَّكَّرُ إِلاَّ أُوْلُوا الأَلْبَابِ

But those among them who are well-grounded
in knowledge, and the believers, believe in what
hath been revealed to thee and what was revealed
before thee: And (especially) those who establish
regular prayer and practise regular charity and
believe in Allah and in the Last Day: To them
shall We soon give a great reward. (Quran 4:162;
translator, Yousuf Ali)

لَـكِنِ الرَّاسِخُونَ فِي الْعِلْمِ مِنْهُمْ وَالْمُؤْمِنُونَ يُؤْمِنُونَ
بِمَا أُنزِلَ إِلَيكَ وَمَا أُنزِلَ مِن قَبْلِكَ وَالْمُقِيمِينَ الصَّلاَةَ
وَالْمُؤْتُونَ الزَّكَاةَ وَالْمُؤْمِنُونَ بِاللّهِ وَالْيَوْمِ الآخِرِ
أُوْلَـئِكَ سَنُؤْتِيهِمْ أَجْرًا عَظِيمًا

The Quran claims that Muhammad was a perfect human
being. Ali and his family members were the protégés of
Muhammad. From the definition of *Ahel-az-Zikr* and *Rasequoona
fil ilm*, it is made apparent that only someone of the status of
Muhammad with an equivalent level of knowledge and intellect
can fit this title. Muhammad and the Quran have identified the
characteristics and attributes of Ahel az Zikr that could only be
present in Muhammad's Ahlul Bayth: Fatima, Ali, Hasan, Husain,
and their progeny.

Muhammad said: "Fatima is a part of me."

The Quran introduces the Ahlul Bayth as follows:

> And stay quietly in your houses, and make not a
> dazzling display, like that of the former Times
> of Ignorance; and establish regular Prayer, and
> give regular Charity; and obey Allah and His
> Messenger. And Allah only wishes to remove
> all abomination from you, ye members of the
> Family, and to make you pure and spotless.
> (Quran 33:33; translator, Yousuf Ali).

إِنَّمَا يُرِيدُ اللَّهُ لِيُذْهِبَ عَنكُمُ الرِّجْسَ أَهْلَ الْبَيْتِ
وَيُطَهِّرَكُمْ تَطْهِيرًا

The last part of the above verse is specifically about the family
of Muhammad characterized as Ahlul Bayth, and most of the
experts of Tafsir agree on this. There is no one in the history of
Islam that qualifies for this status except Muhammad, Fatima,
Ali, and their progeny.

Ahmad bin Muhammad bin Hanbal, the Hanbali Imam (d.
241 AH), in *Musnad* 229:2, quotes Ummu Salamah as saying:

> The Holy Prophet (s) was in my house. Fatimah
> (`a) came to her father holding a stone bowl
> filled with "harirah" (type of food made up of
> flour, milk, and vegetable oil). The Holy Prophet
> (s) stated: 'Invite your husband and two sons to
> come as well.' `Ali, Hasan, and Husayn also came
> there and all sat down to eat "harirah". Then,

the Holy Prophet (s) was sitting on a cloak in his resting place and I was reciting the prayer in the chamber. At this time, Almighty Allah revealed the verse 'Allah only desires to . . .' The Holy Prophet (s) covered `Ali, Fatimah, Hasan, and Husayn (peace be upon them all) with the cloak and then stretched his hand toward the sky and said: 'Allah! These are the Members of my Household, so purify them of all uncleanness'. Ummu Salamah said: 'I asked him: "Am I also with you?" He stated: "You are on good and virtue"' (but did not say that you are a member of my Household).

The tradition known as *Mubahilah* has been recounted in different books of Sirah and history with various wordings. These include those of Tirmidhi (*Sahih* 166:2) which quotes S`ad ibn Abi Waqqas as follows: "When the mubahalah verse was recited, the Holy Prophet (s) summoned `Ali, Fatimah, Hasan, and Husayn and said: `O Allah, these are the Members of my Household." This tradition has been narrated by Hakim Nishapuri *in Al-Mustadrak* 150:3 and Bayhaqi in *Sunan* 63:7. Hakim regards this tradition as authentic.

Fatima's knowledge and intellectual grasp of the socioeconomic, political, philosophic, and administrative aspects of Islam was acquired through the training of Muhammad and Khadija. Fatima was a combination of Muhammad, Khadija, and Ali. She grew up with the Quran and shared everything with Muhammad as Islam started to spread. She was taking care of her father in the battle of Uhad when he was injured. The Quran was her means of communication and way of life from birth.

Ali was in a class unto himself. From his birth to his death, Ali was unique and exceptional. He was born in Kaaba; was raised by Muhammad; was trained by Muhammad; was the first male who accepted Islam; was the organizer and helper of Zul a Sheera, the day of invitation of Islam by Muhammad; and was the lone victor of the war of Khandaq. Ali stands on par with Muhammad with the difference that if Muhammad was the executor of the will of Allah in the form of Islam, Ali was the executive that administered the plans and the processes instituted to develop a robust community adherent to principles set by Allah.

The prophet of Islam, Muhammad, said: "Man kunto Maula fa haza aliun maula."

This is translated as: "Whomsoever I (Muhammad) am maula(master), Ali is also his maula (master)."

Ali was the successful architect of every major war during the time of Muhammad. His non-involvement in wars after Muhammad's death can be viewed as a refusal to engage in nondefensive wars that he did not agree with. From the first war of Badar to Uhad, Khandaq, and Khaiber, Ali carried a streak of victories with an unblemished record. Ali was never found running away or hiding from the battlefield as many others had, blatantly defying the orders of the Quran.

His intellectual dexterity radiates from his sermons, letters, and advisory notes to his appointees and followers. His philosophic attributes he presented to the community were later developed into laws and principles of philosophy that Aveceena, Arabi, and others took to levels still considered as the basis of modern Islamic philosophy.

A small portion of his sermons, letters, and notes demonstrate the masterpieces that only Ali was capable of. These collections are published in book form under the title *Nehjul Balagha*. This level of knowledge belonged to Ali, Fatima, and their progeny. It is impossible to find an equal of Ali in the history of Islam. Muhammad was certain that after him, the community would accept only Ali as his vicegerent.

Following is a portion of one of his supplications that demonstrates the unique expression of the attributes of Allah presented to define terms exclusively applicable to the creator of the universe:

> Allah! I beseech Thee by Thy mercy which
> encompasses all things And by Thy power by
> which Thou overcometh all things and submit to
> it all things and humble before it all things And
> by Thy might by which Thou hast conquered all
> things And by Thy majesty against which nothing
> can stand up. And by Thy grandeur which
> prevails upon all things And by Thy authority
> which is exercised over all things And by Thy
> own self that shall endure forever after all things
> have vanished And by Thy Names which manifest
> Thy power over all things And by Thy knowledge
> which pervades all things And by the light of
> Thy countenance which illuminates everything O
> Thou who art the light! O Thou who art the most
> holy! O Thou who existed before the foremost!
> O Thou who shall exist after the last!

The theoretical dimension to metaphysics is a complex variable of human spirituality, which itself is a dependent variable of the conditioning and sophistication of the development of

mind. The material needs, however, dilute spiritual components. The mysteries of the mind are dimensionless. In a real world, our needs dictate. This clash between spirituality and materialism is real and is usually favorably inclined toward materialism. Islam is different; it is the spiritual world that takes you into unchartered territories to discipline your mind before you turn toward addressing material constituents of human needs. The Quran starts with the belief of the unseen as a prerequisite to total submission to the creator—Allah.

> Let there be no doubt about it is [meant to be] a
> guidance for all the God-conscious. (Quran 2:2;
> translator, Asad).

ذَلِكَ الْكِتَابُ لَا رَيْبَ فِيهِ هُدًى لِّلْمُتَّقِينَ

> Who believe in the Unseen, are steadfast in
> prayer, and spend out of what we have provided
> for them. (Quran 2:3; translator, Yousuf Ali)

الَّذِينَ يُؤْمِنُونَ بِالْغَيْبِ وَيُقِيمُونَ الصَّلَاةَ وَمِمَّا
رَزَقْنَاهُمْ يُنفِقُونَ

Unquestionably, the first principle is to believe in the unseen. The follow-up step is to put one's beliefs into practice. The final phase is to prepare a believer to realize and address the material needs of others to advance the community. The Quran provides a process of evolution of society through sharing to enable sustainable growth of the community and society. These sequences of steps are organized to help promote moral and religious values toward a progressive community. Ali provided

the tools necessary for the potential converts to believe in the unseen.

The Quran invariably talks about the Prophets and Messengers, their experiences, and the lessons they gave that illustrate spirituality as a complementary asset to the materialistic world. The Quran invokes passion, humbleness, morality, forgiveness, tolerance, peace, and love. The Quran condemns all acts that harbor treason, murder, suppression, oppression, immorality, etc; in general, the Quran also condemns acts that undermine peace and love.

Ali was the first after Muhammad that presented the attributes of the creator of the universe that provided a reasoning to the concept of Tawheed. The approach was to eliminate all the manmade deities on the grounds that none of them could stand up to the test of reason created through a range of descriptors both superior and unchallengeable.

> Verily, when He intends a thing, His Command is "be," and it is! (Quran 36:82; translator, Yousuf Ali)

إِنَّمَا أَمْرُهُ إِذَا أَرَادَ شَيْئًا أَنْ يَقُولَ لَهُ كُنْ فَيَكُونُ

It was through Muhammad's training and schooling of Ali in Islamic spirituality and the philosophy behind the concept of Tawheed that Ali was able to share his wisdom effectively in these areas with mankind. It was Ali, Fatima, and their progeny that exclusively provided the tools to the understanding of the holistic image of Islam.

The United Nations report on Arab human development from 2002 quotes Ali's (556–619 AD) statements on knowledge and work from *Nahj Al-Balagha* under the chapter titled "Using Human Capabilities: Towards a Knowledge Society."

Ali Ibn Abi Talib—Knowledge and Work:

- "No vessel is limitless, except for the vessel of knowledge, which forever expands."

- "If god were to humiliate a human being, he would deny him knowledge."

- "No wealth equals the mind, no poverty equals the ignorance, no heritage equals culture, and no support is greater than advice."

- "Wisdom is the believer's quest, to be sought everywhere, even among the deceitful."

- "A person is worth what he excels at."

- "No wealth can profit you more than the mind, no isolation can be more desolate than conceit, no policy can be wiser than prudence, no generosity can be better than decency, no heritage can be more bountiful than culture, no guidance can be truer than inspiration, no enterprise can be more successful than goodness, and no honour can surpass knowledge."

- "Knowledge is superior to wealth. Knowledge guards you, whereas you guard health. Wealth decreases with expenditure, whereas knowledge multiplies with dissemination. A good material deed vanishes as the material resources behind it vanish whereas to knowledge

we are indebted forever. Thanks to knowledge, you command people's respect during your lifetime, and kind memory after your death. Knowledge rules over wealth. Those who treasure wealth perish while they are still alive, whereas scholars live forever; they only disappear in physical image, but in hearts, their memories are enshrined."

- "Knowledge is the twin of action. He who is knowledgeable must act. Knowledge calls upon action; if answered it will stay; otherwise, it will depart."

(United Nations Development Program: Arab Human Development Report 2002, page 82.)

An exhaustive search has demonstrated that there is no equal of Muhammad, Fatima, Ali, and the Imams from Muhammad's progeny in the history of Islam and mankind that has what it takes to become Ahel az Zikr or Rasequoona fil Ilm. This challenge remained unanswered for the last 1,400 years.

1. Umar said: "I swear to God Ali was the most deserving of all the people to become Khalif."[2]

2. Umar said: "If Ali was not there, Umar would perish."[3]

Ali Ibn Abi Talib, in his sermons and letters to his governors and state representatives, provided guidance and encouraged people to be sensitive toward the needs of others and to practice, preach, and implement Islamic laws to enable the creation of a healthy, just society in which no one is left without help. Ali wanted to create an ideal Islamic culture that promoted peace, love, goodwill, and growth. The following is another quotation from the "United Nations Development Program: Arab Human

Development Report 2002," under a chapter titled "Liberating human capabilities: Governance, human development and the Arab World." It is quoted from *Nahj Al-Balagha,* and the author is Ali Ibn Abi Talib.

Ali Ibn Abi Talib On Governance:

"He who has appointed himself an Imam of the people must begin by teaching himself before teaching others, his teaching of others must be first by setting an example rather than with words, for he who begins by teaching and educating himself is more worthy of respect than he who teaches and educates others."

- "Your concern with developing the land should be greater than your concern with collecting taxes, for the latter can be obtained by developing; whereas he who seeks revenue without development destroys the country and the people."

- "Seek the company of the learned and the wise in search of solving the problems of your country and the righteousness of your people."

- "No good can come in keeping silent as to government or in speaking out of ignorance."

- "The righteous are men of virtue, whose logic is straightforward, whose dress is unostentatious, whose path is modest, whose actions are many and who are undeterred by difficulties."

- "Choose the best among your people to administer justice among them. Choose someone who does not easily give up, who is unruffled by enmities, someone who will not persist in wrongdoing, who will not hesitate to pursue right

once he knows it, someone whose heart knows no greed, who will not be satisfied with a minimum of explanation without seeking the maximum of understanding, who will be the most steadfast when doubt is cast, who will be the least impatient in correcting the opponent, the most patient in pursuing the truth, the most stern in meting out judgment, someone who is unaffected by flattery and not swayed by temptation and these are but few."

(United Nations Development Program: Arab Human Development Report 2002, page 107.)

It is worth noting that from the very inception of Islam, even before the revelation of the Quran, there were two groups with two different philosophies, viewpoints, beliefs, interpretation schemes, and understandings of Islam. These two groups developed into seventy or more sectarian divisions after Muhammad's time. The group that took the material value of the movement stayed focused on the material aspect of it through conquests and expansion as their interpretation of the propagation process. Khilaphat was the focus that later went through different stages, eventually turning into monarchy and dictatorship. The second group that focused on the moral and spiritual values of Islam produced Fatima, Ali, Hasan, and Husain.

Chapter 9, Note 1

Translation of Full Speech by Fatima Binte Muhammad in Masjid-e-Nabawi

Fatima (SA) felt grieved by Abu Bakr's actions and was so displeased with him that when she learned of his attempt to seize Fadak, she accompanied a group of women to the mosque. There she sat down and delivered the following speech:

Praise be to Allah for that which He bestowed (upon us); And thanks be to Him for all that which He inspired; and commended in His Name for that which He Provided: Form prevalent favors which He created, And abundant benefactions which He offered and perfect grants which He presented; (such benefactions) that their number is much too plentiful to compute; Bounties too vast to measure; Their limit was too distant to realize; He recommended to them (His creatures) to gain more (of His benefaction) by being grateful for their continuity; He ordained Himself praiseworthy by giving generously to His creatures; I bear witness that there is no God but Allah Who is One without partner, a statement which sincere devotion is made to be its interpretation; hearts guarantee its continuation, and illuminated in the minds is its sensibility. He Who can not be perceived with vision; neither be described with tongues; nor can imagination surround His state.

He originated things but not from anything that existed before them, and created them without examples to follow. Rather, He created them with His might and dispersed them according to His will; not for a need did He create them; nor for a benefit (for Him) did He shape them, But to establish His wisdom, Bring attention to His obedience, manifest His might, lead His creatures to humbly venerate Him, and to exalt His decrees. He then made the reward for His obedience, and punishment for his disobedience, so as to protect

His creatures from His Wrath and amass them into His Paradise.

I too bear witness that my Father, Muhammad, is His Slave and Messenger, Whom He chose prior to sending him, named him before sending him; when creatures were still concealed in that which was transcendental, guarded from that which was appalling, and associated with the termination and nonexistence. For Allah the Exalted knew that which was to follow, comprehended that which will come to pass, And realized the place of every event. Allah has sent him (Muhammad) as perfection for His commands, a resolution to accomplish His rule, and an implementation of the decrees of His Mercy. So he found the nations to vary in their faiths; Obsessed by their fires, Worshipping their idols, And denying Allah despite their knowledge of Him. Therefore, Allah illuminated their darkness with my Father, Muhammad, uncovered obscurity from their hearts, and cleared the clouds from their insights. He revealed guidance among the people; So he delivered them from being led astray, led them away from misguidance, guided them to the proper religion, and called them to the straight path.

Allah then chose to recall him back in mercy, love and preference. So, Muhammad is in comfort from the burden of this world, he is surrounded with devoted angels, the satisfaction of the

Merciful Lord, and the nearness of the powerful King.

So may the praise of Allah be upon my Father, His Prophet, Trusted one, the chosen one from among His creatures, and His sincere friend, and may peace and blessings of Allah be upon him.

Fatima (SA) then turned to the crowd and said:

Surely you are Allah's slaves at His command Prohibition; You are the bearers of His religion and revelation; You are Allah's trusted ones with yourselves; and His messengers to the nations. Amongst you does He have righteous authority; A covenant He brought unto you, and an heir He left to guard you; That is The eloquent book of Allah; The truthful Quran; The brilliant light; The shining beam; Its insights are indisputable; Its secrets are revealed; Its indications are manifest; and its followers are blessed by it. (The Quran) leads its adherents to goodwill; and Hearing it leads to salvation; with it are the bright divine authorities achieved, His manifest determination acquired, His prohibited decrees avoided; His manifest evidence recognized; His satisfying proofs made apparent, His permissions granted, and His laws written.

So Allah made belief to be purification for you from polytheism.

He made Prayer, An exaltation for you from conceit.

Alms -A purification for the soul and a (cause of) growth in subsistence.

Fasting an implantation of devotion.

Pilgrimage -A construction of religion.

Justice -A harmony of the hearts; obeying us (Ahlul-Bayt)—Management of the nation.

Our leadership (Ahlul-Bayt), Safeguard from disunity.

Jihad (struggle)—a strengthening of Islam.

Patience -A helping course for deserving (divine) reward.

Ordering goodness (Amr Bil Maruf)—Public welfare.

Kindness to the parents—A safeguard from wrath.

Maintaining close relations with one's kin —A cause for a longer life and multiplying the number of descendants.

Retaliation (Qesas) —For sparing blood (souls).

Fulfillment of vows—subjecting oneself to mercy.

Completion of weights and measures —A cause for preventing the neglect of others' rights.

Forbiddance of drinking wines an exaltation from atrocity.

Avoiding slander —A veil from curse.

Abandoning theft—a reason for deserving chastity.

Allah has also prohibited polytheism so that one can devote himself to His Lordship.

Therefore; Fear Allah as He should be feared, and die not except in a state of Islam;

Obey Allah in that which He has commanded you to do and that which He has forbidden, for surely those truly fear among His servants, who have knowledge.'

Lady Fatima Zahra (A) then added:

O People! Be informed that I am Fatima, and my father is Muhammad I say that repeatedly and initiate it continually; I say not what I say mistakenly, nor do I do what I do aimlessly.

Now hath come unto you an Apostle from amongst yourselves; It grieves him that you should perish; Ardently anxious is he over you; To the believers he is most kind and merciful. Thus, if you identify and recognize him, you shall realize that he is my father and not the father of any of your women; the brother of my cousin (Ali (A)) rather than any of your men. What an excellent identity he was, may the peace

and blessings of Allah be upon him and his descendants Thus, he propagated the Message, by coming out openly with the warning, and while inclined away from the path of the polytheists, (whom he) struck their strength and seized their throats, while he invited (all) to the way of his Lord with wisdom and beautiful preaching He destroyed idols, and defeated heroes, until their group fled and turned their backs. So night revealed its dawn; righteousness uncovered its genuineness; the voice of the religious authority spoke out loud; the evil discords were silenced; The crown of hypocrisy was diminished; the tightening of infidelity and desertion were untied,

So you spoke the statement of devotion among a band of starved ones; and you were on the edge of a hole of fire;(you were) the drink of the thirsty one; the opportunity of the desiring one; the fire brand of him who passes in haste; the step for feet; you used to drink from the water gathered on roads; eat jerked meat. (Lady Fatima (A) was stating their lowly situation before Islam) You were despised outcasts always in fear of abduction from those around you. Yet, Allah rescued you through my father, Muhammad after much ado, and after he was confronted by mighty men, the Arab beasts, and the demons of the people of the Book Who, whenever they ignited the fire of war, Allah extinguished it; and whenever the thorn of the devil appeared, or a mouth of the polytheists opened wide in defiance, he would strike its discords with his

brother (Ali, (A)), who comes not back until
he treads its wing with the sole of his feet, and
extinguishes its flames with his sword. (Ali is)
diligent in Allah's affair, near to the Messenger
of Allah, A master among Allah's worshippers,
setting to work briskly, sincere in his advice,
earnest and exerting himself (in service to Islam);
While you were calm, gay, and feeling safe in your
comfortable lives, waiting for us to meet disasters,
awaiting the spread of news, you fell back during
every battle, and took to your heels at times of
fighting. Yet, When Allah chose His Prophet
from the dwell of His prophets, and the abode of
His sincere (servants); The thorns of hypocrisy
appeared on you, the garment of faith became
worn out, The misguided ignorant(s) spoke out,
the sluggish ignorant came to the front and
brayed. The he camel of the vain wiggled his tail
in your courtyards and the your courtyards and
the Devil stuck his head from its place of hiding
and called upon you, he found you responsive to
his invitation, and observing his deceits.

He then aroused you and found you quick (to
answer him), and invited you to wrath, therefore;
you branded other than your camels and
proceeded to other than your drinking places.
Then while the era of the Prophet was still near,
the gash was still wide, the scar had not yet
healed, and the Messenger was not yet buried.
A (quick) undertaking as you claimed, aimed at
preventing discord (trial), Surely, they have fallen

into trial already! And indeed Hell surrounds the unbelievers. How preposterous! What an idea!

What a falsehood! For Allah's Book is still among you, its affairs are apparent; its rules are manifest; its signs are dazzling; its restrictions are visible, and its commands are evident. Yet, indeed you have casted it behind your backs! What! Do you detest it? Or according to something else you wish to rule? Evil would be the exchange for the wrongdoers! And if anyone desires a religion other than Islam (submission to Allah), it never will it be accepted from him; And in the hereafter, he will be in the ranks of those who have lost. Surely you have not waited until its stampede seized, and it became obedient. You then started arousing its flames, instigating its coal, complying with the call of the misled devil, quenching the light of the manifest religion, and extinguished the light of the sincere Prophet. You concealed sips on froth and proceeded toward his (the Prophet) kin and children in swamps and forests (meaning you plot against them in deceitful ways), but we are patient with you as if we are being notched with knives and stung by spearheads in our abdomens, Yet-now you claim that there is not inheritance for us! What! Do they then seek after a judgment of (the Days of)ignorance? But How, for a people whose faith is assured, can give better judgment than Allah? Don't you know? Yes, indeed it is obvious to you that I am his daughter.

O Muslims! Will my inheritance be usurped? O son of Abu Quhafa! Where is it in the Book of Allah that you inherit your father and I do not inherit mine? Surely you have come up with an unprecedented thing. Do you intentionally abandon the Book of Allah and cast it behind your back? Do you not read where it says: And Sulaiman inherited Dawood'?

And when it narrates the story of Zakariya and says: `So give me an heir as from thyself (One that) will inherit me, and inherit the posterity of Yaqoob' And: `But kindred by hood have prior rights against each other in the Book of Allah.'

And: Allah (thus) directs you as regards your children's (inheritance) to the male, a portion equal to that of two females' And, If he leaves any goods, that he make a bequest to parents and next of kin, according to reasonable usage; this is due from the pious ones.' You claim that I have no share! And that I do not inherit my father! What! Did Allah reveal a (Quranic) verse regarding you, from which He excluded my father? Or do you say: `These (Fatima and her father) are the people of two faiths, they do not inherit each other?!' Are we not, me and my father, a people adhering to one faith? Or is it that you have more knowledge about the specifications and generalizations of the Quran than my father and my cousin (Imam Ali)? So, here you are! Take it! (Ready with) its nose rope and saddled! But if shall encounter you on the

Day of Gathering; (thus) what a wonderful judge is Allah, a claimant is Muhammad, and a day is the Day of Rising. At the time of the Hour shall the wrongdoers lose; and it shall not benefit you to regret (your actions) then! For every Message, there is a time limit; and soon shall ye know who will be inflicted with torture that will humiliate him, and who will be confronted by an everlasting punishment. (Fatima then turned towards the Ansars and said:) O you people of intellect! The strong supporters of the nation! And those who embraced Islam; What is this short-coming in defending my right? And what is this slumber (while you see) injustice (being done toward me)? Did not the Messenger of Allah, my father, used to say: A man is upheld (remembered) by his children'? O how quick have you violated (his orders)?! How soon have you plotted against us? But you still are capable (of helping me in) my attempt, and powerful (to help me) in that which I request and (in) my pursuit (of it). Or do you say: "Muhammad has perished;"

Surely this is a great calamity; Its damage is excessive its injury is great, Its wound (is much too deep) to heal.

The Earth became darkened with his departure; the stars eclipsed for his calamity; hopes were seized; mountains submitted; sanctity was violated, and holiness was encroached upon after his death. Therefore, this, by Allah, is the great affliction, and the grand calamity; there is not an

affliction-which is the like of it; nor will there be a sudden misfortune (as surprising as this).

The Book of Allah-excellent in praising him-announced in the courtyards (of your houses) in the place where you spend your evenings and mornings; A call, A cry, A recitation, and (verses) in order. It had previously came upon His (Allah's) Prophets and Messengers; (for it is) A decree final, and a predestination fulfilled: "Muhammad is not but an Apostle: Many were the apostles that passed away before him. If he died or was slain, will ye then turn back on your heels? If any did turn back on his heels, not the least harm will he do to Allah; but Allah (on the other hand) will swiftly reward those who (serve Him) with gratitude." O you people of reflection; will I be usurped the inheritance of my father while you hear and see me?! (And while) You are sitting and gathered around me? You hear my call, and are included in the (news of the) affair? (But) You are numerous and well equipped! (You have) the means and the power, and the weapons and the shields. Yet, the call reaches you but you do not answer; the cry comes to you but you do not come to help? (This) While you are characterized by struggle, known for goodness and welfare, the selected group (which was chosen), and the best ones chosen by the Messenger for us, Ahlul-Bayt. You fought the Arabs, bore with pain and exhaustion, struggled against the nations, and resisted their heroes. We were still, so were you in ordering you, and you in obeying us. So that

Islam became triumphant, the accomplishment of the days came near, the fort of polytheism was subjected, the outburst of was subjected, the outburst of infidelity calmed down, and the system of religion was well-ordered. Thus, (why have you) become confused after clearness? Conceal matters after announcing them? Turned on your heels after daring? Associated (others with Allah) after believing? Will you not fight people who violated their oaths? Plotted to expel the Apostle and became aggressive by being the first (to assault) you? Do ye fear them? Nay, it is Allah Whom ye should more justly fear, if you believe!

Nevertheless, I see that you are inclined to easy living; dismissed he who is more worthy of guardianship (Ali (A)); You secluded yourselves with meekness and dismissed that which you accepted. Yet, if you show ingratitude, ye and all on earth together, yet, Allah free of all wants, worthy of all praise. Surely I have said all that I have said with full knowledge that you intent to forsake me, and knowing the betrayal that your hearts sensed. But it is the state of soul, the effusion of fury, the dissemination of (what is) the chest and the presentation of the proof. Hence, Here it is! Bag it (leadership and) put it on the back of an ill she camel, which has a thin hump with everlasting grace, marked with the wrath of Allah, and the blame of ever (which leads to) the Fire of (the wrath of Allah kindled (to a blaze), that which doth mount (right) to

the hearts; For, Allah witnesses what you do, and soon will the unjust assailants know what vicissitudes their affairs will take! And I am the daughter of a warner (the Prophet) to you against a severe punishment. So, act and so will we, and wait, and we shall wait.

(The end of Lady Fatima's speech.)

It appears from recorded historical events, that Lady Fatima (A) was successful at the beginning in persuading Abu Bakr to hand back Fadak to her; listen to part of a speech he (according to some historians) delivered after hearing Fatima's speech. He said:

O daughter of the Messenger of Allah . . . Surely the Prophet is your father, not anyone else's, the brother of your husband, not any other man's; he surely preferred him over all his friends and (Ali) supported him in every important matter, no one loves you save the lucky and no one hates you save the wretched. You are the blessed progeny of Allah's Messenger, the chosen ones, our guides to goodness our path to Paradise, and you-the best of women-and the daughter of the best of prophets, truthful is your sayings, excelling in reason. You shall not be driven back from your right . . . But I surely heard your father saying: "We the, group of prophets do not inherit, nor are we inherited Yet, this is my situation and property, it is yours (if you wish); it shall not be concealed from you, nor will it be stored away from you. You are the Mistress of your father's nation, and the blessed tree of your

descendants. Your property shall not be usurped against your will nor can your name be defamed. Your judgment shall be executed in all that which I possess. This, do you think that I violate your father's (will)?"

Fatima then refuted Abu Bakr's claim that the Prophet had stated that prophets cannot be inherited, and said:

Glory be to Allah!! Surely Allah's Messenger did not abandon Allah's Book nor did he violate His commands. Rather, he followed its decrees and adhered to its chapters. So do you unite with treachery justifying your acts with fabrications? Indeed this-after his departure-is similar to the disasters which were plotted against him during his lifetime. But behold! This is Allah's Book, a just judge and a decisive speaker, saying:

"One that will (truly) inherit Me, and inherit the posterity of Yaqub," (19:6)

She went on to say, "And Sulaiman inherited Dawood" (27:16).

Thus, He (Glory be to Him) made clear that which He made share of all heirs, decreed the amounts of inheritance allowed for males and females, and eradicated all doubts and ambiguities (pertaining to this issue which existed with the bygones).

"Nay!

But your minds have made up a tale (that may pass) with you, but (for me) patience is most fitting against that which ye assert; it is Allah (alone) whose help can be sought."

It is apparent that Abu Bakr changed the mode in which he addressed Lady Fatima (A) after delivering her speech. Listen to his following speech; which is his reply to Fatima's just reported speech.

Abu Bakr said:

> Surely Allah and His Apostle are truthful, and so has his (the Prophet's) daughter told the truth. Surely you are the source of wisdom, the element of faith, and the sole authority. May Allah not refute your righteous argument, nor invalidate your decisive speech. But these are the Muslims between us-who have entrusted me with leadership, and it was according to their satisfaction that I received what I have. I am not being arrogant, autocratic, or selfish, and they are my witnesses.

Upon hearing Abu Bakr speak of the people's support for him, Lady Fatima Zahra (A) turned toward them and said the following:

> O people, who rush toward uttering falsehood and are indifferent to disgraceful and losing actions!

> Do you not earnestly seek to reflect upon the Quran, or are your hearts isolated with locks? But on your hearts is the stain of the evil, which you committed; it has seized your hearing and your sight, evil is that which you justified cursed is that which you reckoned, and wicked is what you have taken for an exchange! You shall, by Allah,

find bearing it (to be a great) burden, and its consequence disastrous. (That is) on the day when the cover is removed and appears to you what is behind it of wrath. When you will be confronted by Allah with that which you could never have expected, there will perish, there and then, those who stood on falsehoods.

Although parts of Abu Bakr's speeches cannot be verified with authentic evidence, and despite the fact that we have already mentioned part of the actual speech, which Abu Bakr delivered after Lady Fatima's arguments, it appears certain that Abu Bakr was finally persuaded to submit Fadak to her.

Nevertheless, when Fatima was leaving Abu Bakr's house, Umar suddenly appeared and exclaimed, "What is it that you hold in your hand?"

Abu Bakr replied by saying, "A decree I have written for Fatima in which I assigned Fadak and her father's inheritance to her."

Umar then said, "With what will you spend on the Muslims if the Arabs decide to fight you?!"

Umar then seized the decree and tore it up!

Sunni references:

- *Seerah al Halabiyah,* vol 3 p 391–400

- *Fadak in History,* Murtaza Muttaheri, p 85

- *Fatimah the Gracious,* Abu Muhammad Ordoni, 217–240

References for the Notes Section

1. Ibn Sa'd, *At-Tabaqat*. Vol. III, pt I, p50-55; Al-Tabari. *Tabari*. Vol. I, p2998-3025; Ibn Athir, *Al-Kamil*. Vol III, p167-180; *Sharh*. Ibn Abi'l Hadid. Vol II, p144-161.

2. Al-Yaqubi, *Tahrikh-i-Yaqubi*. Vol. II, p103-106; Abil Fida, *Tahrikh-i-Abil Fida*. Vol I, p156, 166; *Muruj al Dhahab*. Vol. II p307, 352; *Sharh*. Ibn Abi'l Hadid Vol. I p17, 134.

3. Ibn Sa'd, *At-Tabaqatul Kubra*. Vol. II, p339; As-Sawa'iqul Muhriqa.

APPENDIX 1

Sunni references – Ghadir Khumm:

1. *Asbab al-nuzul*, Al Imam al-Wahidi, p 150

2. *Al Tafsir al Kabir*, Al Imam Abu Ishaq al-Talabi,

3. *Shawahid al-Tanzil li qawa'id al-Tafil*, Al-Hakim al-Hasakani, Vol 1, p187.

4. *Al-Durr al-manthur fi al-Tafsir bi al-Ma'thur*, Jalal al-Din al-Suyuti, Vol III, 117.

5. *Al-Tafsir al-Kabir*, Al-Fakhr al-Razi, Vol XII, p50.

6. *Tafsir al-Manar*, Muhammad Rashid Rida, Vol II, p86; Vol VI, p463.

7. *Ta'rikh Dimashq*, Abu Asakir al-Shafi'I, Vol II, 86.

8. *Fath al-Qadir*, Al-Shawkani, Vol II, p60.

9. *Matalib al-Sa'ul*, Ibn Talhah al-Shafi'I, Vol I, p44.

10. *Al-Fusul al-Muhimmah*, Ibn Sabbagh al-Maliki, p25.

11. *Yanabi al_Mawaddah*, Al-Qunduzi al-Hanafi, p120.

12. *Al-Milal wa al-Nihal*, Al-Shahristani, Vol I, p163.

13. *Kitab al-Wilayah*, Ibn Jarir al-Tabari.

14. *Umdat al-qari fi Sharh al-Bukhari*, Vol VIII, p 584.

15. *Tafsir al-Quran*, Abd al-Wahhab al-Bukhari.

16. *Ruh ma'ani*, al-Alusi, Vol II, p384.

17. *Kitab al-Wilayah*, Ibn Sa'id al-Sijistani.

18. *Fara'id al-simtayn*, Al-Hamwini, Vol I, p185

19. *Fath al-bayan fi maqasid al-Quran*, Al-Sayyid Siddiq Hasan Khan, Vol III, 63.

20. *Nuzul al-Quran*, Al-Hafiz Abu Nu'aym.

APPENDIX 2

Hadith al-Thaqalayn:

Sunni references:

1. *Kitab Fada'il Ali Ibn Abi Talib*, Sahih Muslim, Vol II, p122.

2. *Sahih al-Tirmidhi"*, Vol V, p328.

3. *Al-Kasa'is*, al-Nasa'I, p21.

4. *Musnad*, Ahmad Ibn Hanbal, Vol III, p17.

5. *Mustadrak,* al-Hakim, Vol III, p109.

6. *Kanz al-Ummal*, Vol I, p154.

7. *Al-Tabaqat al-Kubra*, Ibn Sa'd, Vol II, p 194.

8. *Jami al-Usul*, Ibn al-Athir, Vol I, p 187.

9. *Al-Jami al-Saghir*, Al- Suyuti, Vol I, p 353.

10. *Majma al-Zawa'id*, Al-Haythani, Vol IX, 163.

11. *Al-Fath al-Kabir*, Al-Nabhani, Vol I, p451.

12. *Usd al-ghabah fi ma'rifath al-Sahabah*, Ibn- Athir, Vol II, p12.

13. *Tarikh*, Ibn Asakir, Vol V, p463.

14. *Tafsir Ibn Kathir*, Vol IV, p113.

15. *Al-Taj al-Jami li al-Usul*, Vol III, P 308.

APPENDIX 3

1. Quran 33:33, Yousuf Ali, Published by Tahrike Tarsile Quran, New York, note 3715, p 1116.

2. Muslim in his *Sahih,* in "The Chapter on the Merits of the Prophet's household": Vol. 2, p. 368.

3. Al- Tirmidhi in his *Sahih;* Vol. *5,* p. 30.

4. *Al-Musnad,* Ahmed Ibn Hanbal; Vol. 1, p. 330.

5. *A1-Mustadrak,* At- Hakim; Vol. 3, p. 123.

6. *A1-Khas'ais,* Al-Nasa'i; p. 49

7. *Talkhis,* Al-Dhahabi; Vol.2, p. 150.

8. *Mulam,* Al-Tabrani; Vol. I, p. 65.

9. *Shawahid al-Tanzil,* Hakim al-Haskani; Vol. 2, p. II.

10. *History of Bukhari*, Al-Bukhari; Vol. 1, p. 69.

11. *Al-Isaba,* lbn Hajar al-Asqalani; Vol. 2, p. 502.

12. *Tadhkira al-Khawas,* Ibn al-Jawzi; p. 233.

13. *Tafsirofal-Fakhral-Razi;* Vol.2, p. 700.

14. *The Fountains of Love,* al-Qanduzi al-Hanafi; p. 107.

15. *Manaqib* of al-Khawarizmi, p. 23.

16. *Al-Sira* of al-l-lalabi, Vol. 13, p. 212.

17. *Al-Sira* of al-Dihlaniya; Vol. 3, p. 329.

18. *Asadal-Ghaba,* lbn al-Athir; Vol. 2, p. 12.

19. *Tafsir* of al-Tabari; Vol. 22. p. 6.

20. *Al-Dur al-Manthur,* al-Suyuti; Vol. 5, p. 198.

21. *Ta'rikh* of lbn Asakir; Vol. 1, p. 185.

22. *Tafsiral-Kashshaf,* al-Zamakhshari; Vol. 1, p. l93

23. *Ahkam al-Qur'an,* lbn at-Arabi; Vol. 2, p. 166.

24. *Tafsir* al-Qurtubi, Vol. 14, p. 182.

25. *Al-Sawa'iq al-Muhriqa* of Ibn 1-lajar, p. *85.*

26. *Al-Isti'ab,* lbn Abd al-Barr; Vol. 3, p. 37.

27. *Al-'Aqdal-Farid,* lbn 'Abd Rabbih; Vol.4, p.311

28. *Muniakhab Kan: al-'Ummal;* Vol. 5, p. 96.

29. *Masabih al-Sunna,* al-Baghawi, Vol. 2, p. 278.

30. *Asbab al-Nuzul,* al-Wahidi; p. 203.

31. *Tafsir* of lbn Kathir; Vol. 3, p. 483.

ACKNOWLEDGEMENTS

I owe my deceased parents everything that I have accomplished in my life. My father, Dr. Syed Muhammad Jafer Rizvi, and my mother, Yousuf Zehra Begum Rizvi, trained me to be a good Muslim, which automatically transformed me into a decent human being. Moral, ethical, humanistic, and religious aspects played a central role throughout my life. My father provided me the foundations of Islam on firm grounds during the last two years or so of his life. Almost every night before going to bed, he would talk about the important events from Islamic history, and these talks usually ended with discussions about a unique revolutionary movement in Karbala in the year 61 Hijri and its impact on the future of Islam. I remember him saying "Son, curiosity will lead you to the truth provided that your efforts are sincere. Discover Islam through research and you will be thrilled to learn and appreciate its greatness. Karbala will open new doors for you every day." He would then smile with an air of confidence. As a ten year old, I didn't quite realize that this would have a profound impact on my life.

Majalis (lectures and sermons) had a powerful influence on my life as well. Although I was busy as a research scientist, manager, and director, I made sure to find time to benefit from the lectures of *Zakireen* (speakers) and *Ulema* (religious authorities). Zakireen and Ulema provided me the basis to establish the religio-social components of my life. Rasheed Turabi's majalis were inspirational and had a tremendous influence on me. Similarly inspiring were the lectures of the following Ulemas, whom I had the opportunity to hear in person in India: Ali Naqui, Aulad Husain, Kalb-e-

Sadiq, Zeshaan Haider, Tahir Jarvali. In the United States, I heard Sakhawath Husain; Syed Muhammad Rizvi; Mehboob Mehdi; Muntezir Mehdi; Syed Zaki; Husham Husaini; Amir Mukhtar Faizi; Akeel Gharavi; and more recently, Safdar Razi provided vitality to my *Eeman* (piety and devotion to Islam).

My brother Syed Asad Rizvi, who is one of the two founders of the IEC Husaini Association of Chicago, and my other brothers, Syed Bizaath Husain Rizvi and Syed G. Husain Rizvi, have always been inspirational. I also owe my father-in-law, Dr. M. M. Taqui Khan, for the discussions I had with him for many years. My special thanks go out to my mother-in-law, Dr. Badar Taqui Khan, for her encouragement in my pursuit for the truth.

I would also like to thank Kristopher Kmitta for his support in helping to bring this book to fruition, and our editor Zack DePew for his invaluable input and suggestions in the final stages of this book, as well as Katie Schneider who was integral in the publishing of this book.

Above all, I would not have been able to take up this task and be able to finish it had it not been for the support of my wife, Dr. Zehra Begum Rizvi, and my son Asghar Rizvi, who would put up with my idiosyncrasies and sit and listen to my informal discussions about various parts of this book. My son Khasim Rizvi, who is the coauthor of this book, made many sacrifices to carry this project to completion. I owe him for that.

REFERENCES

Introduction

1. Carter, Jimmy. *Our Endangered Values*. Simon and Schuster, 2005. p116-133.

2. Al-Tabari. *Last Years of the Prophet*. Vol. IX. State University New York   Press, 1990. p188, 202.; Ayoub, Mahmoud. *The Crisis of Muslim History*.   Oneworld-Oxford University Press, reprint 2005. p19.; Qutayba, Ibn. Volume I. p29-30.

3. Muhadethseen: Collectors/compilers of ahadith

4. Hadith: Hadith is a tradition that is a collection of the events, actions, and sayings of Muhammad. The six most important compilations for Sunnis are known as Sahih sitha.

5. Sunnah: Actions and practices. Transmission of information from narrators who were witness to the actions of Muhammad.

6. Hudud, Amina. *Quran and Women*. Oxford University Press, 1999.

7. Barlas, Asma. *Believing Women in Islam*. Austin: University of Texas Press, 2002.

Chapter 1   Under Siege

1. Born 615 AD. Died from severe wounds from the attack on her home led by Abu Bakr and Umar in the year 632 AD, six months after the death of her father, Muhammad, the last prophet of Islam.

2. *Al Tabari* 2:244

3. al Athir, Ibn. *Tarikh.* 2:320

4. Ibn Hambal. *Masnad.* vol IV, p172 ; Tirmidhi, vol 5, p699 ; Al Mustadrak; Sunan Ibn Majah; Ibn Hhajr Hayaami chapter 11, section 3 p292

5. Ibn Qutayba. *Al Imama Wa al Siyasa.* p12

6. Ibn Qutayba. *Al Imama Wa al Siyasa.* Dhikr Bayya Abu Bakr. p18-30.

7. Al Tabari. *History of Tabari.* Vol IX p186-187, State University of New York, 1990.

8. Al Tabari. *History of Tabari.* Vol. II, p233 ; Ibn Hadeed. *Sharah Nahjul Balaga.* Vol. VI p47-48 .

9. Al Tabari. *Tarikh Tabari.* Vol III ; Kanzul Ummal. *Tarikh Khulafa.* Vol III ; Bar, Ibn Abdul. *Isteeab.*

10. *Al Bidayah*, Vol VIII, p131.

11. Madelung, Wilferd. *The Succession of Muhammad.* Pg 60-61, Press Syndicate of the University of Cambridge, 1997.

12. Al Tabari. *History of Tabari.* Vol. II, p235.

13. Al Tabari. *History of Tabari*. Vol IX, p189.

14. Bukhari. *Sahih Al-Bukhari*. Vol. V tradition 232 ; Muslim. *Sahih Muslim*. Vol. IV tradition 2493.

15. *At Taj Al Jami lil Ossool*. Vol. III, p353 ;Bukhari. *Sahih Al-Bukhari*. Vol. V, p83 Tradition 232; Muslim. *Sahih Muslim*. Vol. IV, p1902, tradition 2493.

16. Buldan, Maujam-ul. *Dhikr Fadak*. Vol. XIV. p239.

17. Tabari. Vol VIII, Pg 123 *Al-Tabari—The victory of Islam*, Translator; Michael Fishbein, University of California, LA.

18. Ibn Ishaaq. *Sirat Rasul Allah*. Translator, A.Guillaume, p117.

19. Ibn Kathir. *Al Bidayah Wa N-nihayah*. Vol. V, p209. ; Lings, Martin. *Muhammad*. p335.

20. Bukhari. *Sahih Al-Bukhari*. Vol. V, p5; Muslim. *Sahih Muslim*. Vol. II, p72; Hanbal, Ahmed. *Musnad*. Vol.I, p6; Al-Tabari. *Tarikh Tabari*. Vol. II, p236; *Kifayatat-Talib*. p266; Al-Bayhaqi. *Sunan*. Vol VI, p300.

21. Stowasser, Barbara. *Women in the Quran, Tradition and interpretation*. p59-60, 80.

22. Bukhari. *Sahih Bukhari*. Vol. V, p83 tradition 232 .

Chapter 2   Ground Rules

1. Carter, Jimmy. *Palestine: Peace Not Apartheid*. Simon & Schuster, NY, 2006. p217-241.

2. Rai, Anita. *An affair of the heart*.

3. *Sahih Bukhari; Sahih Muslim; Tirmidi; Usul-e-kafi.*

4. Razi, Fakhru'd-Din. *Tafsir Kabir.* Vol. II, p271.

Chapter 3   The Foundations and Establishment

1. Ibn Ishaq. *The Life of Muhammad.* Translator A. Guillaume, Oxford Press, p116-118.

2. Ibn Ishaq. *The Life of Muhammad.* Translator A. Guillaume, Oxford Press, p118.

3. Ibn Ishaq. *The Life of Muhammad.* Translator A. Guillaume, Oxford Press, p120.

4. Hambal, Ibn Ahmed. Following is a translation from Ahmed Ibn Hambal:

The Prophet stood up among them and said: "O descendants of Abdu'l-Muttalib! Allah Almighty has sent me as a messenger to the whole of creation in general and to you in particular. I invite you to make two statements that are light and easy for the tongue, but on the scale of action they are heavy. If you make the two statements, you will be masters of the lands of the Arabs and the non-Arabs. Through them you will go to Paradise and will obtain immunity from Hell. These two expressions are: first, to bear witness to Allah's Oneness, and second, to bear witness to my prophethood. The one who first of all acknowledges my call and helps me in my mission is my brother, my helper, my heir, and my successor after me."

The Prophet repeated the last sentence three times, and each time none except Ali responded to him, saying, "I will aid

and help you, O Prophet of Allah!" So the Prophet declared: "This Ali is my brother, and he is my successor and Caliph among you."

5. Ibn Ishaq. *The Life of Muhammad*. Translator A. Guillaume, Oxford Press. p79-80. 1967.

6. Ibn Ishaq. *The Life of Muhammad*. Translator A. Guillaume, Oxford Press. p289-360. 1967.

7. Ibn Ishaq. *The Life of Muhammad*. Translator A. Guillaume, Oxford Press, p298-310, 337. 1967.

8. Ibn Ishaq. *The Life of Muhammad*. Translator A. Guillaume, Oxford Press, p381. 1967. ;Haykal, Muhammad Husein. *The life of Muhammad*. American Trust Publications 1976, p266.; Madelung, Wilferd. *The Succession to Muhammad*. Cambridge University,1997, p79.

9. Bukhari. *Sahih Bukhari*. Vol. IV, Bk. 51, Nr. 28.

10. Haykal, Muhammad Husein. *The life of Muhammad*. American Trust Publications. p267. 1976 .

11. Ibn Ishaq. *The Life of Muhammad*. Translator A. Guillaume, Oxford Press. p455-456. 1967.

12. Al-Tabari. *The History of Tabari*. Vol. VIII. Translated Michael Fishbein, State University of New York, 1997, p116-124.

13. Ibn Ishaq. *The Life of Muhammad*. Translator A. Guillaume, Oxford Press, p381. 1967.

14. Ibn Ishaq. *The Life of Muhammad*. Translator A. Guillaume, Oxford Press. 1967, p515-516.

15. Mufid. *Al-Irshad*. p.33; Al-Tabari. *The History of Tabari*. Vol. IX, State University of New York, 1990, p77-78 .

16. Al-Ghazaliin, Abu Hamid. *Sirr Al-Alamin*. p5. ; Hanbal, Ibn Ahmed. *Musnad*. Vol IV, p281; Al-Tabari. *Tafsir*. Vol III, p428.

17. Hanbal, Ibn Ahmed. *Musnad*. Vol. IV. p281; Al Tabaiin. *Tafsir*.; Al Razi. *Al Tafsir-Al Kabir*. Vol III, p636.

18. Bukhari. *Ta'rikh*. Vol.I, p375; Hanbal, Ibn Ahmed. *Musnad*. Vol. IV, p281, 371; Ibn Jauzi, Yusuf Sibt. *Tadhkiratu'l-Khasa'isu'l-Umma*. p17.

19. Abu Ja'far Muhammad Bin Jarir Tabari (died 310 A.H.), gives complete details of the hadith of Ghadir in his book 'Kitabu'l-Wilaya' and has narrated it through a chain of seventy-five transmitters.

20. *Al Bidayah Aa'l-Nihayah*. Vol V, p208 & Vol VII, p346 , p79.

21. Bahrani has cited eighty-nine Sunni and seven Shia sources. *Shi'ite Islam* , Muhammad Husain Tabatabai, translator Seyyed Hossein Nasr, State University of New York Press .

22. Al-Tabari. *The History of al Tabari*. Vol. IX, The State University of New York, 1900, p174-175.

23. Bukhari. *Sahih al Bukhari*. 3:138 ; *Sahih al Bukhari*. 1:37; *Kanz al Ummal*, 3:138 ; Tabari. *The Last Years of the Prophet*. State University of New York, Vol. IX , p174-175 .

24. Haykal, Muhammad Husein. *The Life of Muhammad*. American Trust Publications, p498-500, 1976.

25. Al-Tabari. *The Last Years of the Prophet.* State University of New York, Vol IX, p179. ; Al-Tabari. *The Last Years of the Prophet.* State University of New York, Vol IX, p161-189 .

Chapter 4   The Coup at Saquifa

1. List of Sunni scholars. Appendix 1.

2. Madelung, Wilferd. *The succession to Muhammad.* Cambridge University Press, 1997. p253.

3. Al-Tabari. *The Last Years of the Prophet.* The State University of New York, 1990. p186-198.

4. *Taqwa:* See Glossary

5. Immamath: Immamath was a title first awarded to Abrahim Quran (2:124) after he had fulfilled the task of delivering the message after suffering at the hands of the disbelievers and upon maintaining the highest degree of commitment and ascending to the expectation of Allah. The Imam who went beyond this was Husain Ibn Ali in Karbala, as predicted in the Quran (37:107: And We ransomed him with a tremendous sacrifice). The verses of the Quran that foretell this sacrifice are 37:104–107.

6. An-Na'im, Abdullahi. *Toward an Islamic Reformation.* Syracuse University Press, 1990. p76.

7. Al-Tabari. *The History of Tabari.* Vol IX, 1990. p168-174.

8. Al-Tabari. *The History of Tabari.* Vol. IX, State University New York, 1990. p201.

9. Ibn Qutaybah. *Al Imamah Wa Al-Siyasah*. Vol. I, p25.

10. Husayn, Taha. *Al-Fitna Al-Kubra*. Cairo:Dal al-Ma'arf, 1966; Ayoub, Mahmoud. *The Early Crisis of Muslim History*. Oneworld Oxford, 2005, p39.

11. Al Tabari and Ibn Al Athir describe his (Abu Bakr's)condition before death: "Ask Those Who Know", Muhammad Al Tajani al Samawi, Ansariyan Publications, Qum, Iran, p241.

12. El Fadl, Khaled Abou. *Islam and the Challenge of Democracy*. Princeton University Press, 2004. p17, 39.

13. *Sahih Bukhari*. Vol. VIII, Bk 82, Nr 817.

Then he uttered, 'The Prophet has said that he should not be worshipped in the same manner as it was done in the case of Jesus, son of Mary. Concerning me you all can say that I am a servant of God and the Prophet *('Abd Allah wa Rasaal)*. I have been informed that some of you have said that before 'Umar dies he would do *ba'yat* on the hands of someone. One should not be misled by the *ba'yat-e Abu Sakr* (i.e. vote of allegiance to Abu Bakr). It was unconstitutional *(falta)* and later on it was regularized. Yes, it was so. But God saved us from its evil consequences. Of you none is like Abu Bakr to whom people may submit. Whosoever receives *ba'yat* without consulting the Muslimeen should not be followed nor the person who did *ba'yat* with such a person, lest there be rift and fight among the Muslims.'

14. *Nahjul Balagha*. Translated by Syed Ali Raza. Tahreek'e Tarsile Quran, Elmhurst, NY, Ed. 1996. p1011; Masudi. *Isbath-e-Waseeyeth*. p119.

15. *Tahrikh-i-Yaqubi*. Vol.II, p103-106; *Tahrikh-i-Abil Fida* Vol. I,

p156, 166; *Muruj al dhahab* Vol. II, p307, 352; Ibn Abil Hadid. Vol. I, p17, 134.

In answer to Ibn Abbas's protest Umar said: " I swear to God Ali was the most deserving of all the people to become Khalif, but for three reasons we pushed him aside: (1) he was too young (2) he was attached to the descendents of Abd al-Muttalib (3) People did not like to have prophecy and the Khilafath assembled in one house hold."

16. Ibn Sa'd. *At-Tabaqatul Kubra.* Vol. II, p339; Ibn Hajar. *As-Sawa'iqul Muhriqa*, p127.

17. Madelung, Wilferd. *The Succession to Muhammad.* Cambridge University Press, 1997, p223.; Mas'oudi. *Murooj at-Thahab.* Vol. III, p199.

Chapter 5 From Khilapath to Kingship

1. Williams, Annie and Vivian Head. *Terror Attacks.* The Futura Book, 2006.

2. Adil, Hajjah Amina. *Muhammad —The Messenger of Islam.* Islamic Supreme Council of America, 2002. p133.

3. Mernissi, Fatima. *The Veil and the Male Elite.* Basic Books, 1991, p145, 156-157.

4. Al - Tabari. *The History of Al-Tabari.* The State University of New York, 1997.Vol. VIII, p85.

5. Al -Tabari. *The History of Al-Tabari.* The State University of New York, 1990. Vol. IX, p174-175; *Sahih Bukhari.* Vol. I, p37.

6. Ibn Qutayba. *Al Imama Wes-Siyasa.* p12; *Al-Tabari's Tareekh.* Vol. II, p233; Hadeed, Ibn Abdul. *Sharah Nahjul Balagha.* Vol. VI, p47-48.

7. *Sahih Muslim.* Bk 31, Number 6000 *Bab Fatima Binte Rasul* .

8. *Sahih Bukhari. Vol. V, Bk 57, Nr 61:* Narrated Al-Miswar bin Makhrama.

9. Madelung, Wilferd. *The Succession to Muhammad.* Cambridge University Press, 1997. p71-73.

10. Maududi, Abul A'la. *Khilafath aur Mulukiath* [Urdu]. Islamic Publishers, New Delhi,2001. p97-107.

11. Maududi, Abul A'la. *Khilafath aur Mulukiath* [Urdu]. Islamic Publishers, New Delhi, 2001. p107.

12. Maududi, Abul A'la. *Khilafath aur Mulukiath* [Urdu]. Islamic Publishers, New Delhi, 2001. p142.

13. *Futoohul Buldan.* p44-46; Hadeed, Ibn Abul. *Sharh Nahajul Balagha.* Vol. XVI, p216.

14. Shariati, Ali. *And Once Again Abu Dhar.*

15. Madelung, Wilferd. *The Succession to Muhammad.* Cambridge University Press, 1997. p132.

16. Madelung, Wilferd. *The Succession to Muhammad.* Cambridge University Press, 1997. p195.

17. *Al-Yaqubi.* Vol II, p175; *Al-Kufi.* Vol. II, p255; *Aishah the Beloved of Muhammad.* University of Chicago press,1942. Reprint, New York, Arno Press, 1973. p108; Ayoub, Mahmoud. *The Crisis of Muslim History.* Oneworld Oxford, 2005. p70.

18. Madelung, Wilferd. *The Succession to Muhammad*. Cambridge University Press, 1997. p132.

19. *Sharh Nahajul Balagha*. Vol. IX, p35-36.

20. Talib, Ali Ibn Abi. *Nahjul Balagha*. Translated by Syed Ali Reza. Tahrike Tarsile Quran, New York, 1996. p160.

21. Madelung, Wilferd. *The Succession to Muhammad*. Cambridge University Press, 1997. p123.

22. Russell, Bertrand. *A History of Western Philosophy*. Simon & Schuster, 1972. p421.

23. Maududi, Abul A'la. *Khilafath aur Mulukiath* [Urdu]. Islamic Publishers, New Delhi, 2001. p324.

24. Madelung, Wilferd. *The Succession to Muhammad*. Cambridge University Press, 1997. p173-174.

25. Al-Kufi, Ibn A'tham. *The Accounts of Aisha and Umm Salamah Dialogue*. Vol. II, p160-161; Ayoub, Mahmoud. *The Crisis of Muslim History*. Oneworld Oxford, 2005. p90-91.

26. Al-Tabari. *The History of Al-Tabari*. Translator Michael G. Morony, State University of New York Press, 1987. Vol. XVIII, p122 – 156.

27. Madelung, Wilferd. *The Succession to Muhammad*. Cambridge University Press, 1997. p184.

28. Al Tabari. *The History of Al-Tabari*. Translated by Michael Morony, State University of New York, 1987. Vol. XVIII, p154.

29. Stowasser, Barbara. *Women in the Quran, Traditions, and Interpretation*. Oxford University Press, 1994. p96, 100.

30. Stowasser, Barbara. *Women in the Quran, Traditions, and Interpretation*. Oxford University Press, 1994. p116.

Chapter 6 Quranic Exegesis

1. 'Ahel az Zikr' (- Note 1)

2. Wudud, Amina. *Quran and Women*. Oxford University Press, 1999.

3. Saroush, Abdul Karim. *Reason, Freedom, and Democracy in Islam*. Translated by Mahmud Sadri and Ahmed Sadri, Oxford University Press,2000 .

4. El Fadl, Khalid Abou. *Islam and the Challenge to Democracy*. Princeton University Press.

5. Barlas, Asma. *Believing Women in Islam*. University of Texas Press, 2002.

6. Esposito, John. *Unholy War*. Oxford University Press, 2002. p142-150.

7. Lewis, Bernard. *What Went Wrong*. Oxford University Press, 2002. p85-87.

8. Armstrong, Karen. *Muhammad*. Harper SanFrancisco. p108-133.

9. Al-Tabari. *The Last Years of the Prophet*. Translator Ismail Poonawala, State University of New York, 1990. p164-166.

10. Stowasser, Barbara. *Women in the Quran, Traditions, and Interpretation*. Oxford University Press, 1994. p87.

11. Wudud, Amina. *Quran and Women.* Oxford University Press, 1999. p74-78.

12. Stowasser, Barbara. *Women in the Quran, Traditions, and Interpretation.* Oxford University Press, 1994. p87; Haykal, Muhammad Husein. *The Life of Muhammad.* Islamic Book Trust, Kuala Lumpur. p298.

13. *Al Bidayah Wa'l-Nihayah.* Vol. V, p209; *Dhakha Ir Al-Uqba.* p16; *Al-Fusul Al-Muhimmah.* p22; *Khasa-Is.* p30; *Al-Sawaiq Al-Muhariqah.* p147. In Ghayat al-maram, thirty-nine versions of this hadith have been recorded by Sunni sources.

Chapter 7   Ahadith, Sunnah and History

1. Madelung, Wilferd. *The Succession to Muhammad.* Cambridge University Press, 2001. p195-238; Maududi, Abul Ala. *Khilafath-O- Malookiath* [Urdu]. Islami Publishing, 2001. p125-167.

2. Ibn Athir and Ibn Abi'l-Hadid. *Sharh-Nahju'l-Balagha.* Printed in Egypt. Vol. III, p104.

3. Nadwi. Volume IV, Commentary on Sahaih Muslim.

4. Al Samawi, Muhammad Al-Tejani. *Ask those who know.* Ansariyan Publications, 2001. p339.

5. Hadid, Ibn Abi'l. *Sharh Nahaj ul Balagha.* Vol.I p359: Sharafuddin, Abul Hasan. "Abu Hurayra", Translated by Abdullah al-Shahin, Ansariyan Publications. 2002. p42.

6. Razi, Fakhru'd-Din. *Tafsir Kabir.* Vol. II, p271.

7. Al Samawi, Muhammad Al-Tejani. *Ask those who know.* Ansariyan Publications, 2001. p293-385.

8. *Quran*: Published by Translation and commentaries by Yousuf Ali, Tehrike Tarsile.Quran, New York, 2002, p1115 See related notes in this translation.

9. Ibn Ishaq. *The Life of Muhammad*. Translator A. Guillaume, Oxford Press.

10. Marnissi, Fatima. *The Vail and The Male Elite*. Translated by Mary Jo Lakeland, Basic Books , New York, 1991. p37.

11. Ibn Ishaq. *The Life of Muhammad*. Translator A. Guillaume, Oxford Press, p683, 687.

12. Al-Tabari. *The History of Tabari*. Vol. IX, State University of New York, 1990. p188.

Chapter 8   Inheritance and Women's rights

1. Ibn Ishaq. *The Life of Muhammad*. Translated by A. Guillaume, Oxford University Press, 1955. p523.

Chapter 9   The Statement That Shook the World

1. Refer to Notes in Chapter 6, note 1

2. *Peshawar nights*. English Translation, Zehra Publications, Blanco, Texas, 1986 also available on the internet

3. *Seerah al Halabiyah*. Vol. III, p391-400; Muttaheri, Murtaza, *Fadak in History*. p85; Ordoni, Abu Muhammad, *Fatimah the Gracious*. p217 - 240

4. *Al Hadis Mishkat-ul- Masabih.* Translated by Fazlul Karim, Book 1. Dacca, 1960 p163; Nasr, Seyyed Hossein. *Muhammad Man of God* Kazi publications, 1995. p80.

5. Madelung, Wilferd. *Succession to Muhammad.* Cambridge University Press, 1997. p194.

6. Madelung, Wilferd. *Succession to Muhammad.* Cambridge University Press, 1997. p235. Talib, Ali Ibn Abi. *Nahjul Balagha.* Translator- Sayed Ali Reza, Tahrike Tarsile Quran, New York, 1966. P469.

Chapter 10 Reformists, Modernists and Current Crisis

1. Al-Tabari. *The History of Tabari.* The State University of New York, Vol .III, 1997. p85.

2. An-Na'im, Ahmed. *Toward an Islamic Reformation.* Published by Syracuse University Press 1996. p16-19.

3. Schwartz, Stephen. *Two Faces of Islam.* Published by Double Day, 2002. p57-58.

4. Algar, Hamid. *Wahhabism.* Published by Islamic Publications International 2002. p8-12.

5. El Fadl, Khaled Abou. *The Great Theft.* HarperSanFrancisco, 2007. p56-59.

6. An-Na'im, Ahmed. *Toward an Islamic Reformation.* Published by Syracuse University Press 1996. p130.

7. Nasr,Vali. *The Vanguard of Islamic Revolution.* University of California Press, 1994. p236. See note 23.

8. Nasr,Vali. *The Vanguard of Islamic Revolution*. University of California Press, 1994. p165.

9. Maududi, Abul Ala. *Khilafath aur Mulukiath* [Urdu]. Islamic Publishing, Delhi, 2001, p231-234.

10. Barlas, Asma. *Believing Women in Islam"*.University of Texas Press, Austin 2002, p47.

11. Barlas, Asma. *Believing Women in Islam"*.University of Texas Press, Austin 2002, p47.

Chapter 11   Freedom, Democracy, Education and Islam

1. USINFO, White House Correspondent David McKeeby, 13 June 2007.

2. Reidel, Bruce. *Al Qaeda Strikes Back* Foreign Affairs,", Bruce Reidel, Vol. 86, Number 3, May/June 2007, p28.

3. Schwarts, Stephen. *Two Faces of Islam*. Published by Doubleday (Random House) 2002. p75; Algar, Hamid. *Wahabbisim*. Islamic Publications International, 2002. p24-25.

4. Talbi, Muhammad. *Liberal Islam*, Editor Charles Kurzman, Oxford University press, 1998. p165.

5. Carter, Jimmy. *Palestine peace not Apartheid*, p189.

6. Kabir, Humayun. *Liberal Islam*, Editor Charles Kurzman, Oxford University press, 1998, p149.

7. Sahih (or Jami` or Sunan), al-Tirmidhi (d. 279 AH), p141.

8. Talbi, Muhammad. *Liberal Islam.* Editor Charles Kurzman, Oxford University press, 1998, p164.

9. Chittick, William. *The heart of Islamic Philosophy.* Oxford University Press, 2001. p112.

10. Talib, Ali Ibn Abi. *Nahjul Balagha.* Translated by Sayed Ali Reza, Sermon 90, Tehrike Tarsile Quran, New York, 1996, p225

11. Hawking, Stephen. *A Brief History of Time.* Bantam Books, 1988, p38-39.

12. Talib, Ali Ibn Abi. *Nahjul Balagha.* Translated by Sayed Ali Reza, Sermon 90, Tehrike Tarsile Quran, New York, 1996, p222

13. Hawking, Stephen. *A Brief History of Time.* Bantam Books, 1988. p133.

14. Al Tabari, *The History of Tabari.* Vol III, Translated by Michael Fishbein, State University of New York Press, 1997. p98-115.

Chapter 12   Reflections

1. Stowasser, Barbara. *Women in the Quran, Traditions, and Interpretation.* Oxford University Press, 1994. p59-60, 80.

2. *Tareekh Tabari* Volume II p24; *Kanz al Khitab al Khilafath ma al Maar* Volume III p135; *Al Imama wa al Siyasa* Vol. I p18, *Dhikr Wafaath Abu Bakr.* Murujh al Dhahab, Vol. II p308. Al Fareed, Iqd. *Dhikr Khilafath Abu Bakr*; Vol. II, p208.

3. Al-Tabari, *The History of Tabari*.Vol. III, p223; Ayoub, Mahmoud. *Crisis of Muslim History*. Publisher One world, 2005. p157. Ibn Qutaybah, *History of Khilafath*; Al-Tabari, *Ta'rikh Al-Tabari*. Vol. IV, p52.

4. *Sharh Nahjul Balagha*, Vol. XVI, p216; *Futoohul Buldan*. p46.

5. *Sahih Bukhar.* Vol. V, p5; *Sahih Muslim.* Vol. II, p72; Hambal, Ahmed. *Masnad*.Vol . I, p6; AL Tabari, *The History of Tabari.* Vol. II, p236; *Kifayatat Talib.* p266 and Al Bayhaqi. *Sunan* Vol. VI, p300.

6. AL Tabari. *The last years of the Prophet.* State University of New York Press, 1990, p179-180.

7. Ghosh, Bobby. *TIME.* Article Titled: Sunnis vs.Shias: Why They Hate Each Other, March 5, 2007. p32.

Index

I

Ibne Ziyad 73
Ibn Ishaq 43, 101, 250, 251, 260
Ibn Taiymmiah 146, 147
Ijtehad 78, 194, 203
Iraq ix, x, xxi, xxii, 6, 147, 159, 160,
    161, 166, 172, 173, 186, 189,
    190, 194
Iraq War xxi, xxii, 161
Israel 22

J

Jabir bin 'Abdullah 114
Jacob 35, 84
Jafer-e-Sadiq xii
Jallianwalla Bagh 161
Janath-ul-Baqui 185
Jesus x, 18, 84, 148, 175, 176, 178,
    179, 254
Jihad 100, 154, 189, 224

K

Kaabah xv, 44, 195
Karbala xix, xxii, 73, 84, 85, 138,
    160, 208, 245, 253
Khadija x, xvi, 18, 37, 38, 39, 40,
    175, 199, 202, 212
Khalid ibn Walid 58, 138
Khandaq, battle of 42
Khilafath 3, 4, 5, 6, 12, 13, 15, 29, 30,
    34, 54, 55, 56, 57, 58, 59, 60,
    61, 62, 63, 64, 66, 69, 71, 72,
    73, 74, 86, 87, 101, 122, 139,
    146, 152, 163, 180, 181, 182,
    183, 188, 192, 194, 195, 256,
    257, 259, 262, 263, 264
Khybar, battle of 42
Kitabu'l-Wilaya 45, 252
Kulthum binte Ali 11

L

Lewis, Bernard 78, 100, 188

M

Malik ibn Nuwayra 58
Marwan ibn Hakam 66
Masjid, see *Mosque* x, xx, 5, 15, 16,
    17, 68, 123, 144, 177, 195, 220
Masjid-e-Nabavi x, xi, 123, 132, 202
Maududi, Abul Ala 259, 262
Mernissi, Fatima 64, 101
Middle East 162, 165, 191
Moses vii, x, 44, 84, 157
Mosque x, xx, 5, 16, 68, 123, 144,
    177, 195, 220
Mu'tazilites 93
Muawiah, ibne Abu Sufyan 138, 187
Muhadiseen 6, 196
Muhammad vii, x, xi, xii, xiii, xiv, xvi,
    xix, xxi, 1, 2, 3, 4, 5, 6, 7, 8, 9,
    10, 11, 12, 13, 14, 15, 17, 18,
    19, 23, 24, 25, 26, 27, 29, 31,
    34, 37, 38, 39, 40, 41, 42, 43,
    44, 45, 46, 47, 48, 49, 52, 53,
    54, 55, 56, 57, 59, 60, 63, 64,
    65, 66, 67, 68, 70, 71, 72, 73,
    74, 75, 77, 78, 79, 80, 81, 82,
    83, 84, 85, 86, 87, 90, 92, 93,
    94, 95, 96, 97, 98, 99, 100, 101,
    102, 106, 108, 113, 116, 117,
    118, 119, 120, 121, 122, 123,
    125, 126, 127, 128, 129, 130,
    132, 136, 137, 138, 141, 142,
    143, 144, 145, 148, 149, 151,
    155, 156, 157, 160, 163, 164,
    165, 166, 167, 168, 170, 172,
    175, 176, 177, 178, 179, 180,
    181, 182, 183, 185, 186, 187,
    188, 189, 190, 191, 192, 195,
    196, 197, 198, 199, 201, 202,
    204, 205, 206, 207, 208, 210,
    211, 212, 213, 214, 216, 218,
    220, 222, 225, 226, 230, 231,
    236, 239, 247, 248, 249, 250,
    251, 252, 253, 255, 256, 257,
    258, 259, 260, 261, 262, 263
Mustadrak 92, 212, 241, 243, 248

Printed in the United States
124782LV00004B/319-381/P

9 781438 904221

S0-FMH-961